Teacher's Resource Book

MIDDLE GRADES

MATH*Thematics*

Book 1

3 Statistical Safari

4 Mind Games

The STEM Project

McDougal Littell
A HOUGHTON MIFFLIN COMPANY
Evanston, Illinois • Boston • Dallas

McDougal Littell: www.mcdougallittell.com
Middle School Mathematics: www.mlmath.com

Acknowledgments

Writers

The authors of *Middle Grades Math Thematics, Books 1-3,* wish to thank the following writers for their contributions to the Teacher's Resource Books for the *Math Thematics* program: **Mary Buck, Roslyn Denny, Jean Howard, Sallie Morse, Patrick Runkel, Thomas Sanders-Garrett, Christine Tuckerman.**

Photography

Front Cover Lynda Richarson (t);
Melanie Carr/Southern Stock Photo/Uniphoto International (b);
3-1 Lynda Richarson;
4-1 Melanie Carr/Southern Stock Photo/Uniphoto International;
Back Cover Robert Frerck/Odyssey.

The STEM Project

Middle Grades Math Thematics is based on the field-test version of the STEM Project curriculum. The STEM Project was supported in part by the

 NATIONAL SCIENCE FOUNDATION

under Grant No. ESI-9150114. Opinions expressed in *Middle Grades Math Thematics* are those of the authors and not necessarily those of the National Science Foundation.

ISBN: 0-395-89463-8
   6 7 8 9 10–BMW–06 05

About the Teacher's Resource Book

This Resource Book contains all of the teaching support that you need to teach *Math Thematics*, Book 1, Modules 3 and 4. This teaching support includes the following material:

Spanish Glossary

A Spanish translation of the Glossary from the pupil textbook in blackline master form. The Spanish Glossary is located at the beginning of the Teacher's Resource Book for Modules 1 and 2.

Teaching Commentary

Planning the Module Contains a Module Overview and charts showing Module Objectives, Topic Spiraling, Topic Integration, Materials needed, and Teacher Support Materials. Also included are a Guide for Assigning Homework for regular and block schedules, Classroom Ideas, and a Home Involvement Math Gazette. For more information on the Guide for Assigning Homework and pacing, see pages vii-viii.

Teaching Suggestions Complete and comprehensive teaching suggestions for each section of the module. These include a Section Planner, a Section Overview, Materials List, Section Objectives, Assessment Options, Classroom Examples, Closure Questions, a Section Quiz, and notes on Customizing Instruction. Each page features a two-page pupil edition reduced facsimile for easy visual reference to the pupil textbook.

Blackline Masters

Labsheets Blackline masters used in conjunction with various Exploration questions to present data and extend the scope of the Exploration. Answers are provided at point of use in the annotated Teacher's Edition.

Extended Exploration Solution Guide A comprehensive discussion of the Extended Exploration in the pupil textbook, including how to assess student responses and performance.

Alternate Extended Exploration An extended exploration that can be substituted for the one in the pupil textbook, including teaching notes and assessment procedures.

Warm-Up Exercises and Quick Quizzes A page featuring the Warm-Up Exercises from the annotated Teacher's Edition and the Section Quizzes from the Teaching Suggestions of this Resource Book. Each page is printed in large easy-to-read type and can be used to create an overhead visual or used as a hand-out. Answers for the exercises and the quiz are provided at the bottom of each page.

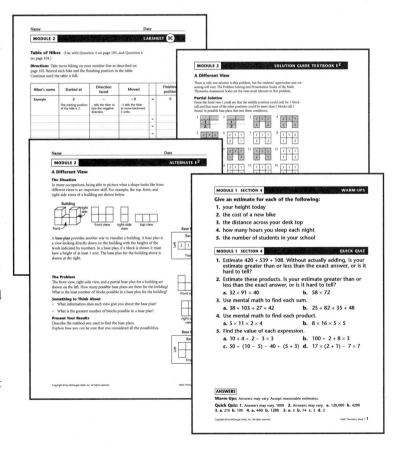

Practice and Applications One to two pages of additional practice for each section of the module. Answers are provided in the Answer section of this Resource Book.

Study Guide Two to three pages of Study Guide for each section of the module. These Study Guide pages feature key concepts, worked-out examples, exercises, and spiral review. They can be used for review and reteaching. Answers are provided in the Answer section of this Resource Book.

Technology Activity A technology activity related to the technology page of each module. Answers are provided in the Answer section of this Resource Book.

Assessment Assessment options include a mid-module quiz and two module tests, Forms A and B. Answers are provided in the Answer section of this Resource Book.

Standardized Assessment A page of standardized multiple-choice questions for each module. Answers are provided in the Answer section of this Resource Book.

Module Performance Assessment A Performance Assessment task for each module. Answers are provided in the Answer section of this Resource Book.

Answers Complete answers to all blackline masters.

Cumulative Test with Answers A cumulative test on both the modules of this Resource Book. Answers to the test follow immediately.

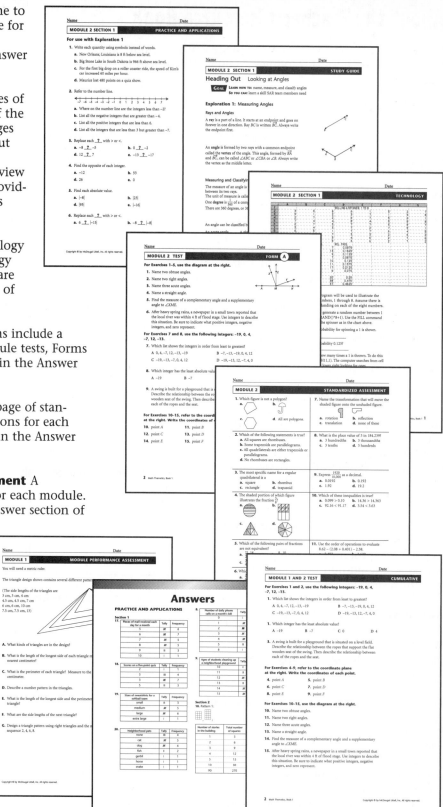

Table of Contents

Pacing and Assigning Homework

Pacing Chart

The Pacing Chart below shows the number of days allotted for each of the three courses: a Core Course, an Extended Course, and a Block Scheduling Course. The Core and Extended Courses require 140 days, and the Block Scheduling Course, 70 days. The time frames include the Module Projects, the Extended Explorations (E^2), and time for review and assessment.

Module	1	2	3	4	5	6	7	8
Core Course	19	18	18	18	16	18	17	16
Extended Course	19	18	18	18	16	18	17	16
Block Scheduling	9	9	9	9	8	9	8	9

Core Course

The Core Course is intended for students who enter with typical, or about average, mathematical skills. The daily assignment provides students with about 20–30 minutes of homework a night taken from appropriate Practice and Application (P&A) exercises. Exercises range from straightforward skill practice, to applications that require reasoning, problem solving, and making connections across mathematical strands. The assignments include all the exercises suggested for use as embedded assessment. Each section's Spiral Review (SR) is included, as are all Reflecting on the Section (ROS) problems. Because of all the elements to be covered, assignments for the one-day sections may take more time. Also, sometimes a lengthy Reflecting on the Section problem (or other essential exercise) may cause an assignment to run longer. These problems have been denoted with a star (*). In such cases, teachers may want to spread the assignment out over more than one day, or may wish to provide class time for students to complete the work.

Extended Course

The Extended Course is designed for students who enter with strong or above average mathematical skills. Daily assignments cover all the essential material in the Core Course, including the embedded assessment exercises, the Spiral Review (SR), and the Reflecting on the Section (ROS) problems. Assignments also contain more difficult problems, including all the Challenge (Chal) and Extension (Ext) exercises. As in the Core Course, each assignment is designed to be completed in about 20–30 minutes. Some Extension or Reflecting on the Section problems may cause assignments to run long. These longer problems are denoted by a star (*).

Block Scheduling Course

The Block Scheduling course is intended for schools that use longer periods, typically 90-minute classes, for instruction. The course covers all eight modules. The assignments range from straightforward application of the material to exercises involving higher-order thinking skills. Daily assignments are designed to provide about 40–50 minutes of homework, and to cover all the essential material in the Core Course, including the embedded assessment exercises, the Spiral Review (SR), and Reflecting on the Section (ROS).

Guide for Assigning Homework

The Guide for Assigning Homework appears on each module's opening pages.
The first chart suggests Core and Extended Assignments. The second chart
offers assignments and pacing for Block Scheduling.

Regular Scheduling (45 min class period)

Section/ P&A Pages	Core Assignment	Extended Assignment	exercises to note		
			Additional Practice/Review	Open-ended Problems	Special Problems
1 pp. 88–93	**Day 1:** 1–8, SR 19–28	1–8, SR 19–28	Sec 1 Ex Prac, p. 92; TB, p. 589	E^2, p. 93	E^2, p. 93
	Day 2: 9, 11–13, 15–16, *ROS 18	9, 11–13, 15–16, Chal 17, *ROS 18		ROS 18; Mod Proj 2	P&A 10, 14; Mod Proj 1–2
2 pp. 102–106	**Day 1:** 1–11, SR 20–29	3–6, 8–11, Chal 12, SR 20–29	Sec 2 Ex Prac, p. 106		
	Day 2: 13–17, ROS 19, Career 30	13–17, Chal 18, ROS 19, Career 30, Ext 32–34		Career 31	Career 31

Additional Practice/Review
Each section contains additional
support and practice for the
objectives:
- **Extra Skill Practice
  (Ex Prac)** A page for each
  section, including exercises
  for each day and a set of
  Standardized Testing or
  Study Skills exercises.
- **Practice and Application
  (P&A)** Exercises beyond the
  20–30 minute homework
  period, covering the same
  skills and concepts as the
  Core Assignment.
- **Toolbox (TB)** Teaching and
  practice for pre-book skills
  applied in this section or in
  upcoming sections.

Open-ended Problems
Included in this category are
exercises where students generate examples, create designs,
or use original ideas. The
Extended Exploration (E^2)
from each module appears here.
It is designed to provide a rich
problem solving experience,
with multiple approaches or
solutions. The listing may
include Reflecting on the
Section (ROS), Career
Connection (Career), Module
Project (Mod Proj), Study
Skills (St Sk), or Standardized
Testing (Std Test) exercises, as
well as other Practice and
Application (P&A) exercises
where appropriate.

Special Problems Exercises in
this category require extra time
or additional materials, such as
a calculator or a newspaper.
All Extended Exploration (E^2)
and Module Project (Mod Proj)
activities are listed, as well as
many Practice and Application
(P&A) exercises labeled Research,
Create Your Own, or Home
Involvement. (The E^2 and the
final Module Project questions
are listed with the sections they
follow.) Although Special
Problems are not included in
the Core Assignment, they are
accessible to all students.
Teachers may allot class time or
extra days for students to complete them.

Block Scheduling (90 min class period)

	Day 1	Day 2	Day 3	Day 4	Day 5	Day 6	Day 7	
Teach	Sec 1	Sec 2 Expl 1–2	Sec 2 Expl 3; Sec 3 Expl 1	Sec 3 Expl 2–3	Sec 4 Expl 1–2	Sec 4 Expl 3; Sec 5	Sec 6	**Allow 2 days** review/assess/projects
Apply/ Assess (P&A)	Sec 1: 3–12, ROS 15, SR 16–27	Sec 2: 2–11, 14–15 SR 33–38	Sec 2: 16–19, 22–25, 31, ROS 32; Sec 3: 2–4	Sec 3: 6, 8–10, 12, ROS 15, SR 16–33	Sec 4: 1–2, 4–5, 8, 10, 12, 15–16, 17–20, SR 43–46	Sec 4: 27, 30, 32, 34, 40 ROS 42; Sec 5: 1, 4, 6, ROS 9, SR 10–15	Sec 6: 1, 2, 5 ROS 7, SR 8–12	
Yearly Pacing	**Mod 1:** 9 days				**Remaining:** 61 days		**Total:** 70 days	

TEACHER'S RESOURCES FOR MODULE 3

MIDDLE GRADES

MATH*Thematics*

MODULE 3

Statistical Safari

- Planning and Teaching Suggestions, p. 3-8
- Labsheets, p. 3-50
- Extended Explorations, p. 3-67
- Blackline Masters, p. 3-70

MODULE 3

STATISTICAL SAFARI

Module Overview

Data about animals are used to explore techniques for displaying information visually and analyzing it numerically. There are opportunities to apply written computation skills, develop mental math and estimation strategies, and use a calculator, as well as to work with metric measurement. Students focus on such themes as fish sampling, dinosaurs, and the work of wildlife biologists in managing sheep populations.

Module Objectives

Section	Objectives	NCTM Standards
1	◆ Sort sets of data using a Venn diagram. ◆ Use benchmarks to estimate metric length and metric mass. ◆ Use appropriate metric units to measure length and mass. ◆ Multiply decimals mentally by special multipliers like 0.001 or 1000. ◆ Convert between metric units of length and between metric units of mass.	1, 2, 3, 4, 7, 8, 13
2	◆ Make predictions from a sample. ◆ Use mental math to find a fraction of a whole number. ◆ Model percents and write percents in fraction or decimal form. ◆ Use hundredths to rename fractions, decimals, and percents. ◆ Become familiar with common fraction/percent equivalents (halves, fourths, fifths, tenths).	1, 2, 3, 4, 5, 6, 10
3	◆ Interpret and make a bar graph. ◆ Find the range of a set of data. ◆ Interpret and make a line plot.	1, 2, 3, 4, 10
4	◆ Use mean, median, and mode to describe data. ◆ Write a fraction as a decimal by using a calculator to divide the numerator by the denominator. ◆ Choose the type of average most appropriate for a set of data. ◆ Round a decimal to a specific place value.	1, 2, 3, 4, 5, 7, 10
5	◆ Divide a decimal by a whole number including appending zeros. ◆ Use compatible numbers to estimate a decimal quotient. ◆ Use front-end estimation to estimate a whole number or decimal sum. ◆ Use trading off to find a whole number or decimal sum mentally.	1, 2, 3, 4, 6, 7
6	◆ Interpret and make a stem-and-leaf plot. ◆ Divide a whole number or a decimal by a decimal.	1, 2, 3, 4, 7, 10

Topic Spiraling

Section	Connections to Prior and Future Concepts
1	Section 1 presents Venn diagrams and metric length and mass. Mental multiplication by 0.01, 1000, and so on is used to convert between metric units. Venn diagrams are applied and decimal multiplication is taught in Module 4. Metric capacity is developed in Module 8.
2	Section 2 uses sampling to introduce fractions of a set. Mental math is used to find fractions of whole numbers. In Module 5 fraction multiplication is used. Percent is introduced with a 100-square grid. Equivalent fractions and the meaning of percent are used to convert between percent, decimal, and fraction form. Section 4 and Modules 4 and 8 extend to other methods.
3	In Section 3 bar graphs and line plots are made, interpreted, and compared. The range of a data set is defined. Bar graphs are revisited in the Module 8 work on misleading graphs.
4	Section 4 explores *mean*, *median*, and *mode* and when each is appropriate. In Module 8 students also consider when averages may be misleading. Students view a fraction as a division, divide with a calculator to write any fraction as a decimal, and round decimals.
5	In Section 5 students divide a decimal or a whole number by a whole number, annexing zeros as needed. Estimation is used to check that quotients are reasonable. Students use mental math and estimation strategies for addition as they explore the effect of extreme values on averages.
6	Section 6 explores stem-and-leaf plots and division by a decimal. Stem-and-leaf plots are used to find averages and are compared to tables. Book 2 Module 5 revisits stem-and-leaf plots.

Integration

Mathematical Connections	1	2	3	4	5	6
algebra (including patterns and functions)		179	192			228
geometry	161–168	179			214	226, 227
data analysis, probability, discrete math	159–160, 165–170	171–173, 177–181	**182–194***	**195–206**	**207–217**	**218–229**

Interdisciplinary Connections and Applications						
social studies and geography	166		189–190		215	
reading and language arts	158			195		
science	158–160, 166, 168, 170	171–173, 175, 177, 179	182–191, 193–194	195–198, 203	207–212	224–225, 230
home economics		178				
health, physical education, and sports			191	203–204		226, 230
architecture, music sales, publishing		178			214	226, 227

* **Bold page numbers** indicate that a topic is used throughout the section.

Guide for Assigning Homework

Regular Scheduling (45 min class period)

Section/ P&A Pages	Core Assignment	Extended Assignment	Additional Practice/Review	Open-ended Problems	Special Problems
			exercises to note		
1 pp. 166–170	**Day 1:** 1–7, SR 41–44	1–7, Chal 8, SR 41–44	Sec 1 Ex Prac, p. 170	P&A 7, Chal 8; St Sk 2, p. 170	
	Day 2: 9–14, 16–19, SR 45–47	9–14, 16–19, SR 45–47, Ext 48–56	P&A 15, 19		
	Day 3: 22–32, 34–36, ROS 40	20–32, 34–39, ROS 40	P&A 20, 30–31		P&A 33
2 pp. 177–181	**Day 1:** 2–6, 10–13, 17, SR 53–60	2–6, 10–13, SR 53–60	Sec 2 Ex Prac, p. 181; P&A 1, 7–9, 14–16	Std Test 2, p. 181	Mod Proj 1–5; Std Test 2, p. 181
	Day 2: 18–20, 25–27, 34–38, 40, 46–49, ROS 52	18–20, 25–27, 34–38, 40–42, 46, 49–50, Chal 51, ROS 52	P&A 21–24, 28–33, 39, 41–45, 50		
3 pp. 189–194	**Day 1:** 1–3, 6–7, 13, SR 23–32	1–7, 12–13, SR 23–32	Sec 3 Ex Prac, p. 193; TB, p. 591; P&A 4–5, 8–12	P&A 7	P&A 9
	Day 2: 14–17, ROS 22	14–21, ROS 22	P&A 18–21	P&A 16, 21; Std Test, p. 193; E^2, p. 194	Mod Proj 6–7; E^2, p. 194
4 pp. 203–206	**Day 1:** 1–5, 7, SR 30–38	1, 5– 7, Chal 8, SR 30–38	Sec 4 Ex Prac, p. 208; TB, p. 596; P&A 6	P&A 7	
	Day 2: 9–14, 18, 21, 22, 24, 26, ROS 29	9–14, 18, 21, 22, 24, 26, 27, ROS 29	P&A 15–17, 19, 20, 23, 25, 27		P&A 28
5 pp. 214–217	**Day 1:** 1–5, 7–9, 12, SR 34–44	1–5, 7–12, SR 34–44	Sec 5 Ex Prac, p. 217; P&A 6, 10, 11, 13–16		Mod Proj 8–9
	Day 2: 17–18, 24–26, 30–31, ROS 33	17–18, 24–26, 30–31, Chal 32, ROS 33	P&A 19–23, 27–29		
6 pp. 224–229	**Day 1:** 1–8	1–8, *Ext 38–41, SR 27–37	Sec 6 Ex Prac, p. 151, P&A 9–12		P&A 7–8
	Day 2: 13–17, 19, 23–24, ROS 26, SR 27–37	13–17, 19, 23–24, Chal 25, ROS 26	P&A 18, 20–22, Career 42–43	Std Test, p. 228	Mod Proj 10–13
Review/ Assess	Review and Assess (PE), Quick Quizzes (TRB), Mid-Module Quiz (TRB), Module Tests— Forms A and B (TRB), Standardized Assessment (TRB)				Allow 5 days
Enrich/ Assess	E^2 (PE) and Alternate E^2 (TRB), Module Project (PE), Module Performance Assessment (TRB)				
Yearly Pacing	**Mod 1:** 18 days	**Mods 1–3:** 55 days	**Remaining:** 95 days		**Total:** 140 days

Key: P&A = Practice & Application; ROS = Reflecting on the Section; SR = Spiral Rev; TB = Toolbox; Ex Prac = Extra Skill Practice; Ext = Extension; * more time

Block Scheduling (90 min class period)

	Day 1	Day 2	Day 3	Day 4	Day 5	Day 6	Day 7	
Teach	Sec 1 Expl 1–2	Sec 1 Expl 3	Sec 2	Sec 3	Sec 4	Sec 5	Sec 6	Allow 2 days review/assess/projects
Apply/ Assess (P&A)	Sec 1: 1–2, 4, 6–7, 9–14, 18–19, SR 41–47	Sec 1: 20–32, 34–39, ROS 40	Sec 2: 2, 10–13, 17–20, 25–27, 34–36, 38, 40, 46, 49, ROS 52, SR 53–60	Sec 3: 1, 2, 6, 7, 14–17, ROS 22, SR 23–32	Sec 4: 1, 5, 7, 9–14, 21, 22, 24, 26, ROS 29, SR 30–38	Sec 5: 1–5, 8, 9, 12, 17, 18, 24–26, ROS 33, SR 34–44	Sec 6: 1–8, 13–14, 17, 19, 23–24, ROS 26, SR 27–37	
Yearly Pacing	**Mod 3:** 9 days		**Mods 1–3:** 27 days		**Remaining:** 43 days		**Total:** 70 days	

Materials List

Section	Materials
1	10 animal cards from Labsheets 1A–1D, 10 index cards, 2 pieces of string each 3 ft long, gram scale, meter stick or metric ruler, Labsheets 1E and 1F and table of prefixes in Exploration 3
2	Labsheets 2A–2D, paper bag, 10 animal cards, base–ten blocks or pennies (optional), Project Labsheet A
3	10 animal cards, statistical graphing software (optional)
4	40 chips, calculator
5	Labsheets 5A and 5B
6	Labsheets 6A and 6B

Support Materials in this Resource Book

Section	Practice	Study Guide	Assessment	Enrichment
1	Section 1	Section 1	Quick Quiz	
2	Section 2	Section 2	Quick Quiz	
3	Section 3	Section 3	Quick Quiz, Mid-Module Quiz	Technology Activity Alternate Extended Exploration
4	Section 4	Section 4	Quick Quiz	
5	Section 5	Section 5	Quick Quiz	
6	Section 6	Section 6	Quick Quiz	
Review/ Assess	Sections 1–6		Module Tests Form A and B Standardized Assessment Module Performance Assessment	

Classroom Ideas

Bulletin Boards:
- pictures and information to match animal cards
- newspaper graphs and statistics
- Venn diagrams using student information
- chart of metric prefixes and their meanings

Student Work Displays:
- student-made graphs and line plots
- newspaper displays from the Module Project
- student reports from the E^2

Interest Centers:
- books on dinosaurs
- string, index cards, and animal cards for making Venn diagrams
- literature center with *The Phantom Tollbooth*, by Norton Juster

Visitors/Field Trips:
- biologist, paleontologist, veterinarian

Technology:
- Module 3 Technology Activity in TRB for PE, p. 185
- spreadsheet software

The Math Gazette
Statistical Safari

Sneak Preview!

Over the next four weeks in our mathematics class, we will be sorting and organizing data, finding fractions and percents, creating and interpreting graphs, exploring statistical averages, reviewing division of decimal skills, and making stem-and-leaf plots while completing a thematic unit on a Statistical Safari. Some of the topics we will be discussing are:

✗ characteristics of animals

✗ sampling trout populations

✗ maximum speeds of animals

✗ average sheep populations

✗ pet preferences

✗ dinosaur data

Ask Your Student

What benchmark can be used to measure one meter? (Sec. 1)

How can you use a sample to make predictions about a population? (Sec. 2)

When might you use a mean, a median, or a mode in real life? (Sec. 4)

What steps are important to remember when dividing decimals? (Secs. 5 and 6)

What can a stem-and-leaf plot tell you about a data set? (Sec. 6)

Connections

Literature:
Students will read an excerpt from *Savage Paradise,* by Hugo van Lawick, that describes a gazelle escaping a lioness in Tanzania. Your students might be interested in reading more about photo safaris.

Students will also read another excerpt from *The Phantom Tollbooth,* by Norman Juster. This excerpt explores the result of interpreting averages too literally. Students may enjoy reading the rest of the book and discussing it with you.

Science:
Students will learn benchmarks for metric measurements and how to convert between metric units. They may be interested in finding out how and why the metric system was developed.

Possible sources include encyclopedias and other reference books.

Students will compare and analyze the food requirements of different types of dinosaurs.

E² Project

Following Section 3, students will have about one week to complete the E² project, *What a Zoo!* Students will analyze data and make decisions regarding stocking a souvenir shop at a zoo.

Statistical Safari

Section Title	Mathematics Your Student Will Be Learning	Activities
1: Animal Facts	◆ using Venn diagrams ◆ estimating metric measures of length and mass ◆ converting between metric units	◆ sort animals according to their characteristics ◆ measure objects to estimate length and mass
2: Something Fishy	◆ finding a fraction of a whole number ◆ writing percents ◆ relating fractions, decimals, and percents	◆ make predictions by using samples ◆ use dot paper to find fractions of numbers ◆ begin Module Project, *Be a Reporter*
3: Amazing Animals	◆ constructing and interpreting bar graphs ◆ constructing and interpreting line plots	◆ create bar graphs and line plots ◆ use statistical software to create a bar graph ◆ work on Module Project ◆ use data about past sales to predict future sales
4: Animal Averages	◆ using mean, median, and mode to describe data ◆ choosing an appropriate average ◆ writing a fraction as a decimal ◆ rounding decimals to a particular place	◆ use chips to model human and animal behavior
5: The Perfect Pet	◆ dividing a decimal by a whole number ◆ estimating averages and using mental math	◆ model division of decimals with 10 × 10 grids ◆ continue work on Module Project
6: Dinosaurs	◆ making and interpreting stem-and-leaf plots ◆ dividing by a decimal	◆ complete the Module Project

Activities to do at Home

◆ Collect several different objects around the house and find their weights in metric units. Have a family member or another person match each object with its weight. (After Sec. 1)

◆ Look for the use of averages in newspapers or magazines. Decide which type of average you think is used. (After Sec. 4)

◆ When shopping for groceries or other items, use front-end estimation to estimate the total cost of the items. Compare the estimate with the actual total. (After Sec. 5)

Related Topics

You may want to discuss these related topics with your student:

 Wildlife reserves

 Journalism

 Population statistics

 Zoology

Section ① Sets and Metric Measurement

Section Planner

DAYS FOR MODULE 3

| 1 | 2 | 3 | 4 | 5 | 6 | 7 | 8 | 9 | 10 | 11 | 12 | 13 |

SECTION 1

First Day
Setting the Stage, *p. 158*
Exploration 1, *pp. 159–160*

Second Day
Exploration 2, *pp. 161–162*

Third Day
Exploration 3, *pp. 163–164*
Key Concepts, *p. 165*

Block Schedule

Day 1
Setting the Stage, Exploration 1, Exploration 2 through Question 16

Day 2
Exploration 3 (starting at Question 17), Key Concepts

RESOURCE ORGANIZER

Teaching Resources
• Practice and Applications, Sec. 1
• Study Guide, Sec. 1
• Warm-Up, Sec. 1
• Quick Quiz, Sec. 1

Section Overview

Students will begin a study of statistics in Module 3 by examining and sorting data. In Exploration 1, they will use a Venn diagram to help sort the data. No formal definitions of set and Venn diagram are given. Instead, students will develop an intuitive understanding of these key terms by separating the data into groups. Students will also develop an intuitive understanding of the relative size of metric units of length and mass. In Exploration 2, the focus is on estimating metric lengths. Students will use familiar lengths as benchmarks to estimate other metric lengths. Then, once students are able to associate a millimeter, a centimeter, and a meter with the lengths of physical objects, they will learn to convert between metric units. The metric prefixes, *kilo, hecto, deka, deci, centi,* and *milli,* are introduced as a tool for determining the relationships between metric units of length and mass.

SECTION OBJECTIVES

Exploration 1
• sort sets of data using a Venn diagram

Exploration 2
• use benchmarks to estimate metric length and metric mass
• use appropriate metric units to measure length and mass

Exploration 3
• multiply decimals mentally by special multipliers like 0.001 or 1000
• convert between metric units of length and between metric units of mass

ASSESSMENT OPTIONS

Checkpoint Questions
• Question 9 on p. 160
• Question 12 on p. 161
• Question 14 on p. 162
• Question 16 on p. 162
• Question 25 on p. 164

Embedded Assessment
• For a list of embedded assessment exercises see p. 3-13.

Performance Task/Portfolio
• Exercise 8 on p. 167 (challenge)
• Exercise 40 on p. 168 (journal)

SECTION 1 MATERIALS

Exploration 1
◆ 10 animal cards from Labsheets 1A–1D
◆ 10 index cards
◆ 2 pieces of string, each 3 ft long

Exploration 2
◆ gram scale
◆ meter stick or metric ruler

Exploration 3
◆ Labsheets 1E and 1F and table of prefixes in Exploration 3

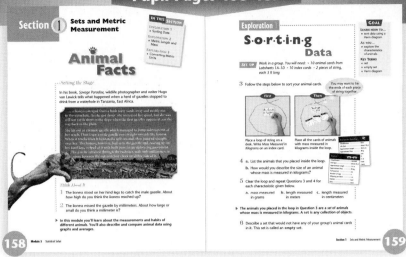

Setting the Stage

MOTIVATE

Have students read *Setting the Stage* as a class or individually. Locate Tanzania, East Africa on a map or globe and discuss with students what they know about the animals of that country or of Africa generally. Tell students that they will learn some facts about animals using mathematics that they know as well as some new mathematics.

Exploration 1

PLAN

Classroom Management This exploration is best performed in groups or pairs. Animal cards from Labsheets 1A–1D will be more manageable if printed on card-stock paper. To save time, consider having the cards cut out before class. Since the cards will be used throughout the module, students should store them in a place where they can easily retrieve them.

GUIDE

Developing Math Concepts
As preparation for their work with Venn diagrams later in the Exploration, students are asked to engage in an activity involving *sets*, especially intersecting sets. John Venn, an English logician of the late 19th and early 20th centuries, devised diagrams consisting of overlapping circles to illustrate logical statements of the form "All F are W," "Some F are W," "Some F are not W," and so on. For example. "Some F are W" was represented by two circles labeled F and W intersecting in a lens-shaped region that contained a small cross to indicate that the overlapping region

was not empty. In recent times, the term "Venn diagram" has been applied, as in this Exploration, to the intersection of sets of objects.

This modern application of Venn's circles has some relationship to its original purpose. For example, examining the diagram on page 160, one may correctly draw the conclusion that "some flying animals are white" (or "some white animals fly") from the appearance of "snowy owl" rather than a cross in the overlapping portion of the diagram.

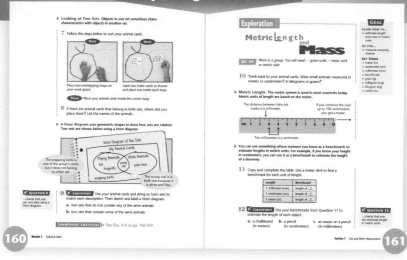

Exploration 1 continued

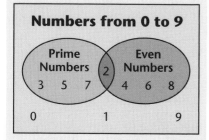

Classroom Examples
Use the Venn diagram to answer the questions below.

Numbers from 0 to 9

Prime Numbers: 3 5 7
2
Even Numbers: 4 6 8

0   1   9

a. Which number(s) are both prime and even?

b. Which number(s) are neither prime nor even?

Answer: a. 2   b. 0, 1, 9

Checkpoint *Question 9* is an informal introduction to the idea that some sets intersect (have members in common) and other sets do not. Sets that have no common members are called *disjoint* sets.

▌ **HOMEWORK EXERCISES** ▶

See the Suggested Assignment for Day 1 on page 3-13. For Exercise Notes, see page 3-13.

Exploration 2

┌─────────────────────────┐
│   **PLAN**   │
└─────────────────────────┘

Classroom Management This exploration is best performed by students in groups. Provide a gram scale and meter stick for each group, if possible. If there is only one scale, place it in a central location and explain how to use it. Students will be asked to think of some *benchmarks* that can play the role of reference objects against which to judge sizes in various length units in the metric system. Therefore, it may be advisable to prepare several objects in advance from which students may choose as their benchmarks, especially for the centimeter and millimeter. Some possibilities include a paper clip, a thick strip of cardboard, a stack of several sheets of paper, coins of several kinds, books of various sizes, and so on.

┌─────────────────────────┐
│   **GUIDE**   │
└─────────────────────────┘

Developing Math Concepts
Discuss with students the main advantage of the *metric system*, namely that it is far easier to convert from one metric unit to another metric unit than from one U.S. unit to another U.S. unit. In the metric system one

need only divide or multiply by 10 or a power of 10 to make a conversion. In the U.S. system, there are various conversion factors that have to be individually remembered, such as the fact that there are 12 inches in a foot and 3 feet in a yard. (Incidentally, you may wish to point out that a meter is a bit more than a yard, that is, about 39.37 inches.)

Checkpoint *Questions 12, 14, and 16* allow students to experience metric measures directly. Emphasize that students need not expect to obtain precise measures. The purpose of estimating the measures is to become familiar with the overall order of magnitude of the units of measures being used, to begin to feel comfortable using the units, and to know for which situations they are best suited.

Exploration 2 continued

Classroom Examples
Find the length of the butterfly in millimeters.

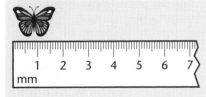

Answer: 1 cm 7 mm, or 17 mm

HOMEWORK EXERCISES

See the Suggested Assignment for Day 2 on page 3-13. For Exercise Notes, see page 3-13.

Exploration 3

PLAN

Classroom Management Each student will need a copy of Labsheets 1E and 1F. Record the answers to *Questions 17(a)*, *18(a)*, and *19* on the overhead projector or board to help students see a pattern. Consider having students complete *Question 19* in written form in order to be better able to check their understanding of the metric terms.

Customizing Instruction

Alternative Approach Conduct a class discussion of why most countries use metric units. (Have students prepare for the discussion in advance by learning how the metric system came into being.) In the discussion raise the question of whether the United States should convert to that system.

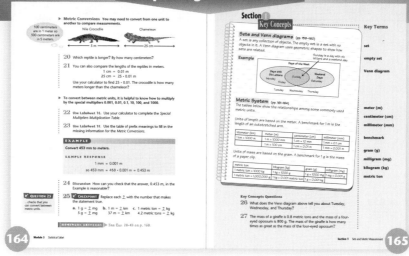

Exploration 3 continued

GUIDE

Developing Math Concepts
As students use Labsheet 1F, they may notice that some of the headings are in light face while others are in bold. This would be a good time to mention that "not all metric units are created equal." Measures that use the prefixes *hecto, deka,* and *deci* are encountered less frequently than are measures that use other prefixes.

Classroom Examples
Convert 25 km to meters.

Answer: 1 km = 1000 m
          so 25 km = 25 • 1000 m
                 = 25,000 m

Checkpoint In *Question 25,* have students explain how they arrived at their answers. You may want groups to report solutions. For students who have difficulty converting from one metric unit to another, ask them to explain what they are thinking. Point out that a larger unit has more of a smaller unit of the same kind so that, for example, you will use more millimeters than centimeters when measuring the length of a pencil.

▌HOMEWORK EXERCISES ▶

See the Suggested Assignment for Day 3 on page 3-13. For Exercise Notes, see page 3-13.

CLOSE

Closure Question Explain some advantages and disadvantages of using Venn diagrams and metric measurement.
Sample Response: Venn diagrams are useful to show how different characteristics or amounts of sets are related. However, numerical values are not displayed so that they can quickly be compared. Metric measurement is useful because its measurements are calculated in multiples of 10, which makes calculations and conversion of units easier. If you are not familiar with the meaning of metric measurements, understanding it at first may be somewhat of a challenge.

Customizing Instruction

Home Involvement Those helping students at home will find the Key Concepts on page 165 a handy reference to the key ideas, terms, and skills of Section 1. Students can also measure objects at home and bring the information to class to be shared verbally or displayed in the classroom.

Absent Students For students who have been absent for all or part of this section, the blackline Study Guide for Section 1 may be used to present the ideas. The Key Concepts on page 165 also provide a good overview of the key ideas, terms, and skills of Section 1.

Extra Help For students who need additional practice, the blackline master Practice and Applications for Section 1 provides additional exercises that may be used to confirm the skills of Section 1. The Extra Skill Practice on page 170 also provides additional exercises.

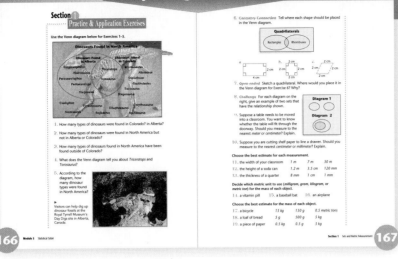

SUGGESTED ASSIGNMENT

Core Course

Day 1: Exs. 1–7, 41–44
Day 2: Exs. 9–14, 16–18, 45–47
Day 3: Exs. 22–32, 34–36, 40

Extended Course

Day 1: Exs. 1–8, 41–44
Day 2: Exs. 9–14, 16–18,
       45–47, 50–56
Day 3: Exs. 20–32, 34–40

Block Schedule

Day 19: Exs. 1, 2, 4, 6, 7, 9–14,
         18, 19, 45–47
Day 20: Exs. 20–32, 34–40

EMBEDDED ASSESSMENT

These section objectives are tested by the exercises listed.

Sort sets of data using a Venn diagram.

Exercises 1, 2, 4, 6, 7

Use benchmarks to estimate metric length and metric mass.

Exercises 12, 13, 18, 19

Use appropriate metric units to measure length and mass.

Exercises 9, 10

Multiply decimals mentally by special multipliers like 0.001 or 1000.

Exercises 21–24

Convert between metric units of length and between metric units of mass.

Exercises 28, 30, 32, 34, 36

Practice & Application

EXERCISE NOTES

Developing Math Concepts
Exs. 6–8 illustrate three possible relationships that can occur between two sets.

1. Two sets may *intersect.*
2. A special case of intersecting sets occurs when one set is a *subset* of another set. This happens if all of its elements are also elements of the other set.
3. Two sets may be *disjoint.*

Geometry Challenge After students have answered *Exs. 6* and *7*, have them consider relationships between other pairs of quadrilaterals. For example, which of the three diagrams that represent set relationships on page 167 best represents the set of rectangles and the set of parallelograms?

Challenge In *Ex. 8*, students are asked to give examples of two sets that have the two relationships shown. Encourage them to find not only geometric examples but some non-geometric one as well.

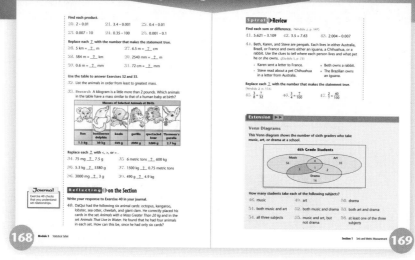

Practice & Application

Research *Ex. 33* mentions that a kilogram is a little more than 2 pounds. If a little more precision is needed, mention that a kilogram is about 2.2 pounds. If even more precision is required, then mention that a kilogram is about 2.2046 pounds. When used by people in daily life, for example at a European supermarket, it is common to refer to the weight of an item in "kilos."

Closing the Section

The students have acquired an understanding of how to use a Venn diagram to show relationships among elements of different sets. They have also learned more about metric units of measure. In the Reflecting on the Section exercise on page 168, students test their understanding of relationships between sets by analyzing how two sets of animals are related.

QUICK QUIZ ON THIS SECTION

Use the Venn diagram shown for Exercises 1 and 2. "W" is the set of white vegetables and "U" is the set of vegetables grown underground .

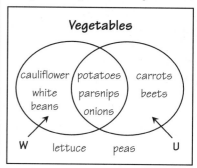

1. Which white vegetables do not grow underground?

2. What does the Venn diagram tell you about peas and lettuce?

3. Replace ____?____ with the number that makes the statement true:
   16 cm = ____?____ m

4. Replace ____?____ with <, >, or =:
   60 g ____?____ 0.6 kg

5. Which metric unit would you use to measure the mass of the family dog?

For answers, see Quick Quiz blackline on p. 3-70.

3-14

Section ② Fractions and Percent

Section Planner

DAYS FOR MODULE 3

`1 2 3 4 5 6 7 8 9 10 11 12 13`

SECTION 2

First Day
Setting the Stage, *p. 171*
Exploration 1, *pp. 172–173*

Second Day
Exploration 2, *pp. 174–175*
Key Concepts, *p. 176*

Block Schedule

Day 3
Setting the Stage, Exploration 1,
Exploration 2, Key Concepts

RESOURCE ORGANIZER

Teaching Resources
• Practice and Applications, Sec. 2
• Study Guide, Sec. 2
• Warm-Up, Sec. 2
• Quick Quiz, Sec. 2

Section Overview

In Section 2, students will study a population sample as a bridge to their study of fractional parts of whole numbers. Once students have chosen a sample from a population, they will use a fraction to describe the relationship between the sample size and the population size. Then they will be able to use the fraction to make a prediction about the sample size of a larger population of similar subjects. Students will practice finding fractional parts by counting and by using mental math.

Exploration 2 extends the discussion of fractional parts of whole numbers by relating the fractions to decimals and percents. Since conversions between fractions and percents require an understanding of equivalent fractions, the treatment of equivalent fractions in Module 2 on page 114 should be reviewed if necessary. A review of compatible numbers on page 50 of Module 1 before they begin the mental math activities in this section may also benefit the students.

Practice and Application Exercise 49 provides visual learners with a geometric model of percents.

SECTION OBJECTIVES

Exploration 1
• predict from a sample
• use mental math to find a fraction of a whole number

Exploration 2
• model percents, and write percents in fraction or decimal form
• use hundredths to rename fractions, decimals, and percents
• become familiar with common fraction/percent equivalents (halves, fourths, fifths, tenths)

ASSESSMENT OPTIONS

Checkpoint Questions
• Question 7 on p. 173
• Question 12 on p. 174
• Question 18 on p. 175

Embedded Assessment
• For a list of embedded assessment exercises see p. 3-19.

Performance Task/Portfolio
• Exercise 18 on p. 178
• Exercise 23 on p. 178
• Exercise 42 on p. 178 (interpreting data)
• Exercise 50 on p. 179
• Exercise 51 on p. 179 (challenge)
• Exercise 52 on p. 179 (oral report)
• Module Project on p. 180
• Standardized Testing on p. 181

SECTION 2 MATERIALS

Setting the Stage
◆ Labsheet 2A
◆ paper bag

Exploration 1
◆ Labsheet 2B
◆ 10 animal cards

Exploration 2
◆ Labsheets 2C and 2D

Practice & Application Exercises
◆ Labsheet 2C
◆ base–ten blocks or pennies (optional)

Module Project on page 180
◆ Project Labsheet A

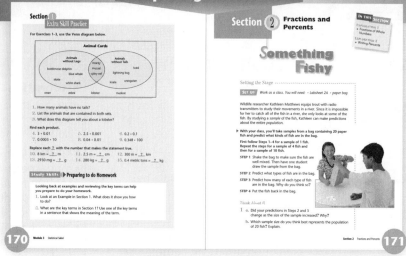

Setting the Stage

MOTIVATE

Tell the class that they are going to use a method actually followed by professional wildlife experts to estimate the fish population of a lake. It is a method based on sampling. For the class demonstration, you will need two copies of the fish cards on Labsheet 2A (card-stock paper works best) and a paper bag to hold the cards. Have students read *Setting the Stage* individually or in small groups. Everyone will need a piece of paper to record results. Choose a student to draw samples from the bag and another student to record the results of all the samplings. After the students read and record the results of the first sampling (one card), have students record their prediction for Steps 2 and 3. Have the students record their prediction again after a sample of 4 fish cards and again after a sample of 10 cards. While students are doing this, discuss the meaning of *sample size*. After the discussion, show the students all the cards and have them compare the sampling results with their predictions and also with the actual population.

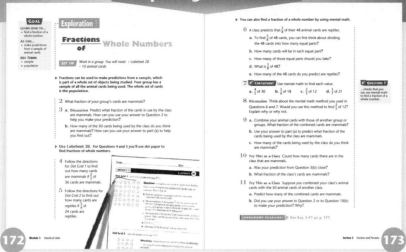

Exploration 1

PLAN

Classroom Management Since the total number of animal cards is 50, it is possible to have as many as five groups to conduct Exploration 1. Have each group randomly select 10 of the animals cards from Labsheets 1A through 1D. Each student should have a copy of Labsheet 2B in order to obtain experience in finding a fraction of a whole number. Each group will use its own set of 10 cards to predict what fraction of the 50 cards consists of mammals. When groups combine their cards with those of other groups in *Question 9*, monitor the care with which students are keeping a record of the results.

GUIDE

Developing Math Concepts
As students study the results of the activity of this Exploration, they should pay close attention to how closely the results of their own group compare to those of groups with which they combine their own results. They will certainly notice that the more groups that are combined, the closer the results approximate the actual number of mammals in the 50 cards. Of course, if all 50 cards were distributed among the groups, then the combined results of all groups must exactly equal the number of mammals.

Checkpoint As students use mental math to solve the four parts of *Question 7*, encourage them also to mentally check whether their answers are reasonable. For example, since 3 is a bit less than half of 7, it is reasonable to expect $\frac{3}{7}$ of 21 to be a bit less than half of 21. Thus, 9 not only is the correct answer, it is also a *reasonable* answer, since it is a bit less than half of 21.

HOMEWORK EXERCISES

See the Suggested Assignment for Day 1 on page 3-19. For Exercise Notes, see page 3-19.

Customizing Instruction

Alternative Approach After students have answered *Question 11* by predicting how many of the combined cards of two classes are mammals, have two classes actually combine their results. Then determine the effect of combining the classes. Students should notice an improvement in the agreement of the predictions with the actual number of mammals. Have students recall their earlier predictions in *Setting the Stage* when they increased the size of their samples first from 1 to 4 and finally to 10.

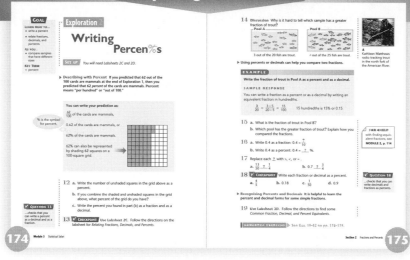

Exploration 2

PLAN

Classroom Management This exploration is best performed by students individually with periodic checking and discussions with the entire class. Every student will need a copy of Labsheets 2C and 2D.

GUIDE

Developing Math Concepts
The example on page 175 shows the fraction $\frac{3}{20}$ changed to a percent and a decimal. Have students devise their own examples, using a variety of denominators. They will quickly discover that some fractions are much easier to convert to percents than others. Eventually, they should notice what type of equivalent fraction is most easily converted to a percent or decimal (denominators that are 100 or a whole-number factor of 100).

Classroom Examples
Write the fraction $\frac{24}{25}$ as a percent and as a decimal.

Answer: $\frac{24}{25} = \frac{24 \cdot 4}{25 \cdot 4}$

$\qquad = \frac{96}{100}$

96 hundredths is 96% or 0.96.

Comparing Fractions In *Question 17*, many students will need a hint to help them compare the fractions. Remind them that if two fractions have the same denominator, then the fraction with the greater numerator is the greater fraction. For part *(b)*, suggest that they write 0.7 as a fraction first.

Recognizing Percents and Decimals As students work on Labsheet 2D (*Question 19*), encourage them to memorize the percent equivalents of the fractions on the labsheet if they have not done so already.

Checkpoint The four parts of *Question 18* can all be solved using the method of the Example on page 175. For part *(d)*, you can point out that if students first rewrite 0.9 as 0.90 and then change it to a fraction with a denominator of 100, then the solution will be a little bit faster than if they first write 0.9 as a fraction with a denominator of 10 .

HOMEWORK EXERCISES

See the Suggested Assignment for Day 2 on page 3-19. For Exercise Notes, see page 3-19.

CLOSE

Closure Question State two real-life situations where you would need to find fractions of whole numbers and two real-life situations where you need to relate percents and decimals or percents and fractions.

Sample Response: Fractions of whole numbers: altering a recipe or building a scale model; percents and decimals or fractions: displaying data in a book or report, or calculating a percent discount in a store

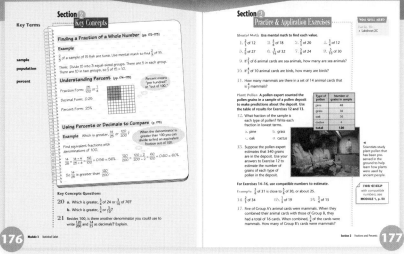

SUGGESTED ASSIGNMENT

Core Course

Day 1: Exs. 2–6, 10–13, 17, 53–60

Day 2: Exs. 18–20, 25–27, 34–38, 40, 46–49, 52

Extended Course

Day 1: Exs. 2–6, 10–13, 53–60

Day 2: Exs. 18–20, 25–27, 34–38, 40–42, 49–52

Block Schedule

Day 21: Exs. 2, 10–13, 17–20, 25–27, 34–36, 38, 40, 46, 49, 52–60

EMBEDDED ASSESSMENT

These section objectives are tested by the exercises listed.

Predict from a sample.

Exercises 12, 13

Use mental math to find a fraction of a whole number.

Exercises 2, 10, 11

Model percents, and write percents in fraction or decimal form.

Exercises 18–20

Use hundredths to rename fractions, decimals, and percents.

Exercises 25–27, 34, 36, 40

Learn common fraction/percent equivalents. (halves, 4ths, 5ths, 10ths)

Exercises 38, 40, 46, 49

Practice & Application

EXERCISE NOTES

Developing Math Concepts In *Exs. 1–8*, students use mental math to find the products of fractions and whole numbers. Encourage them to use whatever approach that they find easiest. For some students this may not always mean first dividing the whole number by the denominator of the fraction and then multiplying by the numerator. For example, some students may find it easier to do *Ex. 8* by first mentally changing $\frac{5}{10}$ to $\frac{1}{2}$ or to 0.5 before multiplying.

Customizing Instruction

Home Involvement Those helping students at home will find the Key Concepts on page 176 a handy reference to the key ideas, terms, and skills of Section 2.

Absent Students For students who have been absent for all or part of this section, the blackline Study Guide for Section 2 may be used to present the ideas. The Key Concepts on page 176 also provide a good overview of the key ideas, terms, and skills of Section 2.

Extra Help For students who need additional practice, the blackline Practice and Applications for Section 2 provides additional exercises that may be used to confirm the skills of Section 2. The Extra Skill Practice on page 181 also provides additional exercises.

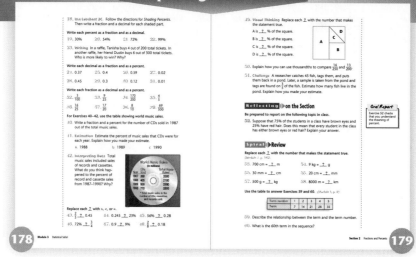

Practice & Application

Developing Math Concepts
Exs. 43–48 can each be solved in more than one way, since all that is required is to determine the greater number. The simplest way will usually be to change both numbers to a fraction with a common denominator, usually 100. Remind students that in a true inequality, the tip of the inequality symbol points to the lesser number.

Challenge *Ex. 51* asks students to estimate the number of fish in the pond when it is known that the relationship of the 45 tagged fish to the total number of fish is probably in the ratio of 3 to 5. The natural approach to this problem would be to set up a proportion but students have not yet learned how to work with this method of solving problems. However, the problem can be solved by using "common sense." If 45 represents $\frac{3}{5}$ of the total number of fish, then $\frac{1}{5}$ of the fish must be represented by $\frac{1}{3}$ of 45, or 15 fish. Next, find the fraction that represents all the fish. This is $5 \times \frac{1}{5}$, or $\frac{5}{5}$. So, the total number of fish must be 5×15, or 75 fish.

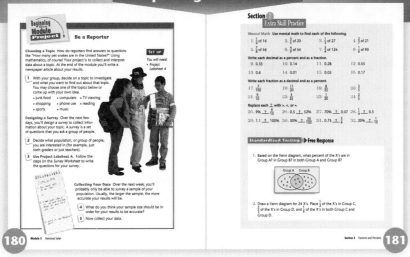

You may want to create a bulletin board with information for working on this module project. This could be a working display in which items are added as they are discussed during the module. The completed display might contain the project pages 180, 192, 216, and 229, examples of newspaper articles, a list of what makes a good article, and possible topics to investigate. Have students recall the importance of having a suitably large sample. You may want to set a minimum number for the sample size. It is useful to have a schedule for students to adhere to. Post the tasks and dates for completion on the project bulletin board. Periodically check students' progress.

Closing the Section

Students have used simulation sampling, dot grids, and 10×10 grids to model fractions, decimals, and percents. First, they learned the importance of having an adequate sample size as they conducted the simulation of a fish-tagging activity. They applied what they learned to a similar activity involving the number of mammals represented on their collection of animal cards. Having applied their ability to multiply a fraction and a whole number to that activity, they proceeded to learn how to represent a fraction as a percent. In the Reflecting on the Section exercise on page 179, they applied their knowledge to the interpretation of a survey of the hair color and eye color of students in a class.

QUICK QUIZ ON THIS SECTION

1. Use mental math to find $\frac{5}{6}$ of 180.

2. Write as a fraction in lowest terms and as a decimal: 18%

3. Which is greater, $\frac{2}{3}$ of 78 or $\frac{3}{5}$ of 80?

4. Which is greater, $\frac{38}{50}$ or $\frac{222}{300}$?

5. Use the measurements on the figure to calculate what percent of the total area of the rectangle is in each of the regions A, B, and C.

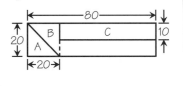

For answers, see Quick Quiz blackline on p. 3-71.

Section ③ Bar Graphs and Line Plots

Section Planner

DAYS FOR MODULE 3

| 1 | 2 | 3 | 4 | 5 | 6 | 7 | 8 | 9 | 10 | 11 | 12 | 13 |

SECTION 3

First Day
Setting the Stage, *p. 182*
Exploration 1, *pp. 183–184*

Second Day
Exploration 2, *pp. 186–187*
Key Concepts, *p. 188*

Block Schedule

Day 4
Setting the Stage, Exploration 1, Exploration 2, Key Concepts

RESOURCE ORGANIZER

Teaching Resources
• Practice and Applications, Sec. 3
• Study Guide, Sec. 3
• Assessment, Sec. 3
• Technology Activity, Sec. 3
• Warm-Up, Sec. 3
• Quick Quiz, Sec. 3

Section Overview

Students will continue their study of statistics in Section 3 by organizing their data in visual displays for easier interpretation. Key terms used are bar graphs, range, and line plot. Students will study the components of a bar graph, such as its title, numerical scale, and scale numbers, that make the graph easy to read. They will examine the effects of different scales on the appearance of a bar graph and how the range of data can help determine the scale. of bar graphs and line plots. As students practice drawing their own bar graphs and line plots, they will examine the data on the graphs and plots and draw inferences from them.

A review of rounding whole numbers can be found in the Toolbox on page 591. Some students may need to review this topic since these skills will be needed in this section.

SECTION OBJECTIVES

Exploration 1
• interpret and make a bar graph
• find the range of a set of data

Exploration 2
• interpret and make a line plot

ASSESSMENT OPTIONS

Checkpoint Questions
• Question 5 on p. 184
• Question 8 on p. 184
• Question 13 on p. 187

Embedded Assessment
• For a list of embedded assessment exercises see p. 3-26.

Performance Task/Portfolio
• Exercise 7 on p. 189 (interpreting data)
• Exercises 9–12 on p. 190
• Exercises 18–21 on p. 191
• Exercise 22 on p. 192 (research)
• Module Project on p. 192
★ Extended Exploration on p. 194

★ = a problem solving task that can be assessed using the Assessment Scales

SECTION 3 MATERIALS

Exploration 1
◆ 10 animal cards
◆ statistical graphing software for technology page

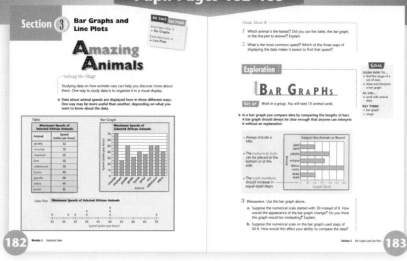

Setting the Stage

MOTIVATE

Tell the students that in this section they are going to organize information from their animal cards in ways that will help them to understand the animals better. For example, on page 182 the running speeds of various animals are presented in three formats. Have each student read and answer *Questions 1* and *2* in *Setting the Stage*. Then ask students to share their responses and discuss the three displays.

Exploration I

PLAN

Classroom Management This exploration is best performed by students working in groups. After students have created their bar graphs in *Question 6*, ask them to prepare a second bar graph limited to a category of their own selection, for example *The Lengths of Sea Animals* or *The Masses of Land Animals*.

GUIDE

Developing Math Concepts In *Question 3(a)* students are asked to discuss the effect of starting the numerical scale with 30 rather than zero. Discuss under what circumstances beginning a numerical scale with a number greater than zero can be justified and when it cannot be justified. (Sample response: It would not be justified in an advertisement for a product if the truncated bars mislead the reader or viewer about the product. It would be justified if it is done to save space in a presentation to a viewer who is not likely to be influenced by the shortened bars. This might be the case in a financial publication, for example.)

Common Error Some students are not careful about how they place the scale numbers on a graph. For example, students may write them between the tick marks rather below. Three other common errors are to omit the scale numbers entirely, to omit the descriptive labels for the two scales, or to omit the title of the graph.

MODULE 3 ◆ SECTION 3

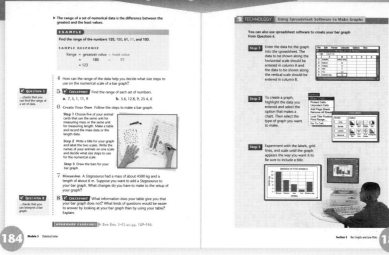

Exploration I continued

Developing Math Concepts

The *range* of a set of data is discussed on page 184. It is the simplest measure of how data are dispersed. There are more mathematically useful measures of dispersion than the range, such as the *standard deviation*. However, for many purposes, the range is perfectly serviceable and, unlike the more sophisticated measures, it is easily calculated and depends only on two easily identified numbers. It is, for example, a quick method of determining how a class as a whole did on a quiz. A disadvantage with the range is that occasionally an isolated item that is very high or low distorts the results. In that event, an "adjusted range" can be used that is based on all of the data except for two items: the very least and the very greatest.

Classroom Examples

Find the range of the numbers 48, 76, 91, 88, 79, and 62.

Answer:
Range
$$= \text{greatest value} - \text{least value}$$
$$= 91 - 48$$
$$= 43$$

Checkpoint For *Question 8*, students should be able to see the advantages that a table and a bar graph each has over the other. As an extension, ask students to write questions based on their bar graph and have other students answer the questions. The questions students write may reveal how much they have learned about bar graphs as well as their skill in formulating good questions.

HOMEWORK EXERCISES

See the Suggested Assignment for Day 1 on page 3-26. For Exercise Notes, see page 3-26.

Customizing Instruction

Technology If statistical graphing software is available, consider using it for class demonstration of some of the bar graphs. For example, with *Question 3*, you can demonstrate the effect of changing the scale so that it starts at 30 and then change the starting point of the scale repeatedly back and forth between 0 and 30. This should impress students with how the change from 0 to 30 alters the visual effect.

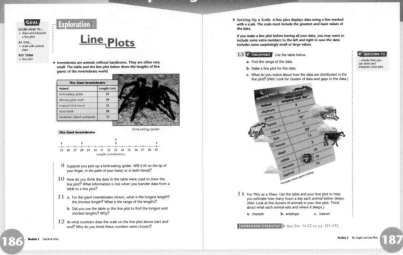

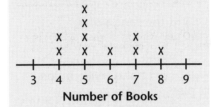

Exploration 2

PLAN

Classroom Management
Questions 9–12 can be completed by students in small groups or individually. In *Question 13(b)*, check whether students are drawing their lines wide enough to accommodate all of the data.

GUIDE

Developing Math Concepts
A line plot has some distinct advantages in displaying data. For example, the range is easily visualized as are the regions where most of the data tend to congregate. Some other advantages will become evident in Section 4, which covers measures of *central tendency*, such as the mean, median, and mode. The mode is particularly easy to read from a line plot and the median is relatively easy to read also.

Classroom Examples
Use the line plot below.

Number of Books Read
in One Month

```
            X
            X
   X    X        X
   X    X    X   X    X
 --+----+----+---+----+--
   3  4  5  6  7  8  9
```

Number of Books

a. What is the range of the data in the line plot?

b. What number is selected the most?

Answer: a. 4   b. 5

Checkpoint For *Question 13*, students may use graph paper. To ensure that the profile of the graph is not distorted, have them prepare each column of X's in a uniform manner by inserting each X between two horizontal grid lines.

HOMEWORK EXERCISES

See the Suggested Assignment for Day 2 on page 3-26. For Exercise Notes, see page 3-26.

CLOSE

Closure Question State the similarities and differences between bar graphs and line graphs.

Sample Response: Both graphs display numerical data, have a title, and have a scale. Bar graphs display numeric values for categories, but exact values are not always readable from the graph. Line graphs display exact values, but specific categories for the values are not displayed.

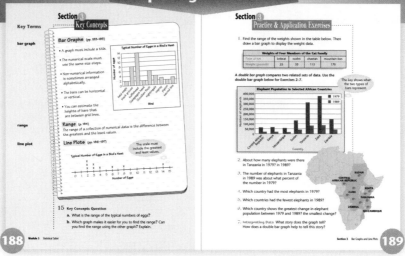

SUGGESTED ASSIGNMENT

Core Course

Day 1: Exs. 1–3, 6, 7, 13, 23–32
Day 2: Exs. 14–17, 22

Extended Course

Day 1: Exs. 1–7, 12, 13, 23–32
Day 2: Exs. 14–22

Block Schedule

Day 22: Exs. 1, 2, 6, 7, 14–17,
22–32

EMBEDDED ASSESSMENT

These section objectives are
tested by the exercises listed.

**Interpret and make a bar
graph.**

Exercises 1, 2, 6, 7

**Find the range of a set of
data.**

Exercise 1

**Interpret and make a line
plot.**

Exercises 14–17

Practice & Application

EXERCISE NOTES

Real-World Connection In
Exs. 2–7, students examine a
change in the elephant population in several African countries.
There was a significant decrease
in the number of elephants
there in the decade following
1979. In the years since 1989,
some African countries have sta-
bilized the situation. Have students find out which countries
have been successful in dealing
with the elephant issue and
which have not. Mention that
Asia also has large elephant populations. Have interested students find out how the elephant
population has changed in India
and other parts of Asia in the
last 10 years.

Customizing Instruction

Home Involvement Those helping students at home
will find the Key Concepts on page 188 a handy reference to the key ideas, terms, and skills of Section 3.
Students can also measure objects at home and bring
the information to class to be shared verbally or displayed in the classroom.

Absent Students For students who have been absent
for all or part of this section, the blackline Study Guide
for Section 3 may be used to present the ideas. The
Key Concepts on page 188 also provide a good
overview of the key ideas, terms, and skills of Section 3.

Extra Help For students who need additional practice, the blackline Practice and Applications for Section
3 provides additional exercises that may be used to
confirm the skills of Section 3. The Extra Skill Practice
on page 193 also provides additional exercises.

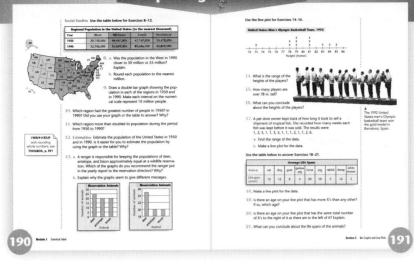

Practice & Application

Developing Math Concepts In *Exs. 14–16*, students examine the heights of the members of the United States Men's Olympic Basketball Team for 1992. In the line graph of these heights, one entry is significantly lower than any of the other entries. A solitary entry such as this that lies on the far left or far right portion of the line plot is called an *outlier*. Ask students what they think is the significance of the outlier in this instance. (Responses will vary. Sample response: Even though most of the players are well over six feet tall, it is still possible for a much shorter person to be a successful basketball player.)

Developing Math Concepts In *Exs. 19* and *20*, students are asked questions concerning how the entries are distributed in the line plot. You might anticipate the material of Section 4 by mentioning that the age that has more X's than any other is called the *mode* of the age data (the most frequently occurring age) and that the age of 10 years is called the *median* age of the animals (the age that is exactly in the middle of the list of ages when they are listed in increasing order).

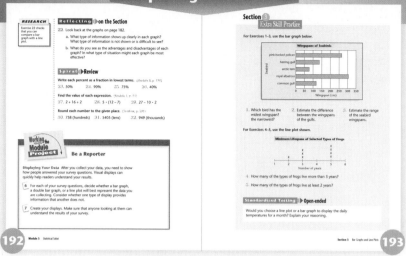

Students will be applying the skills from this section to continue their module project. Point out that each survey question will be represented separately and may even need its own special type of graph. Guide students in choosing an appropriate representation for their survey results. Have students list the advantages and disadvantages of each type of display for each survey question. Encourage each student to participate in the creation of a display.

Closing the Section

Students have successfully constructed bar graphs and line plots and learned to interpret each type of display. In the Reflecting on the Section exercise on page 192, they apply what they have learned by returning to the very first sets of visual displays of data that they encountered when they began the section. They are now able to use their new knowledge to make judgments about the relative effectiveness of the table, bar graph, and line plot of the maximum speeds of African animals.

QUICK QUIZ ON THIS SECTION

Year	Pounds of turkey eaten (per capita)
1980	8.1
1985	9.2
1990	13.9
1995	14.3

1. Use the data above to draw a bar graph.

2. What is the range of the data?

Median Length of Snake Species

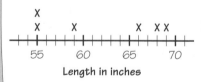

Length in inches

3. What is the range of the data in the line plot above?

4. How many snake species listed in the line plot have a length greater than 60 in.?

For answers, see Quick Quiz blackline on p. 3-72.

Section 4   Mean, Median, Mode

Section Planner

DAYS FOR MODULE 3

| 1 | 2 | 3 | 4 | 5 | 6 | 7 | 8 | 9 | 10 | 11 | 12 | 13 |

SECTION 4

First Day
Setting the Stage, *p. 195*
Exploration 1, *pp. 196–198*

Second Day
Exploration 2, *pp. 199–201*
Key Concepts, *p. 202*

Block Schedule

Day 5
Setting the Stage, Exploration 1,
Exploration 2, Key Concepts

RESOURCE ORGANIZER

Teaching Resources
• Practice and Applications, Sec. 4
• Study Guide, Sec. 4
• Warm-Up, Sec. 4
• Quick Quiz, Sec. 4

Section Overview

Section 4 opens with a discussion of the meaning of average. In the explorations, students will learn how either a mean, a median, or a mode can describe the average number in a data set. They will begin their study of averages by physically modeling the average of a set of data. The method used will recall a line plot, a topic discussed in the previous section. The mode and the median of a data set are defined.

The focus of Exploration 1 is to define and find means medians, and modes, and the focus of Exploration 2 is to determine which average best describes a set of data. Students will use calculators to express fractional parts of means as decimals, and to calculate means and medians. Decimals with many decimal places will require rounding.

SECTION OBJECTIVES

Exploration 1
• use mean, median, and mode to describe data

Exploration 2
• write a fraction as a decimal by using a calculator to divide the numerator by the denominator
• choose the type of average most appropriate for a set of data
• round a decimal to a specific place value

ASSESSMENT OPTIONS

Checkpoint Questions
• Question 9 on p. 198
• Question 20 on p. 201

Embedded Assessment
• For a list of embedded assessment exercises see p. 3-34.

Performance Task/Portfolio
• Exercise 9 on p. 203
• Exercise 19 on p. 204
• Exercise 28 on p. 205 (research)
• Exercise 29 on p. 205 (discussion)

SECTION 4 MATERIALS

Exploration 1
◆ 40 chips

Exploration 2
◆ 11 chips
◆ calculator

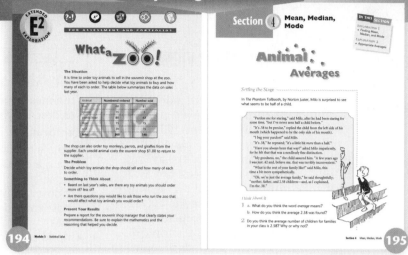

Setting the Stage

MOTIVATE

Read *Setting the Stage* as a whole class and then discuss *Questions 1* and *2* with the students. Instead of reading it yourself, you may wish to have two students read the excerpt with one student playing Milo and another student playing the child. Students may need help answering *Questions 1* and *2*, especially *1(b)* since it requires familiarity with the definition of *mean*, which is introduced in Exploration 1.

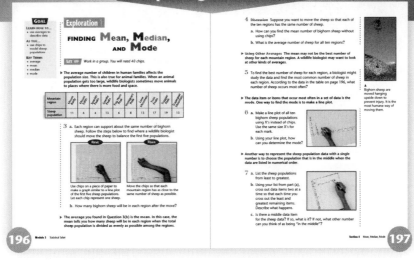

Exploration I

PLAN

Classroom Management The activities of this Exploration are designed to help students appreciate abstract ideas such as *mean* and *median* through concrete experience. For example, students are invited to level the heights of the columns of a line plot by redistributing chips. This procedure effectively conveys the idea of what the *mean* of a set of data is. Try to have students who are keen kinesthetic learners be among those in the group who actually move the chips into their new positions.

GUIDE

Developing Math Concepts
The *mean*, *median*, and *mode* are all *measures of central tendency*, that is, they are all "averages" of a set of data. The median is easier to calculate than the mean and is often more reliable than the mean as an indicator of what most people would expect of an "average." If the family incomes of five neighboring houses are $32,000, $28,000, $37,000, $30,000, and $280,000, then the median income, $32,000, probably provides a better idea of the financial condition of the neighborhood than does the mean, which is $81,400. In this example, there is no mode. Point out to students that a set of data may have no mode, one mode, or even more than one mode.

MODULE 3 ◆ SECTION 4

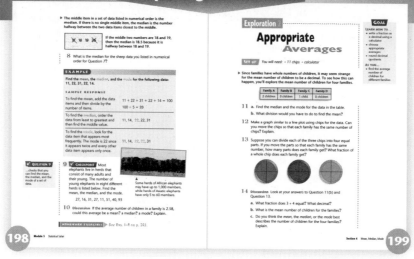

Exploration 1 continued

Classroom Examples
Find the mean, the median, and the mode for the following data: 11, 18, 12, 14, 12, 17.

Answer:
Mean:
11 + 18 + 12 + 14 + 12 + 17 = 84
84 ÷ 6 = **14**
The mean is 14.

Median:
11, 12, 12, 14, 17, 18
13 is halfway between the middle values of 12 and 14.
The median is 13.

Mode:
11, **12, 12**, 14, 17, 18
The mode is 12.

Checkpoint *Question 9* allows students to apply what they have learned about various kinds of averages. Devise a few extra examples that cover cases not already illustrated. For example present data in which the median is a data item (not the mean of two items) and that is not also a mode. Also, present a set of data that has no mode and another set of data that has two modes. An example of the latter follows: 10, 13, 13, 15, 21, 21, 26.

HOMEWORK EXERCISES

See the Suggested Assignment for Day 1 on page 3-34. For Exercise Notes, see page 3-34.

Exploration 2

PLAN

Classroom Management This exploration can be done by students working individually or in pairs. Each person or pair should have 11 chips to create a graph similar to the bighorn sheep line plot in Exploration 1. As students work on *Questions 11–15*, they may spend too much time trying to equalize the four parts in the graph of the distribution of three children over four families on page 199; this cannot be done using three chips. Have them concentrate on the five parts in the graph of the distribution of 11 children over five families (page 200) using 11 chips. This can be *approximately* done (two chips for each part). Keep the students moving to the realization that the use of chips as a model for representing the idea of "average" has served mainly to explain how an average family can have 2.58 children (on page 195) or 0.75 children (page 199) or 2.2 children (page 200).

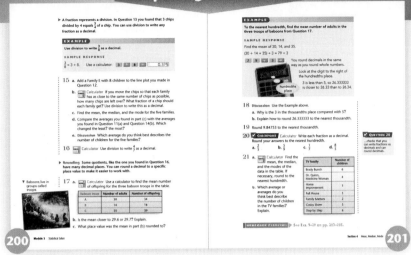

Exploration 2 continued

GUIDE

Classroom Examples
Use division to write $\frac{5}{16}$ as a decimal.

Answer:
$$\frac{5}{16} = 5 \div 16$$

| 5 | ÷ | 1 | 6 | = |

| 0.3125 |

Developing Math Concepts In this exploration, students frequently use their calculators to find decimal equivalents for fractions. In the Example on page 201, students will notice the repeat of the digit 3 in the number 26.333333. Ask students whether the 3 repeats indefinitely. Students can confirm that it does by dividing 79 by 3 using pencil and paper. Mention that they can show the decimal exactly by writing it as 26.333333... rather than as 26.333333. Ask them to study the calculator display when 4 is divided by 7 in **Question 16**.

Does the decimal repeat? A 10-digit display will show 0.571428571, which suggests that the decimal repeats. Have students compare this with the answer to **Question 20(c)**: 1 ÷ 7 = 0.14285714... . Help students to see that when *any* whole number is divided by 7 then the quotient contains the sequence 142857, which repeats indefinitely.

Classroom Examples
To the nearest hundredth, find the mean for 55, 89, and 71.

Answer:
$(55 + 89 + 71) \div 3 = 215 \div 3$

| 2 | 1 | 5 | + | 3 | = |

| 71.66666667 |

6 is greater than 5, so 71.66666667 is closer to 71.67 than 71.66. The mean is 71.67.

Checkpoint In **Question 20**, students should remember to round the number up if the block of digits to be dropped begins with a digit that is equal to or greater than 5.

HOMEWORK EXERCISES

See the Suggested Assignment for Day 2 on page 3-34. For Exercise Notes, see page 3-34.

CLOSE

Closure Question How are the mean, median, and mode alike? How are they different? Which values may need to be rounded off?

Sample Response: All three measure averages of data, or give you a value that approximates the center of the data values. The mean is calculated by adding the data values and then dividing by the number of items in the data set. You may need to round the mean, and it is not always one of the data values. The median is the middle value of the data when the values are ordered from least to greatest, or the average of the two middle values if the data in a set have an even number of values. The median does not need to be rounded off. The mode is the most frequently occurring data value, and may or may not exist in a data set. It is never rounded off.

MODULE 3 ◆ SECTION 4

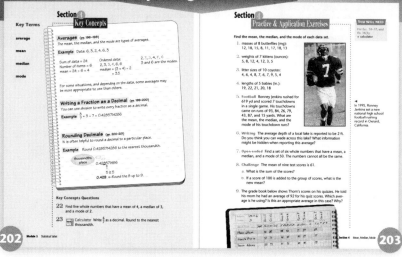

SUGGESTED ASSIGNMENT

Core Course

Day 1: Exs. 1–5, 7, 30–38
Day 2: Exs. 9–14, 18, 21, 22, 24, 26, 29

Extended Course

Day 1: Exs. 1, 5–8, 30–38
Day 2: Exs. 9–14, 18, 21, 22, 24, 26, 27, 29

Block Schedule

Day 23: Exs. 1, 5, 7, 9–14, 21, 22, 24, 26, 29–38

EMBEDDED ASSESSMENT

These section objectives are tested by the exercises listed.

Use mean, median, and mode to describe data.

Exercises 1, 5, 7

Write a fraction as a decimal by using a calculator to divide the numerator by the denominator.

Exercises 10, 11, 14

Choose the type of average most appropriate for a set of data.

Exercise 9

Round a decimal to a specific place value.

Exercises 21, 22, 24, 26

Practice & Application

EXERCISE NOTES

Ongoing Assessment For *Exs. 5* and *7*, you may want to suggest that students keep their answers for their portfolio work to show their progress in understanding the mean, median, and mode of a set of data.

Writing *Ex. 6* provides another opportunity to bring out the fact that an average does not summarize all that a person may need to know about a situation. Ask students what other statistical measure (studied in Section 3) might allow them to wade across the lake safely. (If a person knew that the *range* of the lake depths were, say, 3.2 feet, he or she might be able to wade across safely.)

Problem Solving In *Ex. 7*, students find a set of numbers, not all the same, that have a mean, median, and mode that are equal. Some students may solve the problem using trial-and-error. Discuss how they might use reasoning to solve the problem methodically.

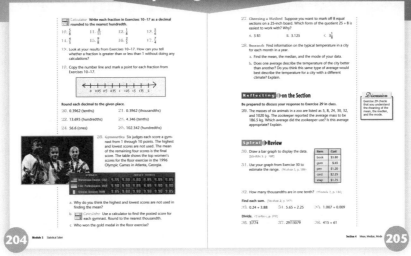

Practice & Application

Rounding Decimals In *Ex. 22*, check to see that students write their answer as 13.70 and not as 13.7. Remind them that since the rounding is to the nearest *hundredth* (not the nearest tenth), they must insert the zero to indicate the higher degree of precision.

Closing the Section

Students have learned that to use three measures of central tendency, or "averages." They engaged in "hands-on" activities that modeled real-life settings, for example the mean number of children in a typical family. They learned that for some situations the mean is the best average to use and sometimes another measure, such as the median, is the better choice. In the Reflecting on the Section exercise on page 205, they faced that decision directly, choosing the median over the mean as the more appropriate choice for this particular situation.

QUICK QUIZ ON THIS SECTION

Find the mean, median, and mode for the following data.

1. length of selected raccoons (inches): 26, 29, 30, 29, 36

2. weight of selected black bears (pounds): 280, 340, 410, 220, 500, 280

Write each fraction as a decimal rounded to the nearest hundredth.

3. $\frac{4}{7}$ 4. $\frac{5}{12}$

Round each decimal to the given place.

5. 100.419 to the nearest tenth

6. 42.6782 to the nearest thousandth

For answers, see Quick Quiz blackline on p. 3-73.

Customizing Instruction

Home Involvement Those helping students at home will find the Key Concepts on page 202 a handy reference to the key ideas, terms, and skills of Section 4.

Absent Students For students who have been absent for all or part of this section, the blackline Study Guide for Section 4 may be used to present the ideas. The Key Concepts on page 202 also provide a good overview of the key ideas, terms, and skills of Section 4.

Extra Help For students who need additional practice, the blackline Practice and Applications for Section 4 provides additional exercises that may be used to confirm the skills of Section 4. The Extra Skill Practice on page 206 also provides additional exercises.

Section ⑤ Dividing Decimals, Estimation, and Mental Math

Section Planner

DAYS FOR MODULE 3

| 1 | 2 | 3 | 4 | 5 | 6 | 7 | 8 | 9 | 10 | 11 | 12 | 13 |

SECTION 5

First Day
Setting the Stage, *p. 207*
Exploration 1, *pp. 208–210*

Second Day
Exploration 2, *pp. 210–212*
Key Concepts, *p. 213*

Block Schedule

Day 6
Setting the Stage, Exploration 1,
Exploration 2, Key Concepts

RESOURCE ORGANIZER

Teaching Resources
• Practice and Applications, Sec. 5
• Study Guide, Sec. 5
• Warm-Up, Sec. 5
• Quick Quiz, Sec. 5

Section Overview

Students will begin Section 5 by investigating the mean weights of small pets. This activity will introduce them to division of a decimal by a whole number. Students will first use a 10 × 10 grid to perform the divisions. Then they will use compatible numbers to check the reasonableness of a quotient and to estimate a quotient. Students will also explore division problems that have remainders.

As students continue to explore the weights of pets in Exploration 2, they will learn how to use two mental math techniques, front-end estimation and trading off, to estimate the sum of decimals. Students will learn how front-end estimation focuses on the digits with the greatest value and how trading off balances rounding up with subtraction.

As they estimate mean weights of pets, students will decide whether a mean, a median, or a mode represents the best average for a set of weights. This activity will prepare them for the Module Project in this section, which will require the students to choose the average that best summarizes the data from their surveys.

SECTION OBJECTIVES

Exploration 1
• divide a decimal by a whole number including appending zeros
• use compatible numbers to estimate a decimal quotient

Exploration 2
• use front-end estimation to estimate a whole number or decimal sum
• use trading off to find a whole number or decimal sum mentally

ASSESSMENT OPTIONS

Checkpoint Questions
• Question 6 on p. 208
• Question 8 on p. 209
• Question 10 on p. 210
• Question 14 on p. 212
• Question 16 on p. 212

Embedded Assessment
• For a list of embedded assessment exercises see p. 3-41.

Performance Task/Portfolio
★Exercises 27–29 on p. 215 (writing)
• Exercises 30–31 on p. 215 (estimation)
• Exercise 33 on p. 216 (visual thinking)
• Module Project on p. 216

★= a problem solving task that can be assessed using the Assessment Scales

SECTION 5 MATERIALS

Exploration 1
◆ Labsheets 5A and 5B
◆ base-ten blocks

Beginning the Module Project
◆ Project Labsheet A

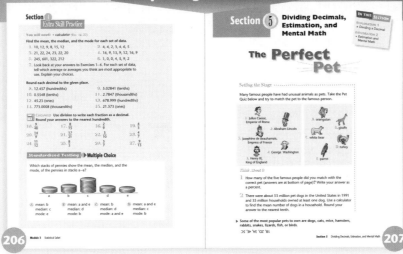

Setting the Stage

MOTIVATE

Before beginning the section, engage students' interest by informing them that they will be performing activities that involve pets. Start by having students read *Setting the Stage* individually or as a whole class and then answer the two questions. If you have them work as a class, you may find that it encourages students to talk about their own pets, especially if the pet is unusual.

MODULE 3 ◆ SECTION 5

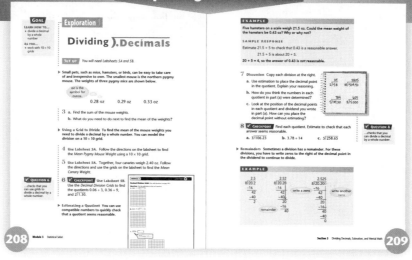

Exploration 1

PLAN

Classroom Management
Prepare Labsheets 5A and 5B for each student. This exploration is best performed individually. Students have been dividing by whole numbers already, most recently in Section 5 while calculating the mean of a number. Therefore, Labsheets 5A and 5B should go smoothly. They serve mainly to reinforce the meaning of what it means to divide a decimal by a whole number. Thus, it is important to verify not only that the answers to the labsheet exercises are correct but also that the grids are filled in properly.

GUIDE

Developing Math Concepts
The skill for estimating a quotient may take a good deal of practice but the time that students spend on it is worthwhile. Students who acquire good estimation skills develop "number sense" and consequently tend to make fewer errors. As a result, they gain a feeling of confidence that is based on accomplishment.

Spend some time on the division algorithm illustrated in the Example on page 209. The examples and exercises of this section and later sections focus on divisors and dividends that produce quotients that eventually *terminate*, that is, that have a zero remainder. Nevertheless, students will inevitably experiment with some divisors, such as 3, 6, 7, and 9, that can result in a quotient that does not terminate. Point out to students that, if this occurs, then they should stop work at a convenient place. Then they will have to decide whether to round up the last digit in the uncompleted quotient.

Classroom Examples
Six books on a scale weigh 11.4 lb. Could the mean weight of the books be 1.9 lb? Why or why not?

Answer:
Estimate 11.4 ÷ 6 to check that 1.9 is a reasonable answer.
11.4 ÷ 6 is about 12 ÷ 6.

12 ÷ 6 = 2, so the answer of 1.9 is reasonable.

Historical Note
Our current method of performing "long division" began in the fifteenth century. The first example of this method to appear in print was the division of 53,497 by 83 in Calandri's book on arithmetic published in 1491.

Classroom Examples
Find the quotient: 4)54.3

$$
\begin{array}{r}
13.575 \\
4\overline{)54.300} \\
-4 \\
\hline
14 \\
-12 \\
\hline
2\,3 \\
-2\,0 \\
\hline
30 \\
-28 \\
\hline
20 \\
-20 \\
\hline
0
\end{array}
$$

Answer: 13.575

Checkpoint *Questions 8* and *10* both make a point of having students verify that the results of their calculations are reasonable. Students may do this by rounding the divisor or dividend (or both), dividing and then deciding whether the actual quotient and the approximate quotient are approximately equal. Another approach is to round the divisor and the *quotient* and multiply back to see how close the result is to the dividend. For example the answer to *Question 8(a)*, 35.41, may be checked by rounding 35.41 to 35 and mentally multiplying by 3 to get 105, which is close to the dividend 106.23.

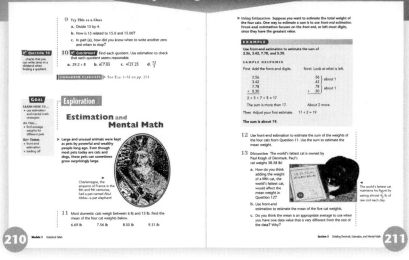

Exploration 1 continued

HOMEWORK EXERCISES

See the Suggested Assignment for Day 1 on page 3-41. For Exercise Notes, see page 3-41.

Exploration 2

PLAN

Classroom Management This exploration can be completed by students individually or in groups. Monitor students' progress by asking them whether their answers are exact or approximate. Help students understand the difference between the Example on page 211 and the Example on page 212. In the first Example, there is no attempt to arrive at an exact answer. In the second Example, the answer is exact because the "trading-off" method exactly compensates the two addends by the same amount.

GUIDE

Developing Math Concepts In *Question 13*, an issue raised in Section 4 is revisited: Which of the two measures of tendency is more useful, the mean or the median? If forced to choose, most people are probably better off with the median. It is easier to determine than the mean and, by definition, the median is always found right where you want it to be, in the middle of the other data items. Furthermore, in most situations of practical importance, the mean and the median turn out to have about the same value. Professional mathematicians usually prefer the mean, since it is easier to work with in the statistical formulas, but for most people, the median is the more practical choice.

Classroom Examples

Use front-end estimation to estimate the sum of 7.34, 6.62, 4.91, and 8.86.

Answer:

First Add the front-end digits.

$$7.34$$
$$6.62$$
$$4.91$$
$$+ \ 8.86$$

$$7 + 6 + 4 + 8 = 25$$
The sum is more than 25.

Next Look at what is left.

.34	about 1
.62	
.91	about 1
+ .86	about 1

About 3 more.

Then Adjust your first estimate.
$$25 + 3 = 28$$
The sum is about 28.

MODULE 3 ◆ SECTION 5

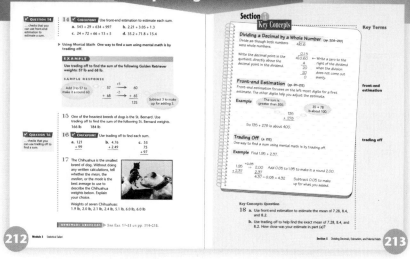

Exploration 2 continued

Checkpoint In *Questions 14* and *16*, students show whether they can use front-end estimation and trading off to find the sum of two or three numbers. In *Question 14(a)*, some students may attempt to use 540, 20, 630, and 990 as the starting point for the front-end estimation (instead of 500, 600, and 900), since the Example on page 211 does not provide guidance on the issue. For that reason, you may wish to have students do parts *(b)–(d)* first.

Classroom Examples
Use trading off to find the sum of the following weights: 122 lb and 143 lb.

Answer:

$$
\begin{array}{rcl}
122 - 2 & \rightarrow & 120 \\
+\,143 + 2 & \rightarrow & +\,145 \\
\hline
& & 265
\end{array}
$$

▶ **HOMEWORK EXERCISES**

See the Suggested Assignment for Day 2 on page 3-41. For Exercise Notes, see page 3-41.

CLOSE

Closure Question Why are estimation and mental math important when dividing a decimal?

Sample Response: When dividing a decimal, the answer is also a decimal. You can use estimation and mental math to check that your answer is reasonable.

Customizing Instruction

Alternative Approach Have students create a list of numbers for other students or groups to practice front-end estimation. Students can then explain how they went about performing the estimation.

Home Involvement Those helping students at home will find the Key Concepts on page 213 a handy reference to the key ideas, terms, and skills of Section 5. Students can also measure objects at home and bring the information to class to be shared verbally or displayed in the classroom.

Absent Students For students who have been absent for all or part of this section, the blackline Study Guide for Section 5 may be used to present the ideas. The Key Concepts on page 213 also provide a good overview of the key ideas, terms, and skills of Section 5.

Extra Help For students who need additional practice, the blackline Practice and Applications for Section 5 provides additional exercises that may be used to confirm the skills of Section 5. The Extra Skill Practice on page 217 also provides additional exercises.

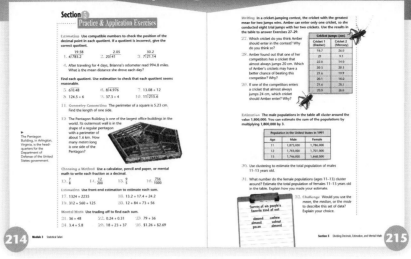

SUGGESTED ASSIGNMENT

Core Course

Day 1: Exs. 1–5, 7–9, 12, 34–44
Day 2: Exs. 17, 18, 24–26, 30, 31, 33

Extended Course

Day 1: Exs. 1–5, 7–12, 34–44
Day 2: Exs. 17, 18, 24–26, 30–33

Block Schedule

Day 24: Exs. 1–5, 8, 9, 17, 18, 24–26, 33–44

EMBEDDED ASSESSMENT

These section objectives are tested by the exercises listed.

Divide a decimal by a whole number including appending zeros.

Exercises 4, 5, 8, 9, 12

Use compatible numbers to estimate a decimal quotient.

Exercises 1–3

Use front-end estimation to estimate a whole number or decimal sum.

Exercises 17, 18

Use trading off to find a whole number or decimal sum mentally.

Exercises 24–26

Practice & Application

EXERCISE NOTES

Estimation In *Ex. 4*, students are asked to find the mean distance traveled in 4 days. Even though the exercise is perfect for using estimation, there was no instruction to use estimation either as a check or otherwise. Ask students by a show of hands how many of them used estimation to help solve the problem even though they were not required to do so. This will give an indication of which students really accept estimation as an integral part of the process of calculation.

Ongoing Assessment For *Exs. 10, 20,* and *26* you may wish to suggest that students keep their answers for their portfolio work to show their progress in understanding division of decimals, front-end estimation, and mental math.

Choosing a Method In *Exs. 13–16,* encourage students first to use mental math, if possible, then to check their answer with pencil and paper, and finally with a calculator.

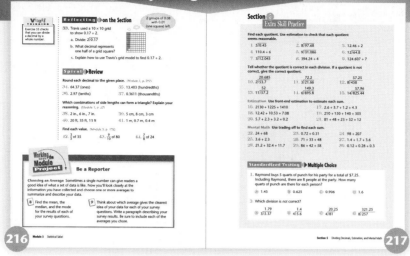

You should mention to students that they need answer Project Questions 8 and 9 only for survey results that are numbers. However, the paragraph that they write should cover all of the survey results, both numerical and non-numerical.

Closing the Section

Students have used the weights of house pets as a starting point for learning several important skills. They began by dividing decimals by whole numbers to obtain the mean weights of three or four animals. As they did so, they continued their work on estimation and mental math that they began in Module 1. Finally, in the Reflecting on the Section exercise on page 216, they extended what they learned about dividing decimals to a grid model in which they needed to interpret the meaning of half a grid square.

QUICK QUIZ ON THIS SECTION

Find each quotient.

1. $8\overline{)211.36}$ 2. $3\overline{)7.83}$

3. Use front-end estimation to estimate the sum:
$1.78 + 15.32 + 20.81$

4. Use trading off to find the sum:
$$\begin{array}{r} 132 \\ + \ 98 \\ \hline \end{array}$$

5. Write as a decimal: $\frac{123}{300}$

6. Selena got $30 for baby-sitting 8 hours one Saturday night. How much does she get paid per hour?

For answers, see Quick Quiz blackline on p. 3-74.

Section 6 — Stem-and-Leaf Plots and Dividing by a Decimal

Section Planner

DAYS FOR MODULE 3

1 2 3 4 5 6 7 8 9 10 11 **12 13**

SECTION 6

First Day
Setting the Stage, *p. 218*
Exploration 1, *pp. 219–220*

Second Day
Exploration 2, *pp. 221–222*
Key Concepts, *p. 223*

Block Schedule

Day 7
Setting the Stage, Exploration 1,
Exploration 2, Key Concepts

RESOURCE ORGANIZER

Teaching Resources
- Practice and Applications, Sec. 6
- Study Guide, Sec. 6
- Assessment, Sec. 6
- Warm-Up, Sec. 6
- Quick Quiz, Sec. 6

Section Overview

In Section 6, Module 3's final connection between statistics and decimals will be presented. The key concepts are stem-and-leaf plots and dividing by decimal. At this point, students should understand how the range of a data set affects its average. They will see how a stem-and-leaf plot shows the spread of a wide range of data. Attention will be called to the fact that a stem-and-leaf plot displays only data. The data labels included in a table are lost when the plot is constructed. Students will interpret stem-and-leaf plots to determine the range, the mode, and the median of the plotted data.

In Exploration 2, division grids will help students find the quotient of two decimals. The students will compare related quotients, looking for a pattern that will help them determine a method for dividing a decimal or a whole number by a decimal.

The Extension exercise on page 227 will introduce students to back-to-back stem and leaf plots for comparing two sets of related data.

SECTION OBJECTIVES

Exploration 1
- interpret and make a stem-and-leaf plot

Exploration 2
- divide a whole number or a decimal by a decimal

ASSESSMENT OPTIONS

Checkpoint Questions
- Question 7 on p. 220
- Question 10 on p. 221
- Question 14 on p. 224

Embedded Assessment
- For a list of embedded assessment exercises see p. 3-47.

Performance Task/Portfolio
- Exercises 4–8 on p. 224 (writing)
- Exercise 26 on p. 226 (journal)
- ★ Standardized Testing on p. 228
- ★ Module Project on p. 229

★ = a problem solving task that can be assessed using the Assessment Scales

SECTION 6 MATERIALS

Exploration 1	Exploration 2
◆ Labsheet 6A	◆ Labsheet 6B

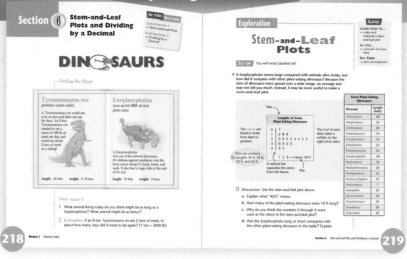

Setting the Stage

MOTIVATE

Most students do not need to be motivated to learn information about dinosaurs. Tell students that they will be studying the sizes and weights of several dinosaurs and organizing that information in a form that is easy to follow. After students have answered *Questions 1* and *2*, ask them what they think is the largest land or sea animal alive today. (The blue whale is the largest animal that has ever lived. Blue whales have been known to reach 100 feet in length and to weigh as much as 120 tons. However, in recent times whales even as heavy as 80 tons are now rather rare.)

Help students with the pronunciation of *Euoplocephalus* (Yoo-o-plo-SEF-a-lus) and *Tyrannosaurus rex* (Ti-ran-o-SOR-us rex).

Exploration 1

PLAN

Classroom Management Since students are probably not familiar with stem-and-leaf plots, this exploration is best performed with the entire class. Each student should have his or her own copy of Labsheet 6A. Help students to prepare their stem-and-leaf plots of plant-eating dinosaurs by stressing the need to keep track of their table entries. Stress the importance of using pencils of different colors (or using different marks) as students move from one stem to another. Some students may be more successful if they prepare each stem in two stages. The first stage would be to write the leaves in the order in which they appear in the table. The second would be to reorder the leaves from least to greatest.

GUIDE

Developing Math Concepts
After discussing *Question 3* with the students, have them practice reading the plot. Ask questions such as "What does the zero after the 2-stem mean?" Emphasize the ease with which the modes and median of the dinosaur weights are found after the data have been transferred to a stem-and-leaf plot.

Classroom Examples
Use the stem-and-leaf-plot below to answer the questions.

**Number of Miles
Driven on Vacation**

```
50 | 1 2 6
49 | 0
48 | 3 3
47 | 1 1 1 2 7 9
46 | 2 3 5
45 |
44 | 1 4
```

44 | 1 → means 441 mi

a. Find the median and the mode of the set of data.
b What is the range of the data?

Answer: a. 471; 471   b. 65

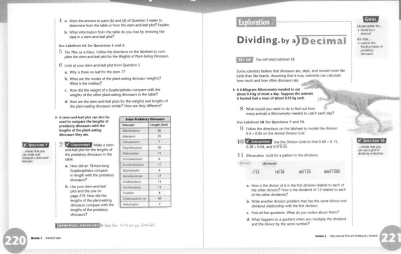

Exploration I continued

Common Error Regarding *Question 6(a)*, some students may be bothered by the fact that there is no stem for 1. They may want to "fill the gap" with a stem of 1 followed by a leaf of 0 "to show that there is nothing there." Point out that doing so would actually introduce the data item 1.0, which does not exist. Mention that there is no need to fill the gap between the stems 0 and 2.

Checkpoint If students understand the process for constructing a stem-and-leaf plot, they will be able to complete *Question 7* with few questions or none at all.

HOMEWORK EXERCISES

See the Suggested Assignment for Day 1 on page 3-47. For Exercise Notes, see page 3-47.

Exploration 2

PLAN

Classroom Management
Prepare Labsheet 6B for each student. Provide graph paper or paper with 10×10 grids for additional practice in modeling division by a decimal.

GUIDE

Background Information The small animals that the *Microvenator* hunted were not composed entirely of edible material. So, the *Microvenator* would probably need to capture more than 8 such animals to satisfy its minimum daily requirement of food.

Developing Math Concepts
As you discuss *Question 11* with the students, you may want to bring out the point of the discussion by rewriting the division problems as equivalent improper fractions, that is as:
$$\frac{12}{6}, \frac{12 \times 3}{6 \times 3}, \frac{12 \times 10}{6 \times 10}, \text{ and } \frac{12 \times 100}{6 \times 100}.$$
This shows that to maintain the value of the quotient (or of the fraction), the dividend and divisor must be multiplied by the same number, just as the numerator and denominator of a fraction must be multiplied by the same number.

Classroom Examples
Find $0.04 \overline{)2.62}$.

$0.04 \overline{)2.62} \rightarrow 4\overline{)262.0}$
$\times 100 \quad \times 100$

Answer: $\dfrac{65.5}{4\overline{)262.0}}$

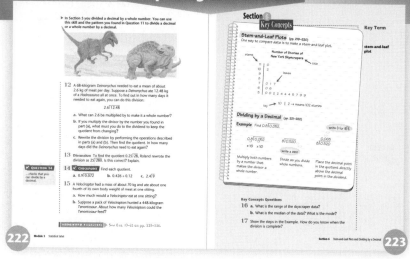

Exploration 2 continued

Checkpoint *Questions 10* and *14* ask students to divide a decimal by a decimal, first with the aid of a division grid and then without. Monitor closely the students' work on the lead-in question, *Question 9*. They may need guidance in understanding that 0.4 of the grid is 40 grid squares, that is, forty hundredths, or 0.40 of the grid. Then help them see that 0.05 is represented by 5 grid squares. Dividing the shaded area into 8 equal-sized groups should then quickly follow.

HOMEWORK EXERCISES

See the Suggested Assignment for Day 2 on page 3-47. For Exercise Notes, see page 3-47.

CLOSE

Closure Question Compare reading a stem-and-leaf plot with reading a line plot, and dividing by a decimal with dividing a decimal. How are they alike? How are they different?

Sample Response: Both stem-and-leaf plots and line plots display data so that the range, median, and mode are relatively easy to find. A stem-and-leaf plot is usually more useful with a wider range of data values. In both plots, the category in which each data value belongs is lost. When dividing by a decimal, the first step is to multiply the dividend and the divisor by a number that makes the divisor a whole number. After that, the two processes are the same.

Customizing Instruction

Home Involvement Those helping students at home will find the Key Concepts on page 223 a handy reference to the key ideas, terms, and skills of Section 6. Students can also measure objects at home and bring the information to class to be shared verbally or displayed in the classroom.

Absent Students For students who have been absent for all or part of this section, the blackline Study Guide for Section 6 may be used to present the ideas. The Key Concepts on page 223 also provide a good overview of the key ideas, terms, and skills of Section 6.

Extra Help For students who need additional practice, the blackline Practice and Applications for Section 6 provides additional exercises that may be used to confirm the skills of Section 6. The Extra Skill Practice on page 228 also provides additional exercises.

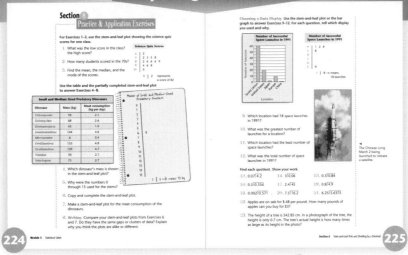

SUGGESTED ASSIGNMENT

Core Course

Day 1: Exs. 1–8
Day 2: Exs. 13–17, 19, 23, 24, 26–37

Extended Course

Day 1: Exs. 1–5, 7, 8, 27–33
Day 2: Exs. 13–17, 19, 23–26, 34–41

Block Schedule

Day 25: Exs. 1–8, 13, 14, 17, 19, 23, 24, 26–37

EMBEDDED ASSESSMENT

These section objectives are tested by the exercises listed.

Interpret and make stem-and-leaf plots.

Exercises 1, 2, 5–8

Divide a whole number or a decimal by a decimal.

Exercises 13, 17, 19, 23, 24

Practice & Application

EXERCISE NOTES

Developing Math Concepts
Ex. 1 illustrates another advantage of displaying data in the form of a stem-and-leaf plot. As mentioned earlier, the median and mode are easily identified. As shown in *Ex. 1*, it is also easy to find the *range* of the data from the maximum and minimum scores: $100 - 62 = 38$.

Writing *Ex. 8* illustrates still *another* advantage of stem-and-leaf plots over a table; by comparing the two stem-and-leaf plots for *Exs. 6* and *7*, you can see at a glance that the larger the dinosaur, the greater the daily consumption of meat.

Ongoing Assessment For *Exs. 1–8*, you may wish to suggest that students keep their answers for their portfolio work to show their progress in understanding how to make and interpret stem-and-leaf plots.

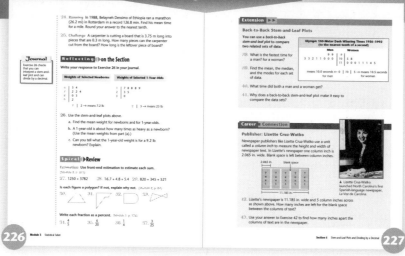

Closing the Section

Students have used stem-and-leaf plots to organize data about dinosaurs into a form that allows them to make revealing comparisons about the animals. For example, the plots show clearly something that is not so clear from the tabulated data: plant-eating dinosaurs are longer from head to tail than are meat-eating dinosaurs. Students also use the division of one decimal by another to determine the hunting habits of some dinosaurs. Finally, in Reflecting on the Section on page 226, students use their new skills to compare the relationship between the weights of newborn babies and 1-year-old infants.

QUICK QUIZ ON THIS SECTION

For Exercises 1–4 use the stem-and-leaf plot below.

**Weights of Selected
12-year-olds**

7	2 5 5 8
8	4 7 9
9	2 2 3 6 9
10	0 1 5 8
11	4 7
12	0 5

8 | 4 → means 84 lb

1. What is the range of the data?

2. What are the modes?

3. What is the median?

4. What percent of the children have weights between 80 and 110 lb?

Find each quotient.

5. $2.6\overline{)18.46}$ 6. $0.3\overline{)521.7}$

7. $12.1\overline{)0.48037}$

For answers, see Quick Quiz blackline on p. 3-75.

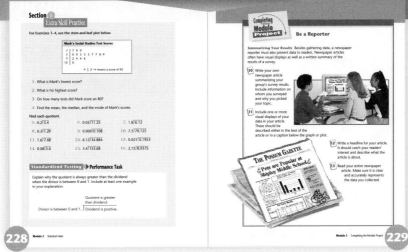

Completing the Module Project

In this final phase of the module project, you may wish to have each student write an article that includes a display about one of the survey questions. Then combine the articles into a group paper that includes a summary of the results from each group. The result should be considered as unedited manuscript. Have students edit one another's work and, where necessary, rewrite material that is unclear, too long, or not well organized. There are several software packages that can be used to produce final copy in newspaper form. If allowed to use computers to create their final copy, students will be able to share their articles with classmates, other classes, and perhaps the entire school.

Name _____ Date _____

Animal Cards

(See instructions on page 3-117.)

African Elephant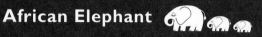

Classification	mammal
Life Span	about 60 yr
Approximate Length	6.8 m
Approximate Mass	7.5 metric tons
Tail (yes/no)	yes
Number of Legs	4
Offspring per Birth	1
Habitat	land
Diet	plants

Jaguar

Classification	mammal
Life Span	about 22 yr
Approximate Length	1.4 m
Approximate Mass	90 kg
Tail (yes/no)	yes
Number of Legs	4
Offspring per Birth	1–4
Habitat	land
Diet	meat

Blue Whale

Classification	mammal
Life Span	about 40 yr
Approximate Length	30 m
Approximate Mass	115 metric tons
Tail (yes/no)	yes
Number of Legs	0
Offspring per Birth	1
Habitat	water
Diet	meat

Striped Skunk

Classification	mammal
Life Span	about 8 yr
Approximate Length	69 cm
Approximate Mass	3.2 kg
Tail (yes/no)	yes
Number of Legs	4
Offspring per Birth	2–10
Habitat	land
Diet	both

European Starling

Classification	bird
Life Span	about 18 yr
Approximate Length	20.5 cm
Approximate Mass	80 g
Tail (yes/no)	yes
Number of Legs	2
Offspring per Birth	4–6
Habitat	land
Diet	both

MODULE 3   **LABSHEET** **1B**

Animal Cards

(See instructions on page 3-117.)

English Sole

Classification · · · · · · · · · · fish
Life Span · · · · · · · · · · about 14 yr
Approximate Length · · · · 35 cm
Approximate Mass · · · · · 550 g
Tail (yes/no) · · · · · · · · · yes
Number of Legs · · · · · · · 0
Offspring per Birth · · · · 0.3–1.5 million
Habitat · · · · · · · · · · · · water
Diet · · · · · · · · · · · · · · meat

Northern Copperhead

Classification · · · · · · · · · reptile
Life Span · · · · · · · · · · about 20 yr
Approximate Length · · · · · 1.12 m
Approximate Mass · · · · · · not available
Tail (yes/no) · · · · · · · · · · yes
Number of Legs · · · · · · · · 0
Offspring per Birth · · · · · 2–10
Habitat · · · · · · · · · · · · both
Diet · · · · · · · · · · · · · meat

Black Widow Spider

Classification · · · · · · · · · · · arachnid
Life Span · · · · · · · · · · · · about 2 yr
Approximate Length · · · · · · 1.27 cm
Approximate Mass · · · · · · · not available
Tail (yes/no) · · · · · · · · · · · no
Number of Legs · · · · · · · · 8
Offspring per Birth · · · · · · 250–750
Habitat · · · · · · · · · · · · · land
Diet · · · · · · · · · · · · · · meat

Winter Flounder

Classification · · · · · · · · · · fish
Life Span · · · · · · · · · · · about 11 yr
Approximate Length · · · · · 46 cm
Approximate Mass · · · · · · 875 g
Tail (yes/no) · · · · · · · · · · yes
Number of Legs · · · · · · · · 0
Offspring per Birth · · · · · 0.5–3.3 million
Habitat · · · · · · · · · · · · water
Diet · · · · · · · · · · · · · meat

Domestic Guinea Pig

Classification · · · · · · · · · · mammal
Life Span · · · · · · · · · · · about 6 yr
Approximate Length · · · · · 30 cm
Approximate Mass · · · · · · 750 g
Tail (yes/no) · · · · · · · · · · yes
Number of Legs · · · · · · · · 4
Offspring per Birth · · · · · 1–8
Habitat · · · · · · · · · · · · land
Diet · · · · · · · · · · · · · plants

MODULE 3   **LABSHEET** **1C**

Animal Cards

(See instructions on page 3-117.)

Gila Monster

Classification · · · · · · · · · · ·	reptile
Life Span · · · · · · · · · · · ·	about 17 yr
Approximate Length · · · · ·	54 cm
Approximate Mass · · · · · ·	1.5 kg
Tail (yes/no) · · · · · · · · ·	yes
Number of Legs · · · · · · ·	4
Offspring per Birth · · · · · ·	1–8
Habitat · · · · · · · · · · · ·	land
Diet · · · · · · · · · · · · ·	meat

Snow Hare

Classification · · · · · · · · · ·	mammal
Life Span · · · · · · · · · · ·	about 9 yr
Approximate Length · · · · ·	58 cm
Approximate Mass · · · · · · ·	2.75 kg
Tail (yes/no) · · · · · · · · ·	yes
Number of Legs · · · · · · · ·	4
Offspring per Birth · · · · · ·	1–5
Habitat · · · · · · · · · · · ·	land
Diet · · · · · · · · · · · · · ·	plants

Monarch Butterfly

Classification · · · · · · · · · ·	insect
Life Span · · · · · · · · · · ·	about 3 weeks
Approximate Length · · · ·	3.3 cm
Approximate Mass · · · · · ·	not available
Tail (yes/no) · · · · · · · · ·	no
Number of Legs · · · · · · ·	6
Offspring per Birth · · · · ·	400
Habitat · · · · · · · · · · · ·	land
Diet · · · · · · · · · · · · ·	plants

Royal Albatross

Classification · · · · · · · · · ·	bird
Life Span · · · · · · · · · · · ·	about 45 yr
Approximate Length · · · · · ·	1.14 m
Approximate Mass · · · · · · ·	8.3 kg
Tail (yes/no) · · · · · · · · ·	yes
Number of Legs · · · · · · · ·	2
Offspring per Birth · · · · · · ·	1
Habitat · · · · · · · · · · · · ·	water
Diet · · · · · · · · · · · · · ·	meat

California Grunion

Classification · · · · · · · · · · ·	fish
Life Span · · · · · · · · · · · ·	about 3 yr
Approximate Length · · · · · ·	15 cm
Approximate Mass · · · · · · ·	21 g
Tail (yes/no) · · · · · · · · ·	yes
Number of Legs · · · · · · · ·	0
Offspring per Birth · · · · · ·	1,500–2,500
Habitat · · · · · · · · · · · ·	water
Diet · · · · · · · · · · · · ·	meat

Animal Cards

(See instructions on page 3-117.)

Rock Crab

Classification	invertebrate
Life Span	about 8 yr
Approximate Length	10 cm
Approximate Mass	220 g
Tail (yes/no)	no
Number of Legs	8
Offspring per Birth	4,400–330,500
Habitat	water
Diet	meat

Japanese Flying Squid

Classification	invertebrate
Life Span	about 1 yr
Approximate Length	37 cm
Approximate Mass	400 g
Tail (yes/no)	no
Number of Legs	0
Offspring per Birth	300–4,000
Habitat	water
Diet	meat

Bottlenose Dolphin

Classification	mammal
Life Span	about 25 yr
Approximate Length	3.5 m
Approximate Mass	250 kg
Tail (yes/no)	yes
Number of Legs	0
Offspring per Birth	1
Habitat	water
Diet	meat

Muskrat

Classification	mammal
Life Span	about 4 yr
Approximate Length	30 cm
Approximate Mass	1,200 g
Tail (yes/no)	yes
Number of Legs	4
Offspring per Birth	1–3
Habitat	water
Diet	plants

Giant Panda

Classification	mammal
Life Span	about 30 yr
Approximate Length	1.7 m
Approximate Mass	92 kg
Tail (yes/no)	yes
Number of Legs	4
Offspring per Birth	1–2
Habitat	land
Diet	plants

MODULE 3 | **LABSHEET** **1E**

Special Multipliers Multiplication Table

(Use with Question 22 on page 164.)

Directions Use your calculator to complete the table by filling in the missing products. Then use your table to answer the questions about multiplying decimals by the special multipliers 0.001, 0.01, 0.1, 1, 10, 100, and 1000.

•	0.001	0.01	0.1	1	10	100	1000
3		0.03			30		3000
0.6				0.6	6		600
4.9	0.0049		0.49			490	
0.002		0.00002					

a. What happens to a number when you multiply it by 1? by a special multiplier greater than 1? by a special multiplier less than 1?

b. Complete each statement below to describe what happens to the decimal point of a number when you multiply by each of the special multipliers.

- **10**   When I multiply by 10, the decimal point moves

- **100**   When I multiply by 100, the decimal point moves

- **1000**   When I multiply by 1000, the decimal point moves

- **0.1**   When I multiply by 0.1, the decimal point moves

- **0.01**   When I multiply by 0.01, the decimal point moves

- **0.001**   When I multiply by 0.001, the decimal point moves

Name _____   Date _____

Metric Conversions (Use with Question 23 on page 164.)

Directions Use the table of prefix meanings to fill in the missing information for the metric conversions.

Prefix	**kilo**	hecto	deka	**meter/gram**	deci	**centi**	**milli**
Meaning	1000	100	10	1	0.1 or $\frac{1}{10}$	0.01 or $\frac{1}{100}$	0.001 or $\frac{1}{1000}$

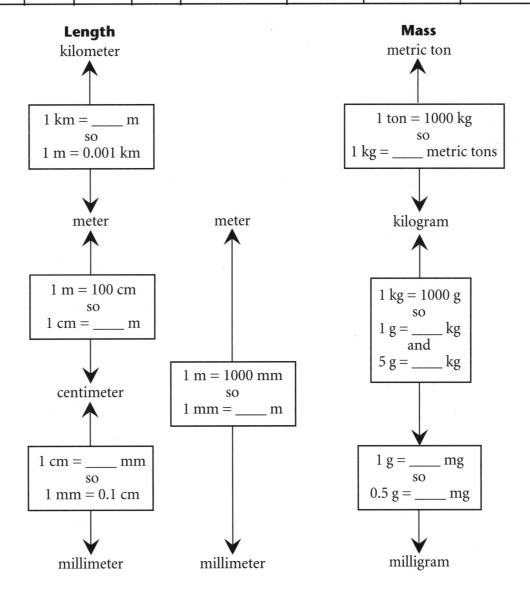

Length
kilometer

1 km = _____ m
so
1 m = 0.001 km

meter

1 m = 100 cm
so
1 cm = _____ m

centimeter

1 cm = _____ mm
so
1 mm = 0.1 cm

millimeter

meter

1 m = 1000 mm
so
1 mm = _____ m

millimeter

Mass
metric ton

1 ton = 1000 kg
so
1 kg = _____ metric tons

kilogram

1 kg = 1000 g
so
1 g = _____ kg
and
5 g = _____ kg

1 g = _____ mg
so
0.5 g = _____ mg

milligram

Name _____ Date _____

20 Paper Fish (Use with the Setting the Stage on page 171.)

Directions Make two copies and cut out the fish.

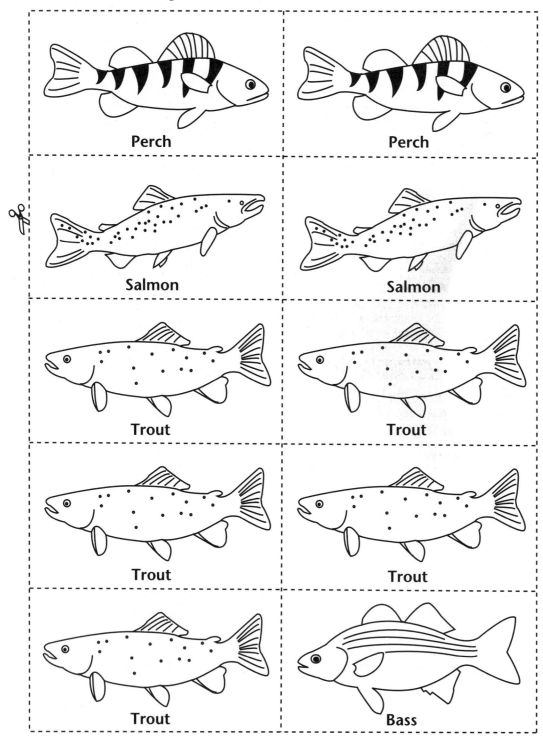

MODULE 3   **LABSHEET** **2B**

Dot Grid 1 (Use with Question 4 on page 172.)

Directions Complete parts (a)–(d) to answer the following:

A class using 36 animal cards predicts that $\frac{2}{3}$ of the cards are mammals. What is $\frac{2}{3}$ of 36?

a. Each dot represents one animal card. How many dots represent all the animal cards?

b. The denominator of the fraction $\frac{2}{3}$ tells you to divide the 36 dots into 3 groups with the same number of dots in each group. Circle groups of dots to divide the 36 dots into 3 equal groups. How many dots are in each group?

c. The numerator of the fraction $\frac{2}{3}$ tells you to consider 2 of the 3 groups. Shade 2 of the 3 groups of dots. How many dots are in two groups?

d. $\frac{2}{3}$ of 36 = _____

e. How many of the 36 animal cards are mammals?

Dot Grid 2 (Use with Question 5 on page 172.)

Directions Complete parts (a) and (b) to answer the following:

A class using 24 animal cards predicts that $\frac{3}{4}$ of the cards are reptiles. What is $\frac{3}{4}$ of 24?

a. Circle groups of dots to divide 24 into 4 equal parts. Then shade $\frac{3}{4}$ of 24.

b. $\frac{3}{4}$ of 24 = _____

c. How many of the 24 animal cards are reptiles?

Name _____   Date _____

Relating Fractions, Decimals, and Percents

(Use with Question 13 on page 174.)

Directions   Write a fraction, a decimal, and a percent for the shaded part of each grid.

a. 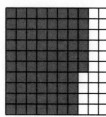   **b.**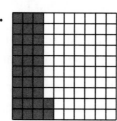

....

Shading Percents   (Use with Homework Exercise 18 on page 178.)

Directions   Shade the part of the grid represented by each percent. Write a fraction and a decimal for the shaded part.

a. 1%   **b.** 10%   **c.** 25%

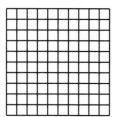   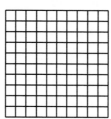   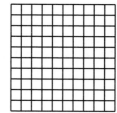

fraction _____   fraction _____   fraction _____

decimal _____   decimal _____   decimal _____

d. 46%   **e.** 67%   **f.** 100%

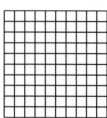   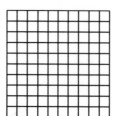   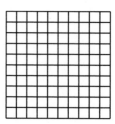

fraction _____   fraction _____   fraction _____

decimal _____   decimal _____   decimal _____

Name _____   Date _____

Common Fraction, Decimal, and Percent Equivalents

(Use with Question 19 on page 175.)

Directions Write each fraction in the table in lowest terms. Use the grids
and any patterns you see to write a percent and a decimal for each fraction.

a.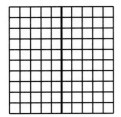

Fraction	Percent	Decimal
$\frac{1}{2}$		
$\frac{2}{2} =$		

b.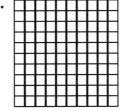

Fraction	Percent	Decimal
$\frac{1}{4}$		
$\frac{2}{4} =$		
$\frac{3}{4}$		
$\frac{4}{4} =$		

c.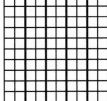

Fraction	Percent	Decimal
$\frac{1}{5}$		
$\frac{2}{5}$		
$\frac{3}{5}$		
$\frac{4}{5}$		
$\frac{5}{5} =$		

d.

Fraction	Percent	Decimal
$\frac{1}{10}$		
$\frac{2}{10} =$		
$\frac{3}{10}$		
$\frac{4}{10} =$		
$\frac{5}{10} =$		
$\frac{6}{10} =$		
$\frac{7}{10}$		
$\frac{8}{10} =$		
$\frac{9}{10}$		
$\frac{10}{10} =$		

Math Thematics, Book 1 **3-59**

MODULE 3 **PROJECT LABSHEET** A

Survey Worksheet (Use with Project Question 3 on page 180.)

Directions Complete parts (a) and (b) on your own. You should work with your group on parts (c)–(e).

a. How might someone answer each of the questions at the right? What types of information would you get from each question?

b. Write one question for your group's survey. As you write your question remember to:

- Be specific. Create a question that will give you enough information about your topic.

- State your question clearly. Make sure that people who take your survey will understand what is being asked.

c. Share your survey question with your group. With your group, rewrite any questions that are not clear.

d. Discuss any other questions that you may want to ask. For example, you could ask about age or grade level.

e. Combine your survey questions onto one sheet of paper. Make sure your group has at least five different questions.

Survey on Pets

1. How many pets do you own?

2. Name each kind of pet you own and how many of each kind you own.

3. What is your favorite pet?

MODULE 3   LABSHEET **5A**

Mean Pygmy Mouse Weight   (Use with Question 4 on page 208.)

Directions Follow the steps below to find 0.90 ÷ 3.

a. The whole grid represents one unit. Each small square is what decimal part of the grid?

b. Shade 0.90 of the grid.

c. Divide the shaded portion into 3 equal-sized groups.

d. 0.90 ÷ 3 = _____

e. What is the mean weight of the three pygmy mice?

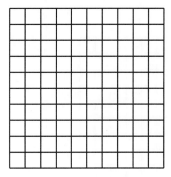

Mean Canary Weight (Use with Question 5 on page 208.)

Directions   Follow the steps below to find 2.40 ÷ 4.

a. Shade 2.40 of the grids. (Shade 2 grids plus 0.40 of another grid.)

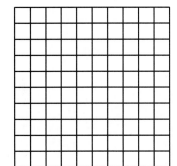 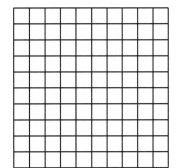 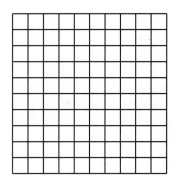

b. Divide the shaded area into 4 equal-sized groups.

c. Each group in part (a) is what part of a whole grid? Write your answer as a decimal.

d. 2.40 ÷ 4 = _____

e. What is the mean canary weight?

MODULE 3   **LABSHEET** **5B**

Decimal Division Grids   (Use with Question 6 on page 208.)

Directions Use the grids below to find each quotient.

a. 0.06 ÷ 3 = ____

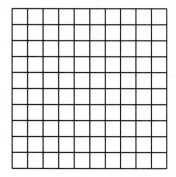

b. 0.36 ÷ 9 = ____

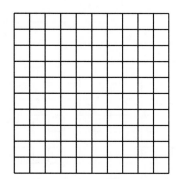

c. 2)‾1̅.̅3̅0̅ = ____      2)‾1̅.̅3̅0̅ means 1.30 ÷ 2.

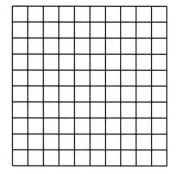   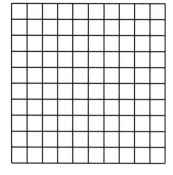

MODULE 3   LABSHEET **6A**

Weights of Plant-Eating Dinosaurs
(Use with Questions 5 and 6 on page 220.)

Directions Complete parts (a)–(d) to make a
stem-and-leaf plot for the weights of the plant-eating
dinosaurs listed in the table.

a. Find the least and the greatest data items in the
table to help you choose the stem numbers. List
each stem in a column from least to greatest on
the blank stem-and-leaf plot below.

b. In the table, place a check next to the data that
have a stem of 3. Use your list to write the leaves
for the stem 3 in order from least to greatest in the
stem-and-leaf plot below. Do this for each stem
using a different mark or color.

c. Fill in the key so that it tells the values represented
by a stem and leaf.

d. Write a title for the stem-and-leaf plot so that
anyone can tell what it is about.

Some Plant-Eating Dinosaurs

Dinosaur	Weight (tons)
Anatosaurus	3.5
Ankylosaurus	5.0
Centrosaurus	2.6
Chasmosaurus	2.2
Corythosaurus	3.7
Edmontonia	3.9
Edmontosaurus	3.9
Euoplocephalus	3.0
Hadrosaurus	3.0
Pachyrhinosaurus	4.0
Panoplosaurus	4.0
Parasaurolophus	3.5
Parksosaurus	0.1
Sauropelta	2.7
Styracosaurus	2.7
Tenontosaurus	2.0
Torosaurus	5.0
Triceratops	5.3

List the stems here.

Title: _____

List the leaves to the
right of each stem.

Key: ☐|☐ means _____

MODULE 3	LABSHEET 6B

Animal Division Grid (Use with Question 9 on page 221.)

Directions Complete parts (a)–(e) to divide 0.4 by 0.05.

A 6-kilogram *Microvenator* needed to eat about 0.4 kg of meat a day. Suppose the animals it hunted had a mass of about 0.05 kg each. To find how many animals a *Microvenator* needed to catch each day, you need to divide 0.4 by 0.05.

You can use a 10 × 10 grid to model the division. Let the grid represent one unit.

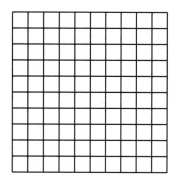

   a.   Shade 0.4 of the grid.

   b.   Divide the shaded area into equal-sized groups with 0.05 in each group.

   c.   How many equal-sized groups are there?

   d.   0.4 ÷ 0.05 = _____

   e.   How many animals did a Microvenator need to catch each day?

Division Grids (Use with Question 10 on page 221.)

Directions Use each grid to find the quotient.

a. 0.60 ÷ 0.15 = _____   **b.** 0.28 ÷ 0.04 = _____   **c.** 0.9)‾0.45‾ = _____

$$0.45 \div 0.9$$

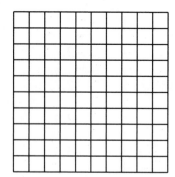 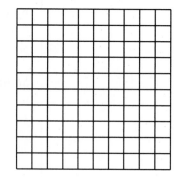 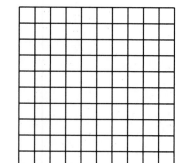

Name _____   Problem _____

 The star indicates that you excelled in some way.

Problem Solving

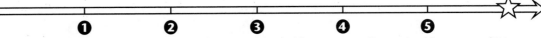

①   **②**   **③**   **④**   **⑤**

You did not understand the problem well enough to get started or you did not show any work.

You understood the problem well enough to make a plan and to work toward a solution.

You made a plan, you used it to solve the problem, and you verified your solution.

Mathematical Language

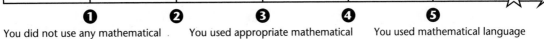

①   **②**   **③**   **④**   **⑤**

You did not use any mathematical vocabulary or symbols, or you did not use them correctly, or your use was not appropriate.

You used appropriate mathematical language, but the way it was used was not always correct or other terms and symbols were needed.

You used mathematical language that was correct and appropriate to make your meaning clear.

Representations

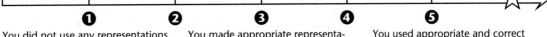

①   **②**   **③**   **④**   **⑤**

You did not use any representations such as equations, tables, graphs, or diagrams to help solve the problem or explain your solution.

You made appropriate representations to help solve the problem or help you explain your solution, but they were not always correct or other representations were needed.

You used appropriate and correct representations to solve the problem or explain your solution.

Connections

①   **②**   **③**   **④**   **⑤**

You attempted or solved the problem and then stopped.

You found patterns and used them to extend the solution to other cases, or you recognized that this problem relates to other problems, mathematical ideas, or applications.

You extended the ideas in the solution to the general case, or you showed how this problem relates to other problems, mathematical ideas, or applications.

Presentation

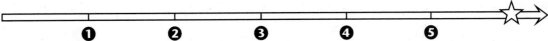

①   **②**   **③**   **④**   **⑤**

The presentation of your solution and reasoning is unclear to others.

The presentation of your solution and reasoning is clear in most places, but others may have trouble understanding parts of it.

The presentation of your solution and reasoning is clear and can be understood by others.

Content Used: _____   Computational Errors: Yes ☐ No ☐

Notes on Errors: _____

_____

Name _____ Problem _____

 **STUDENT** **SELF-ASSESSMENT SCALES**

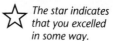 If your score is in the shaded area, explain why on the back of this sheet and stop.

☆ The star indicates that you excelled in some way.

 ## Problem Solving

❶   **❷**   **❸**   **❹**   **❺**

I did not understand the problem well enough to get started or I did not show any work.

I understood the problem well enough to make a plan and to work toward a solution.

I made a plan, I used it to solve the problem, and I verified my solution.

 ## Mathematical Language

❶   **❷**   **❸**   **❹**   **❺**

I did not use any mathematical vocabulary or symbols, or I did not use them correctly, or my use was not appropriate.

I used appropriate mathematical language, but the way it was used was not always correct or other terms and symbols were needed.

I used mathematical language that was correct and appropriate to make my meaning clear.

 ## Representations

❶   **❷**   **❸**   **❹**   **❺**

I did not use any representations such as equations, tables, graphs, or diagrams to help solve the problem or explain my solution.

I made appropriate representations to help solve the problem or help me explain my solution, but they were not always correct or other representations were needed.

I used appropriate and correct representations to solve the problem or explain my solution.

 ## Connections

❶   **❷**   **❸**   **❹**   **❺**

I attempted or solved the problem and then stopped.

I found patterns and used them to extend the solution to other cases, or I recognized that this problem relates to other problems, mathematical ideas, or applications.

I extended the ideas in the solution to the general case, or I showed how this problem relates to other problems, mathematical ideas, or applications.

 ## Presentation

❶   **❷**   **❸**   **❹**   **❺**

The presentation of my solution and reasoning is unclear to others.

The presentation of my solution and reasoning is clear in most places, but others may have trouble understanding parts of it.

The presentation of my solution and reasoning is clear and can be understood by others.

What a Zoo! (E² on textbook page 194)

The Problem Solving, Mathematical Language, Representations, and Presentation Scales of the *Math Thematics* Assessment Scales should be used to assess student work. This open-ended E² will result in a variety of answers.

Students should make a recommendation on how many toy animals to buy using the percent of toy animals sold, the number of toy animals sold, or the difference between what was sold and ordered. Percents (rounded to the nearest percent) of animals sold are: lion 85%, iguana 7%, panda bear 78%, tiger 100%, and seal 63%. For example, all of the 15 tigers ordered were sold and students will probably decide to order more. Students must use critical reasoning to decide how many more tigers to order. Will 15 be the most they can sell? Is it better to buy 200 tigers and not buy other animals? Does each animal cost the same amount? Does each animal sell for the same price? How much money is available to order with? These are the types of questions students should address in this E².

Students may gather other information by conducting a survey about the popularity of real and toy animals.

The survey group should be representative of people who visit the zoo. Students might also create a bar graph or double bar graph to visually show the differences between the number of toy animals bought and sold.

Some questions students might want to ask the director of the zoo or other zoo personnel include:

- Will there be any special events this year, such as *The Silly Seal Show* or a *Love Your Lizard* course?
- Do you expect any new arrivals at the zoo (including transferred animals or births)? If so, which animals?
- Do the prices of the toy animals vary or are they all sold for the same amount?
- Can the souvenir shop keep toy animals rather than send them back?
- Which animal exhibits are the most popular?
- How many people visit the zoo each day? each year?

MODULE 3   **ALTERNATE E²**

Hidden Squares

The Situation

Many designs are more complex than you think. This flag design contains both squares and rectangles. How many squares do you see in the flag? Be careful! There are more than 24.

The Problem

Estimate the number of rectangles in the flag. Then determine the number of rectangles and explain how you found them all.

Something to Think About

*   What problem solving strategies could you use to solve this problem?
*   How could you organize your work to be sure you found all the rectangles?

Present Your Results

Describe the method you used to find all the rectangles. Will your method work for any size checkered flag?

Hidden Squares

All of the *Math Thematics* Assessment Scales should be used to assess student work. Students may make an ordered list or look at a simpler problem to solve this E². All students should get a total of 210 rectangles, but their approaches will vary. The sample response below shows part of a student's solution. It also gives an extension to finding the number of squares from the list of rectangles.

Partial Solution

I made a list of all the rectangles possible by looking at the number of rectangles that could be made in each row. I highlighted the rectangles that are squares to get a total of 50 squares in the flag design.

RECTANGLES

1×1: 6 per row, 4 rows $\rightarrow$ 24 rectangles
1×2: 5 per row, 4 rows $\rightarrow$ 20 rectangles
1×3: 4 per row, 4 rows $\rightarrow$ 16 rectangles
1×4: 3 per row, 4 rows $\rightarrow$ 12 rectangles
1×5: 2 per row, 4 rows $\rightarrow$ 8 rectangles
1×6: 1 per row, 4 rows $\rightarrow$ 4 rectangles

2×1: 6 per row, 3 rows $\rightarrow$ 18 rectangles
2×2: 5 per row, 3 rows $\rightarrow$ 15 rectangles
2×3: 4 per row, 3 rows $\rightarrow$ 12 rectangles
2×4: 3 per row, 3 rows $\rightarrow$ 9 rectangles
2×5: 2 per row, 3 rows $\rightarrow$ 6 rectangles
2×6: 1 per row, 3 rows $\rightarrow$ 3 rectangles

3×1: 6 per row, 2 rows $\rightarrow$ 12 rectangles
3×2: 5 per row, 2 rows $\rightarrow$ 10 rectangles
3×3: 4 per row, 2 rows $\rightarrow$ 8 rectangles
3×4: 3 per row, 2 rows $\rightarrow$ 6 rectangles
3×5: 2 per row, 2 rows $\rightarrow$ 4 rectangles
3×6: 1 per row, 2 rows $\rightarrow$ 2 rectangles

4×1: 6 per row, 1 row $\rightarrow$ 6 rectangles
4×2: 5 per row, 1 row $\rightarrow$ 5 rectangles
4×3: 4 per row, 1 row $\rightarrow$ 4 rectangles
4×4: 3 per row, 1 row $\rightarrow$ 3 rectangles
4×5: 2 per row, 1 row $\rightarrow$ 2 rectangles
4×6: 1 per row, 1 row $\rightarrow$ 1 rectangle

This gives a total of 210 rectangles.

Other Considerations

- **Connections** Expect most students to extend this problem by looking at rectangles of various sizes.

  Some students may see a pattern in the number of rectangles and try to generalize the pattern. "The number of rectangles per row decreases as the rectangle size increases. You can see that for each set of rectangles the number of rectangles per row is 6, 5, 4, 3, 2, and 1. There is another pattern in the number of rows that the rectangles will fit in. A $1 \times n$ rectangle will fit in all 4 rows, a $2 \times n$ rectangle will only fit in 3 rows, a $3 \times n$ rectangle will only fit in 2 rows, and a $4 \times n$ rectangle will only fit in 1 row."

Estimate the length and weight of each animal. Use ounces, pounds, tons, inches, or feet.

1. hamster   2. boa constrictor   3. miniature poodle

4. rhinoceros   5. ostrich   6. lobster

MODULE 3 SECTION 1   **QUICK QUIZ**

Use the Venn diagram shown for Questions 1 and 2. "W" is the set of white vegetables and "U" is the set of vegetables grown underground.

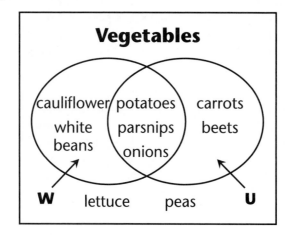

1. Which white vegetables do not grow underground?

2. What does the Venn diagram tell you about peas and lettuce?

3. Replace ___?___ with the number that makes the statement true: 16 cm = ___?___ m

4. Replace ___?___ with >, <, or = : 60 g ___?___ 0.6 kg

5. Which metric unit would you use to measure the mass of the family dog?

ANSWERS

Warm-Ups: Sample responses are given. Accept reasonable estimates.
1. length: 4 in.; weight: 4 oz   **2.** length: 10 ft; weight: 40 lb
3. length: 1.5 ft; weight: 15 lb   **4.** length: 11 ft; weight: 2 tons
5. length: 8 ft; weight: 300 lb   **6.** length: 8 in.; weight 1 lb

Quick-Quiz: 1. cauliflower and white beans   **2.** They are not white and do not grow underground.   **3.** 0.16   **4.** <   **5.** kilogram

Evaluate each expression.

1. 13×8 **2.** 19×7 **3.** 15×15

4. $48 \div 3$ **5.** $102 \div 17$ **6.** $440 \div 11$

MODULE 3 SECTION 2   **QUICK QUIZ**

1. Use mental math to find $\frac{5}{6}$ of 180.

2. Write as a fraction in lowest terms and as a decimal: 18%

3. Which is greater, $\frac{2}{3}$ of 78 or $\frac{3}{5}$ of 80?

4. Which is greater, $\frac{38}{50}$ or $\frac{222}{300}$?

5. Use the measurements on the figure to calculate what percent of the total area of the rectangle is in each of the regions A, B, and C.

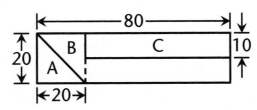

1. How many 8th grade boys are there?

2. How many 6th grade students are there?

3. How many girls are there in all three grades?

4. Which grade has the least number of boys? the most number of girls?

Grade	Boys	Girls
6th	81	124
7th	92	99
8th	101	98

MODULE 3 SECTION 3   **QUICK QUIZ**

1. Use the data to draw a bar graph.

2. What is the range of the data?

Year	Pounds of turkey eaten per capita
1980	8.1
1985	9.2
1990	13.9
1995	14.3

3. What is the range of the data in the line plot?

4. How many snake species listed in the line plot have a length greater than 60 in.?

Median Length of Selected Snake Species

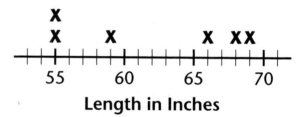

Length in Inches

ANSWERS

Warm-Ups: 1. 101 **2.** 205 **3.** 321 **4.** 6th grade; 6th grade

Quick-Quiz: 1.

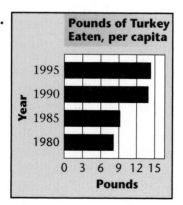

2. 6.2 lb **3.** 14 in. **4.** 3 species

Add.

1. 17 + 45 + 37 + 35
2. 2 + 71 + 14 + 9 + 60
3. 894 + 1216 + 929 + 57
4. 2.1 + 3.4 + 6.2
5. 14 + 3.2 + 5.96 + 7.23
6. 8.441 + 7.42 + 0.019 + 4.2673

Find the mean, median, and mode for the following data.

1. length of selected raccoons (inches): 26, 29, 30, 29, 36
2. weight of selected black bears (pounds): 280, 340, 410, 220, 500, 280

Write each fraction as a decimal rounded to the nearest hundredth.

3. $\frac{4}{7}$

4. $\frac{5}{12}$

Round each decimal to the given place.

5. 100.419 to the nearest tenth
6. 42.6782 to the nearest thousandth

ANSWERS

Warm-Ups: 1. 134 **2.** 156 **3.** 3096 **4.** 11.7 **5.** 30.39 **6.** 20.1473

Quick-Quiz: 1. mean = 30 in.; median = 29 in.; mode = 29 in.
2. mean = 338.3 lb; median = 310 lb; mode = 280 lb **3.** 0.57 **4.** 0.42 **5.** 100.4 **6.** 42.678

Use mental math to divide.

1. $24 \div 6$ **2.** $63 \div 9$ **3.** $24 \div 8$

4. $72 \div 12$ **5.** $10{,}000 \div 100$ **6.** $55 \div 5$

Find each quotient.

1. $8\overline{)211.36}$ **2.** $3\overline{)7.83}$

3. Use front-end estimation to estimate the sum:
$1.78 + 15.32 + 20.81$

4. Use trading off to find the sum: $\begin{array}{r} 132 \\ + \ 98 \\ \hline \end{array}$

5. Write as a decimal: $\dfrac{123}{300}$

6. Selena got \$30 for baby-sitting 8 hours one Saturday night. How much does she get paid per hour?

Use these data values. 3, 9, 8, 6, 6, 5, 4, 6, 8, 2, 7, 5

1. What is the least value?

2. What is the greatest value?

3. What is the range?

4. Order the values from least to greatest.

5. What is the median?

6. What is the mode?

For Questions 1–4 use the stem-and-leaf plot below.

Weights of Selected 12-year-olds

```
 7 | 2 5 5 8
 8 | 4 7 9
 9 | 2 2 3 6 9
10 | 0 1 5 8
11 | 4 7
12 | 0 5
```

$8 \mid 4 \rightarrow$ means 84 lb

1. What is the range of the data?

2. What are the modes?

3. What is the median?

4. What percent of the children have weights between 80 and 110 lb?

Find each quotient.

5. $2.6\overline{)18.46}$ 6. $0.3\overline{)521.7}$ 7. $12.1\overline{)0.48037}$

ANSWERS

Warm-Ups: 1. 2 **2.** 9 **3.** 7 **4.** 2, 3, 4, 5, 5, 6, 6, 6, 7, 8, 8, 9 **5.** 6 **6.** 6

Quick-Quiz: 1. 53 lb **2.** 75 lb and 92 lb **3.** 94.5 lb **4.** 60% **5.** 7.10 **6.** 1739
7. 0.0397

MODULE 3 SECTION 1	PRACTICE AND APPLICATIONS

For use with Exploration 1

1. Sketch and label a Venn diagram showing what students have the kinds of pets indicated below.

Dogs	Cats	Both
Andrea	David	Harry
Jason	Helen	Jean
Kelly		
Stephanie		

2. Use the Venn diagram to answer.

    a. How many girls' names are there? What are they?

    b. How many boys' names are there? What are they?

    c. What does the overlap between the two sets in the diagram mean?

    d. Why is "Spot" outside the sets? Who might have such a name?

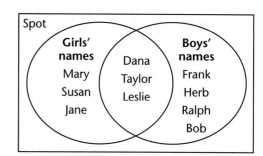

For use with Exploration 2

3. Choose the appropriate metric unit (*meter, centimeter,* or *millimeter*) to estimate the length of each object.

    a. bus   **b.** poster   **c.** paper clip

4. Use the drawing at right to answer the questions.

    a. How long is the goldfish in millimeters?

    b. How long is the goldfish in centimeters?

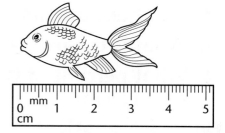

5. Choose the appropriate metric unit (*metric ton, kilogram, gram,* or *milligram*) for measuring each mass.

    a. an apple   **b.** a serving of salt   **c.** a bus

(continued)

MODULE 3 SECTION 1 | PRACTICE AND APPLICATIONS

For use with Exploration 3

6. a. Name a bird whose mass could be measured in kilograms.

    b. Name a bird whose length is measured in millimeters.

7. Replace each __?__ with the number that makes the statement true.

    a. 2 g = __?__ mg

        10 g = __?__ mg

    b. 2 m = __?__ km

        58 m __?__ km

    c. 2 metric tons = __?__ kg

        6.2 metric tons = __?__ kg

8. Find each product.

    a. 8 · 0.01

    b. 7.3 · 0.01

    c. 0.9 · 0.001

    d. 0.003 · 10

    e. 0.29 · 100

    f. 0.01 · 0.1

    g. 4.7 · 0.001

    h. 0.093 · 10

    i. 0.005 · 0.1

9. Replace each __?__ with the number that makes the statement true.

    a. 4 km = __?__ m

    b. 7.1 m = __?__ cm

    c. 325 m = __?__ km

    d. 6310 mm = __?__ m

    e. 0.4 m = __?__ mm

    f. 52 cm = __?__ mm

10. Replace each __?__ with <, >, or =.

    a. 720 g __?__ 7.2 kg

    b. 6000 mg __?__ 6 g

    c. 2000 kg __?__ 0.25 metric tons

    d. 4.9 kg __?__ 4500 g

    e. 38 mg __?__ 3.8 g

    f. 9 metric tons __?__ 900 kg

11. An evergreen tree is 12 m tall. A Bonsai tree is 18 cm tall. Which tree is taller? How much taller?

Name _____   Date _____

For use with Exploration 1

1. Use mental math to find each value.

   a. $\frac{2}{3}$ of 9   **b.** $\frac{4}{5}$ of 20   **c.** $\frac{3}{8}$ of 16

   d. $\frac{3}{4}$ of 28   **e.** $\frac{2}{9}$ of 36   **f.** $\frac{2}{3}$ of 18

2. a. If $\frac{5}{8}$ of 24 marbles are clear, how many marbles are clear?

   b. How many striped marbles are there in a set of 35 marbles that is $\frac{2}{5}$ striped?

For use with Exploration 2

3. Write each decimal as a fraction and as a percent.

   a. 0.35   **b.** 0.2   **c.** 0.17

   d. 0.08   **e.** 0.24   **f.** 0.75

4. Write each fraction as a decimal and as a percent.

   a. $\frac{7}{100}$ **b.** $\frac{4}{25}$ **c.** $\frac{3}{5}$

   d. $\frac{4}{10}$ **e.** $\frac{9}{20}$ **f.** $\frac{140}{200}$

5. Replace each ___?___ with >, <, or =.

   a. $\frac{2}{5}$ ___?___ 0.25   **b.** 0.132 ___?___ 13%   **c.** $\frac{9}{50}$ ___?___ 18%

   d. 48% ___?___ $\frac{1}{2}$ **e.** 20% ___?___ $\frac{2}{5}$ **f.** 0.04 ___?___ 4%

6. a. At the University Bookstore, 2500 textbooks were sold last month. If $\frac{3}{5}$ of the textbooks were science books, how many science books were sold?

   b. Math and science book sales totaled 1800 books. Write a fraction and a percent for the number of math and science books sold out of all the books sold.

Name _____ Date _____

For use with Exploration 1

1. Find the range of each set of numbers.

   a. 8, 6, 2, 9, 7   **b.** 4.9, 10.1, 8.7, 3.8, 6.5

For Exercises 2–5, use the bar graph below.

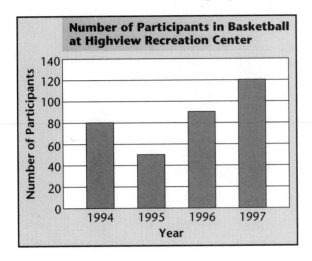

2. In which year was the number of participants the greatest? the least?

3. Estimate the range of the number of participants in basketball at the Recreation Center.

4. Estimate the difference between the number of participants in 1997 and in 1994.

5. About how many participants have there been in basketball from 1994 to 1997?

6. a. Find the range of the weights shown in the table below.

   b. Draw a bar graph to display the weight data.

Weights of Four Types of Dogs

Type of dog	Poodle	Dalmation	Golden Retriever	Great Dane
Weight (in pounds)	20	55	75	110

(continued)

MODULE 3 SECTION 3   PRACTICE AND APPLICATIONS

For use with Exploration 2

Use the line plot for Exercises 7–10.

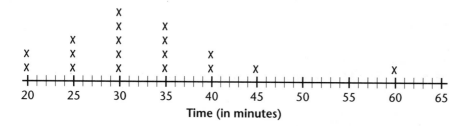

Time Students Spend Exercising in Mr. Tino's Class

7. What is the range of time students spend exercising in Mr. Tino's class?

8. How many students exercise more than 30 minutes?

9. How many students exercise at least 25 minutes?

10. What can you conclude about the amount of time students spend exercising in Mr. Tino's class?

11. The students in Ms. Samuel's class recorded their heights. The heights, in inches, are: 43, 47, 45, 43, 44, 46, 50, 43, 40, 45, 43, 41, 44, 45, 46.

    a. Find the range of the heights.

    b. Make a line plot for the data.

    c. Is there a height on your line plot that has more X's than any other? If so, which height?

    d. Is there a height on your line plot that has the same number of X's to the right of it as there are to the left of it? Explain.

    e. What do you notice about how the data are distributed in the line plot?

MODULE 3 SECTION 4   **PRACTICE AND APPLICATIONS**

For use with Exploration 1

1. Find the mean, the median, and the mode of each data set.

  a. length of 9 hummingbirds (in.): 4, 2, 5, 2, 3, 3, 4, 2, 2

  b. number of eggs of 8 turtles: 14, 16, 23, 8, 28, 12, 11, 16

  c. wingspan of 7 birds (in.): 34, 11, 16, 22, 19, 34, 25

  d. number of birds using a feeder each day for a 5-day period:
     8, 15, 12, 17, 23

2. Calvin was the high scorer in 6 basketball games this season. He
   scored 22, 28, 18, 30, 22, and 24 points in the games. What are the
   mean, the median, and the mode of Calvin's scores?

For use with Exploration 2

3. Emily recorded the amount of snowfall in her backyard for a week
   for a winter science project. The snowfall amounts for the week, in
   inches, were: 9, 3, 0, 4, 18, 1, and 0. Should Emily use the mean, the
   mode, or the median as the average to report the average amount of
   snowfall for the week in her report? Why?

4. Use a calculator to write each fraction as a decimal rounded to the
   nearest hundredth.

  a. $\frac{3}{8}$ **b.** $\frac{3}{5}$ **c.** $\frac{7}{9}$

  d. $\frac{5}{3}$ **e.** $\frac{7}{6}$ **f.** $\frac{2}{7}$

  g. $\frac{5}{12}$ **h.** $\frac{9}{5}$ **i.** $\frac{8}{13}$

5. Write each decimal to the given place.

  a. 0.4829 (tenths)   **b.** 0.1564 (thousandths)

  c. 2.798 (hundredths)   **d.** 3.819 (tenths)

  e. 11.901 (ones)   **f.** 2.7005 (thousandths)

  g. 24.455 (tenths)   **h.** 59.45 (ones)

Name _____   Date _____

For use with Exploration 1

1. Use compatible numbers to check the position of the decimal point in each quotient. If a quotient is incorrect, give the correct quotient.

   a. $8\overline{)32.48}$ (quotient 40.6)

   b. $4\overline{)49.4}$ (quotient 1.235)

   c. $20\overline{)84}$ (quotient 4.2)

2. Find each quotient. Estimate to check the reasonableness of your answers.

   a. $11.32 \div 4$

   b. $5\overline{)15.75}$

   c. $6\overline{)31.35}$

   d. $\dfrac{58}{8}$

   e. $19.8 \div 8$

   f. $12.6 \div 12$

   g. $4\overline{)12.94}$

   h. $6\overline{)30.15}$

   i. $7\overline{)29.33}$

   j. $17.1 \div 5$

   k. $11.8 \div 4$

   l. $18.63 \div 2$

3. Tell whether the quotient is correct in each division. If a quotient is not correct, give the correct quotient.

   a. $4\overline{)145.8}$ (quotient 36.45)

   b. $3\overline{)70.35}$ (quotient 20.345)

   c. $6\overline{)15.9}$ (quotient 26.5)

4. Kristin needs a 13.68 m long piece of lace to use as trim around the edge of a square tablecloth. How long is each side of the tablecloth?

5. Andrew has 3 days to drive to 367.8 miles to Jackson. If he wants to drive the same distance each day, how many miles a day should he drive?

(continued)

MODULE 3 SECTION 5   **PRACTICE AND APPLICATIONS**

For use with Exploration 2

6. Use front-end estimation to estimate each sum.

    a. 7235 + 2148   **b.** 18.6 + 12.3 + 31.8

    c. 216 + 680 + 106   **d.** 14 + 92 + 61 + 72

    e. 3215 + 1145 + 2320   **f.** 5.8 + 2.6 +3.1 + 6.2

    g. 2.8 + 3.4 + 6.1 + 0.3   **h.** 88 + 27 + 31 + 42 + 21

    i. 220 + 160 + 130 + 309   **j.** 3412 + 2335 + 1210

    k. 14.28 + 11.86 + 6.41   **l.** 43 + 18 + 59 + 84

7. Use trading off to find each sum.

    a. 79 + 24   **b.** 0.36 + 0.42

    c. 68 + 47   **d.** 6.3 + 2.9

    e. 27 + 34 + 16   **f.** $1.48 + $3.29

    g. 69 + 27   **h.** 0.34 + 0.75

    i. 74 + 308   **j.** 4.8 + 3.6

    k. 87 + 31 + 59   **l.** 2.3 + 1.6 + 3.7

8. Rebecca buys some markers for $4.37 and some construction paper for $1.48. How much does she spend altogether?

MODULE 3 SECTION 6   **PRACTICE AND APPLICATIONS**

For use with Exploration 1

For Exercises 1-6, use the stem-and-leaf plot showing the spelling test scores for one class.

Spelling Test Scores

```
 6 | 8
 7 | 5 9
 8 | 0 0 2 6 7
 9 | 0 1 1 1 4 4 5 7
10 | 0
```

8 | 2 represents a score of 82

1. What was the low score in the class? The high score?

2. How many students scored in the 80s?

3. How many students took the spelling test?

4. How many students scored 94?

5. How many students scored 85?

6. Find the mean, the median, and the mode of the scores.

For use with Exploration 2

7. Find each quotient.

   a. $0.08\overline{)5.6}$ **b.** $3\overline{)0.09}$ **c.** $0.4\overline{)0.96}$

   d. $0.3\overline{)0.2142}$ **e.** $3.2\overline{)52}$ **f.** $0.6\overline{)2.475}$

   g. $0.5\overline{)3.45}$ **h.** $5.14\overline{)19.018}$ **i.** $0.015\overline{)0.114}$

8. Melissa bought 4.25 lb of peanuts for $2.89. How much is one pound of the peanuts?

9. A carpenter has a piece of wood that is 210.7 cm long. How many 8.6 cm long pieces of wood can be cut from the wood?

Name _____ Date _____

For use with Section 1

1. Use the Venn diagram to answer.

   a. Which months of the year begin
   with a vowel?

   b. Which month of the year begins
   with a vowel and ends with "r"?

   c. How many months end with "r"?

   d. Why are some of the months of
   the year outside of the sets?

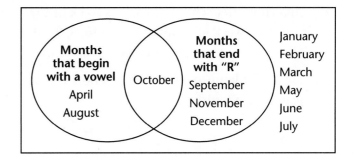

2. Replace each __?__ with the number that makes the statement true.

   a. 6 km = __?__ m

   b. 5.8 m = __?__ cm

   c. 418 m = __?__ km

   d. 5270 mm = __?__ m

   e. 0.3 m = __?__ mm

   f. 75 cm = __?__ mm

For use with Section 2

3. Use mental math to find each value.

   a. $\frac{3}{5}$ of 30

   b. $\frac{5}{8}$ of 56

   c. $\frac{7}{9}$ of 36

4. Write each fraction as a decimal and as a percent.

   a. $\frac{7}{25}$

   b. $\frac{2}{5}$

   c. $\frac{11}{20}$

For use with Section 3

5. Students at Audy School collected aluminum cans for recycling. The
   number of pounds collected by each class were 7, 9, 12, 8, 9, 10, 9, 7,
   6, 9, 10, and 8.

   a. Find the range of the pounds.

   b. Make a line plot for the data.

(continued)

MODULE 3 SECTIONS 1–6   PRACTICE AND APPLICATIONS

For use with Section 4

6. Tina runs after school. She keeps track of the number of miles she runs each week for 2 months: 12, 10, 8, 9, 10, 12, 15, and 10 miles. What are the mean, the median, and the mode of the data?

7. Use a calculator to write each fraction as a decimal rounded to the nearest hundredth.

   a. $\frac{4}{9}$ **b.** $\frac{7}{8}$ **c.** $\frac{1}{6}$

For use with Section 5

8. Find each quotient.

   a. $15.92 \div 4$ **b.** $5\overline{)21.8}$ **c.** $18.6 \div 8$

9. Use front-end estimation to estimate each sum.

   a. $6122 + 1873$ **b.** $13.8 + 11.9 + 27.5$
   c. $411 + 390 + 120$ **d.** $12 + 62 + 51 + 49$

For use with Section 6

10. Use the stem-and-leaf plot showing the geography quiz scores for one class.

Geography Quiz Scores

```
 7 | 6 9
 8 | 3 3 5 6 8 8 9 9 9
 9 | 0 1 2 2 4 6 9
10 | 0 0
```

8 | 5 represents a score of 85

   a. What was the low score in the class? the high score?

   b. Find the mean, the mode, and the median of the scores.

11. Find each quotient.

   a. $2.4\overline{)8.64}$ **b.** $0.006\overline{)0.108}$ **c.** $8.4\overline{)55.02}$

MODULE 3 SECTION 1   STUDY GUIDE

Animal Facts   Sets and Metric Measurement

GOAL **LEARN HOW TO:** • sort data using a Venn diagram
• estimate length and mass in metric units
• convert between metric units

AS YOU: • measure everyday objects
• relate metric prefixes to place values

Exploration 1: Sorting Data

Sets and Venn Diagrams

A **set** is a collection of objects. A set with no objects is called the **empty set**. A **Venn diagram** uses geometric shapes to show how sets are related.

Example

This Venn diagram shows that of the 12 months of the year, there are 4 months whose names end in y and 3 months whose names begin with J. Two of the months have names that end in y and begin with J.

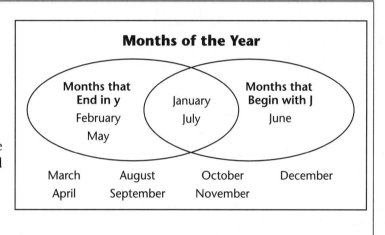

Months of the Year

Months that End in y
February
May

January
July

Months that Begin with J
June

March   August   October   December
April   September   November

Exploration 2 : Metric Length and Mass

Metric Length

The *metric system* of measurement is a decimal system.

Metric units of length are based on the **meter** (m). The names of the other units of length have been chosen to show how these units are related to a meter.

Name of unit	Prefix	Meaning	Relationship to a meter
millimeter (mm)	milli-	thousandth	1 mm = 0.001 m
centimeter (cm)	centi-	hundredth	1 cm = 0.01 m
kilometer (km)	kilo-	thousand	1 km = 1000 m

A **benchmark** is a comparison with a familiar measure. Benchmarks for the metric units of length are: 1 m is about the length of a baseball bat, 1 cm is about the width of a key on a telephone push pad, and 1 mm is about the thickness of a dime.

MODULE 3 SECTION 1   STUDY GUIDE

Metric Mass

Metric units of mass are based on the **gram** (g).
A benchmark for one gram is the mass of a
paper clip.

The table shows the commonly used units
of mass.

Name of unit	Relationship to a gram
milligram (mg)	1 mg = 0.001 g
kilogram (kg)	1 kg = 1000 g
metric ton	1 metric ton = 1,000,000 g

Exploration 3: Converting Metric Units

The prefixes used in the metric system are like place values. They show
how the other units of measure in the system are related to the basic unit.

Prefix	kilo-	hecto-	deka-	basic unit	deci-	centi-	milli-
Meaning	1000	100	10	1	0.1	0.01	0.001

To convert metric units, it is helpful to know how to multiply by special multipliers.

- To multiply by 10, 100, or 1000, move the decimal point to the right as many places as there are zeros in the multiplier.

$562.34 \times 100 = 562.34 = 56,234$

Move the decimal point 2 places to the right.

If there are not enough places to move the decimal point, add extra zeros to the right of the number in order to complete the movement.

34.72×1000

$= 34.720 \leftarrow$ Insert an extra 0 to the right in order to move the decimal point 3 places to the right.

$= 34,720$

- To multiply by 0.001, 0.01, or 0.1, move the decimal point to the left as many places as there are decimal places in the multiplier. If needed, insert zeros to the left of the original number.

16.79×0.001

$= .016.79 \leftarrow$ Insert an extra 0 to the left, in order to move the decimal point 3 places to the left.

$= 0.01679$

Example

The main span of the Brooklyn Bridge is about 486 m. The main span of the old
London Bridge is about 2620 cm. Which bridge has the longer span?

■ Sample Response ■

To make a comparision, both lengths should be expressed in terms of the same unit.

Brooklyn Bridge: 486 m = 48,600 cm   London Bridge: 2620 cm

So the main span of the Brooklyn Bridge is longer than that of the London Bridge.

Name _____ Date _____

Exploration 1

For Exercises 1 and 2, use the Venn diagram at the right, which shows the number of freshmen who are taking a Spanish or a French class at a certain school.

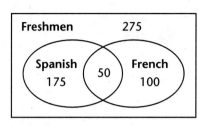

1. How many of the freshmen in the data group are taking

   a. a Spanish class but not a French class?

   b. a French class but not a Spanish class?

   c. both Spanish and French?

   d. neither Spanish nor French?

2. How many freshmen are in the data group?

Exploration 2

Decide which metric unit to use (*meter, centimeter, millimeter,* or *kilometer*) for the length of each item.

   3. a length of carpeting   **4.** the distance covered on an auto trip

   5. the thickness of a nickel   **6.** the length of a page in your textbook

Decide which metric unit to use (*milligram, gram, kilogram,* or *metric ton*) for the mass of each item.

   7. yourself   **8.** a truck   **9.** a feather   **10.** a serving of cereal

Find each product.

   11. 456.13×1000 **12.** 76.4×0.1 **13.** 9.245×0.001

Spiral Review

14. On two consecutive days, the maximum temperatures of Mr. Winters, a hospital patient, were 102.3° F and 99.7° F. The maximum temperatures on those same days of another patient, Mrs. Kumar, were 98.6° F and 101.9° F. Which patient had the greater change in maximum temperature? **(Module 2, pp. 145–146)**

15. For which description is it impossible to draw a trapezoid that fits the conditions? **(Module 2, p. 83)**

   A. contains two right angles   **B.** contains one right angle

   C. has three congruent sides   **D.** has four acute angles

MODULE 3 SECTION 2   **STUDY GUIDE**

Something Fishy   Fractions and Percents

GOAL **LEARN HOW TO:** • find a fraction of a whole number
• write a percent
• relate fractions, decimals, and percents

AS YOU: • make predictions from a sample
• compare samples that have different sizes

Exploration 1: Fractions of Whole Numbers

Finding a Fraction of a Whole

A **sample** is part of a whole set of objects being studied. The whole set is
called the **population**. If you know how many objects are in a population
and what fractional part of that population a sample represents, you can
determine how many objects are in the sample.

Example

Suppose $\frac{3}{5}$ of the 30 fish in an aquarium are guppies. How many of the fish are guppies?

Sample Response

Separate the 30 fish into 5 equal-sized groups. → There are 6 fish in each group.

Find the number of fish in 3 of these groups. → There are 3(6), or 18 fish in 3 groups.

So, $\frac{3}{5}$ of 30 is 18. There are 18 guppies in the aquarium.

Exploration 2: Writing Percents

Understanding Percent

Percent means *per hundred* or *out of 100*. In the 10×10
grid at the right, 40 of the 100 squares are shaded.
In percent form: 40% of the squares are shaded.
In decimal form: 0.40 (or 0.4) of the squares are shaded.

In fraction form: $\frac{40}{100}$ $\left(\text{or } \frac{2}{5}\right)$ of the squares are shaded.

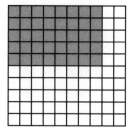

Name _____ Date _____

Using Percents or Decimals to Compare

To compare fractions using percents or decimals, first rewrite the fractions so their denominators are 100.

> ### Example
>
> Which is greater, $\frac{7}{20}$ or $\frac{14}{200}$?
>
> ### Sample Response
>
> Find the equivalent fractions with denominators of 100 so that you can rewrite each fraction as a percent. Then compare the percents.
>
> $$\frac{7}{20} = \frac{7 \cdot 5}{20 \cdot 5} = \frac{35}{100} = 0.35 = 35\% \qquad\qquad \frac{14}{200} = \frac{14 \div 2}{200 \div 2} = \frac{7}{100} = 0.07 = 7\%$$
>
> Since 35% > 7%, therefore $\frac{7}{20} > \frac{14}{200}$.

| **MODULE 3 SECTION 2** | **PRACTICE & APPLICATION EXERCISES** |

Exploration 1

Use mental math to find each value.

1. $\frac{2}{3}$ of 21   **2.** $\frac{3}{4}$ of 24   **3.** $\frac{5}{16}$ of 48   **4.** $\frac{7}{10}$ of 1000

Use compatible numbers to estimate.

5. $\frac{2}{5}$ of 27   **6.** $\frac{5}{7}$ of 29   **7.** $\frac{4}{9}$ of 87   **8.** $\frac{3}{5}$ of 9800

Food Inspection A supermarket purchased a mixture consisting of 4 types of nuts. An inspector examined a sample of the mixture to determine the extent of the variety. Use the table of results for Exercises 9 and 10.

Type of nut	Number of grams in sample
almonds	200
peanuts	800
pecans	400
walnuts	600

9. What fraction of the sample is each type of nut? Write each fraction in lowest terms.

     a. almonds   **b.** peanuts   **c.** pecans   **d.** walnuts

10. In all, there were 50 kilograms of the mixture of nuts. Use your answer to Exercise 9 to estimate the number of kilograms of each type of nut in the mixture.

Name _____   Date _____

Exploration 2

Write each percent as a fraction and as a decimal.

11. 70%   **12.** 38%   **13.** 8%   **14.** 15%

Write each fraction as a decimal and as a percent.

15. $\frac{7}{100}$ **16.** $\frac{11}{25}$ **17.** $\frac{100}{400}$ **18.** $\frac{12}{100}$

Spiral Review

19. Draw a regular pentagon. Show all the lines of symmetry of the figure. **(Module 2, pp. 84–86)**

20. Use the mathematical language scale on page 21 of your book to assess the description below. Explain. **(Module 1, pp. 20, 83)**

This is a trapezoid with a segment connecting the left endpoint of the top base to the bottom base.

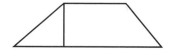

Name _____   Date _____

Amazing Animals   Bar Graphs and Line Plots

GOAL **LEARN HOW TO:** • find the range of a set of data
             • draw and interpret a bar graph
             • draw and interpret a line plot
        AS YOU: • work with data

Exploration 1: Bar Graphs

Range

The **range** of a set of numerical data is the difference between the greatest
and least values.

Example

For the set of numbers 54, 32, 198, 107, and 136,
    Range = greatest value – least value = 198 – 32 = 166.

Bar Graphs

A **bar graph** is used to compare data by comparing the
lengths of bars.

• A bar graph should always include a title.

• The bars can be horizontal or vertical.

• The numerical scale, which can be placed at the bottom
  or on the left, must use the same size steps.

• You can estimate the height (or length) of bars that are
  between grid lines.

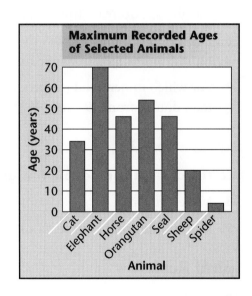

A **line plot** displays data using a line marked with a scale.
The scale must include the greatest and least values of the
data. The line plot shown below models that same data
shown in the bar graph at the right.

Maximum Recorded Ages of Selected Animals

Math Thematics, Book 1 **3-93**

Name _____   Date _____

Exploration 1

For Exercises 1 and 2, use the table.

Animal	Number of teeth
beaver	20
cat	30
elephant	6
horse	40
human	32
turtle	0

1. Find the range of the number of teeth.

2. Draw a bar graph to display the data.

A double bar graph compares two sets of related data. For Exercises 3–8, use the double bar graph.

3. About how many metric tons of copper were produced in the United States

    a. in 1987?   **b.** in 1992?

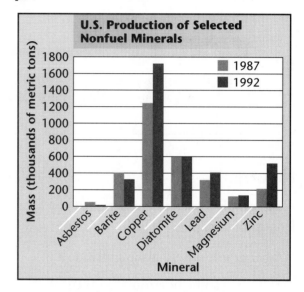

4. For which two minerals was the production of one of them in 1987 about the same as the production of the other in 1992?

5. For which mineral did the production show the greatest decrease from 1987 to 1992?

6. For which two minerals did the production remain unchanged from 1987 to 1992?

7. For which mineral did the production more than double from 1987 to 1992?

Exploration 2

Use the data in the double bar graph shown above.

8. Make a line plot for the data of 1987.

9. Make a line plot for the data of 1992.

Spiral Review

10. Of the following, which is the best estimate for the distance between Los Angeles, California and New York, New York? **(Module 3, p. 161–162)**

    A. 48 km   **B.** 480 km   **C.** 4800 km   **D.** 48,000 km

11. Moshe and Jim have a budget of $200 to buy food and decorations for a party. If they have spent $178.56 on food and $17.35 on decorations, will their budget allow for invitations that would cost $4.02? Explain. **(Module 2, p. 143–146)**

MODULE 3 SECTION 4

Animal Averages   Mean, Median, Mode

GOAL   **LEARN HOW TO:** • use averages to describe data
• write a fraction as a decimal using a calculator
• choose appropriate averages
• round decimal quotients

AS YOU: • find averages for different data sets

Exploration 1: Finding Mean, Median, and Mode

Averages

One method of summarizing data is to calculate an **average** for the set of values. There are three kinds of averages.

Mean: To find the mean, add all the values together and divide the sum by the number of values.

Data set: 30, 41, 32, 46, 37

$$\text{mean} = \frac{30 + 41 + 32 + 46 + 37}{5} = \frac{186}{5} = 37.2$$

Median: To find the median, arrange the values in order and find the middle value. If there are two middle values, the median is the mean of these two values.

Data set: 3, 4, 1, 1, 4, 6

In order, the data is 1, 1, 3, 4, 4, 6.

There are two middle numbers, 3 and 4.

$$\text{median} = \frac{3 + 4}{2} = \frac{7}{2} = 3.5$$

Mode: The mode is the value that occurs most often in a data set. There can be no mode or more than one mode for a data set.

Data set: 4, 3, 1, 1, 3, 1, 3, 4, 5, 6, 9

There are two modes, 1 and 3.

Depending on the situation and the data, one of these three averages may be more representative of the data than the others.

Exploration 2: Appropriate Averages

Writing a Fraction as a Decimal

You can use division to write a fraction as a decimal. For example, to write $\frac{3}{7}$ as a decimal, divide 3 by 7 by using a calculator. $\boxed{3}$ $\boxed{\div}$ $\boxed{7}$ $\boxed{=}$ $\boxed{0.4285714}$

Rounding Decimals

You round decimals in the same way that whole numbers are rounded. If the digit one place to the right of where you are rounding is 5 or greater, round up. Otherwise, leave the digit unchanged. For example, the result of rounding the decimal 2.483 to the nearest tenth is 2.5.

Name _____ Date _____

Exploration 1

Find the mean, the median, and the mode of each data set.

1. masses of 5 marsupial mice (in grams): 8, 5, 7, 6, 4

2. litter sizes of 6 naked mole rats: 25, 12, 12, 12, 10, 13

3. lengths of 10 elephant tusks (in feet): 11, 10, 8, 10, 5, 8, 8, 10, 4, 9

For Exercises 4–6, tell whether the *mean, median,* or *mode* is being used.

4. Half of the houses sold were priced at $180,000 or less.

5. The average number of children in the households studied was 2.7.

6. The most popular women's shoe size is 7.

7. Writing Juan Ruiz owns a large citrus farm from which he has a monthly income of $8000. During the orange-picking season, Mr. Ruiz paid the four Mendez brothers $600, $700, $600, and $800 for part-time work during one month. Which type of average would you use as a fair representation of these 5 monthly incomes? Explain.

8. Challenge On her 5 math tests so far this grading period, Leah has earned grades of 94%, 86%, 92%, 80%, and 78%. The last math test for this grading period was this morning and Leah's mean grade on all 6 tests is 85%. What grade did Leah earn on the test this morning? What strategies did you use to obtain your answer?

Exploration 2

Calculator Write each fraction as a decimal rounded to the nearest hundredth.

9. $\frac{2}{9}$ **10.** $\frac{9}{4}$ **11.** $\frac{11}{8}$ **12.** $\frac{8}{12}$

Round each decimal to the given place.

13. 9.3478 (tenths)   **14.** 0.3857 (hundredths)   **15.** 154.2395 (thousandths)

Spiral Review

16. Write 7.8, 0.078, 7.08, and 0.807 in order from least to greatest. **(Module 2, pp. 136–137)**

17. For which transformation is Figure B the image of Figure A? **(Module 2, pp. 121–123)**

Figure A   Figure B

MODULE 3 SECTION 5   STUDY GUIDE

The Perfect Pet   Dividing Decimals, Estimation, and Mental Math

GOAL   **LEARN HOW TO:** • divide a decimal by a whole number
                                  • use estimation and mental math strategies
        AS YOU: • find averages

Exploration 1: Dividing Decimals

Divide a Decimal by a Whole Number

Divide as though both numbers, the dividend as well as the divisor, were whole numbers.

Write the decimal point in the quotient directly above the decimal point in the dividend.

$$
\begin{array}{r}
8.95 \\
4\overline{)35.80} \\
\underline{32} \\
3\,8 \\
\underline{3\,6} \\
20 \\
\underline{20} \\
0
\end{array}
$$

Add zeros to the right end of ← the dividend as needed to continue the division.

Exploration 2: Estimation and Mental Math

Front-End Estimation

One way to estimate a sum is front-end estimation, a technique that focuses on the left-most digits, since they have the greatest value.

Example

Use front-end estimation to estimate the sum: 3.45 + 2.57 + 4.04.

■ Sample Response ■

1. For a first estimate, focus on the left-most digits.

$$\left.\begin{array}{r} 3.45 \\ 2.57 \\ +4.04 \end{array}\right\} 3 + 2 + 4 = 9$$

2. Look at the decimal parts separately.

$$\left.\begin{array}{r} 0.45 \\ 0.57 \\ +0.04 \end{array}\right\} \text{about } 1$$

3. Adjust your estimate: 9 + 1 = 10. → The sum is about 10.

Trading Off

In this technique, you add an amount to one of the numbers so that the new number is easy to compute with mentally and then subtract the same amount from the other number.

MODULE 3 SECTION 5   STUDY GUIDE

Example

$$
\begin{array}{l}
\begin{matrix} 3.87 \\ +\,1.38 \end{matrix} \rightarrow
\begin{matrix} 3.87 + 0.13 \rightarrow \\ +\,1.38 - 0.13 \rightarrow \end{matrix}
\left. \begin{matrix} 4.00 \\ +\,1.25 \end{matrix} \right\} 5.25 \leftarrow \text{Use mental math.}
\end{array}
$$

MODULE 3 SECTION 5 | PRACTICE & APPLICATION EXERCISES

Exploration 1

For Exercises 1–3, find each quotient. Use estimation to check.

1. $5\overline{)7.25}$ **2.** $24\overline{)21.48}$ **3.** $2.87 \div 14$

4. Eight cans of Pal Dog Food are stacked one upon the other. If the height of the stack is 99.2 cm, find the height of one can.

5. If 5 oranges cost $2.25, what is the cost of 7 oranges? Explain.

Exploration 2

Estimation Use front-end estimation to estimate each sum.

6. $2689 + 4328$ **7.** $16.5 + 18.3$ **8.** $32 + 46 + 78 + 93$

Mental Math Use trading off to find each sum.

9. $27 + 39$ **10.** $0.16 + 0.78$ **11.** $697 + 898 + 207$

Estimation The numbers of male commissioned officers on active duty in the U.S. Army in the years shown in the table *cluster* around 77,000.

12. Use clustering to estimate the total number of male commissioned officers during the 3-year period.

13. Explain how you could use clustering to estimate the total number of female commissioned officers during the 3-year period.

U.S. Army Personnel on Active Duty: Commissioned Officers		
Year	**Male**	**Female**
1990	79,520	11,810
1991	77,489	11,959
1992	74,326	11,627

Spiral Review

For Exercises 14–16, complete each pair of equivalent fractions.
(Module 2, pp. 110–113)

14. $\dfrac{4}{5} = \dfrac{?}{30}$ **15.** $\dfrac{3}{7} = \dfrac{?}{42}$ **16.** $\dfrac{5}{16} = \dfrac{20}{?}$

17. Can three segments of lengths 3 cm, 3 cm, and 6 cm form an isosceles triangle? Explain. **(Module 1, pp. 16–17)**

Name _____   Date _____

Dinosaurs   Stem-and-Leaf Plots and Dividing by a Decimal

GOAL   **LEARN HOW TO:** • make and interpret a stem-and-leaf plot
                              • divide by a decimal
          AS YOU: • compare data

Exploration 1: Stem-and-Leaf Plots

A **stem-and-leaf plot** is used to compare data.

Example

The Baltimore Weather Bureau   46 31 33 42 25 29 37 44 45 36
recorded these daily high temperatures, 35 40 52 48 35 39 40 42 51 29
in °F, for the month of November.   45 30 26 52 44 54 46 43 45 42
Make a stem-and-leaf plot of the data.

Sample Response

To make a stem-and-leaf plot for the data:

Note that the temperatures can be   stems
arranged into 4 groups: the 20's,   2 |
the 30's, the 40's, and the 50's.   3 |
Use the tens digits for the stems.   4 |
                                           5 |

Now use the ones digits for the leaves.   leaves
Read through the data, placing the leaves 2 | 5 9 9 6
next to the corresponding stem in the   3 | 1 3 7 6 5 5 9 0
order that the values appear in the data set. 4 | 6 2 4 5 0 8 0 2 5 4 6 3 5 2
                                           5 | 2 1 2 4

Then rewrite the display with the leaves   2 | 5 6 9 9
in order from least to greatest.   3 | 0 1 3 5 5 6 7 9
                                           4 | 0 0 2 2 2 3 4 4 5 5 5 6 6 8
                                           5 | 1 2 2 4

Finally, write a title above the plot and a key below it.

November Daily High Temperatures in Baltimore

2 | 5 6 9 9
3 | 0 1 3 5 5 6 7 9
4 | 0 0 2 2 2 3 4 4 5 5 5 6 6 8
5 | 1 2 2 4

2 | 5 means 25° F

MODULE 3 SECTION 6   STUDY GUIDE

Exploration 2: Dividing by a Decimal

Example

Find the quotient $175.5 \div 0.25$.

Sample Response

Multiply both numbers by 100 in order
to change the divisor, 0.25, to a whole number.
One zero must be inserted to the right of
the dividend, 175.5, to accomplish this.

$$0.25\overline{)175.50} \atop {\times 100 \,\, \times 100} \;\;\rightarrow\;\; 25\overline{)17550.}$$

Now divide as you would for whole numbers.
Place the decimal point in the quotient directly
above the decimal point in the dividend.

$$\begin{array}{r} 702. \\ 25\overline{)17550.} \\ -175\downarrow\downarrow \\ \hline 050 \\ -\;\;50 \\ \hline 0 \end{array}$$

MODULE 3 SECTION 6 | PRACTICE & APPLICATION EXERCISES

Exploration 1

For Exercises 1–8, use the stem-and-leaf plot.

1. How many people were surveyed?

2. How many people were younger than 25?

3. How many people were younger than 35?

4. How many people were older than 45?

Age Survey at a Movie Screening

```
2 | 1 3 3 6 8 8 9 9
3 | 2 3 5 7 9
4 | 0 1 4 6 8 9
5 | 1 3 4 7 8 9
```

2 | 1 means 21 years

Find the following statistical values for the data.

5. the range   **6.** the mean   **7.** the median   **8.** the mode

**Botany A researcher recorded the heights (in cm)
of one specimen of each of 16 varieties of tulips.
The data set is shown at the right.**

31	42	28	27
35	38	49	19
25	37	43	36
40	41	39	24

9. Make a stem-and-leaf plot for the data.

10. Use your stem-and-leaf plot to find how many of the tulips

a. were shorter than 36 cm.   **b.** were taller than 31 cm.

11. What percent of the tulips were between 20 cm and 29 cm tall?

Name _____   Date _____

Use the stem-and-leaf plot or the bar graph to answer Exercises 12–15. For each question, tell which display you used and why.

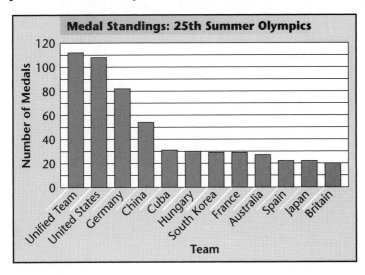

Medal Standings:
25th Summer Olympics

```
 2 | 0 2 2 7 9 9
 3 | 0 1
 4 |
 5 | 4
 6 |
 7 |
 8 | 2
 9 |
10 | 8
11 | 2
```

11 | 2 means 112 medals

12. Which team won 82 medals in the 25th Summer Olympics?

13. What was the greatest number of medals won by any team?

14. Which teams earned the same number of medals?

15. What was the total number of medals won by the 12 teams shown?

Exploration 2

For Exercises 16–19, find each quotient. Show your work.

16. $0.12\overline{)4.824}$ **17.** $1.7\overline{)159.12}$ **18.** $0.08\overline{)24.4}$ **19.** $0.009\overline{)8.127}$

20. The length of the living room in the McArdle house is to be 6.096 m. In the blueprint of the house, the architect has drawn that length as 4.8 cm. How many times the length of the blueprint measure will the actual length of the living room be?

Spiral Review

21. a. Use a calculator to find the decimal equivalents of $\frac{1}{11}, \frac{2}{11}, \frac{3}{11}, \frac{4}{11}$, and $\frac{5}{11}$.

  b. Write a rule to describe the pattern of decimals in part (a). **(Module 3, p. 200)**

22. Using the pattern found in part (b) of Exercise 21, write the decimal equivalent of $\frac{9}{11}$. Use a calculator to check your answer. **(Module 1, p. 3–7)**

MODULE 3   **TECHNOLOGY**

For Use with Section 3

1. The table shown below contains the same information as the table at the
bottom of page 191. Use spreadsheet software to make a table like the one
shown below.

Animal	Life span (years)
cat	12
dog	12
goat	8
guinea pig	4
horse	20
pig	10
rabbit	5
sheep	12
white mouse	3

2. Below are two bar graphs, graph A and graph B, that are based on the
information in the table for Exercise 1.

a. In which bar graph does the difference in life spans between the horse
and the white mouse appear greatest? _____

b. What causes the bar graphs to present the information in different ways?

_____

_____

Graph A

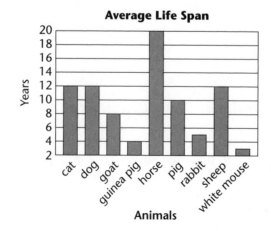

MODULE 3   **TECHNOLOGY**

Graph B

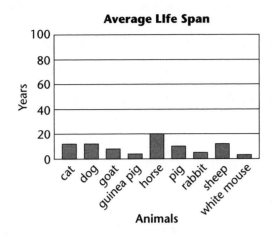

Average Life Span

3. Use the data in the table for Exercise 1 on page 189 to make two bar graphs that display the data in entirely different ways. (Note: To change the appearance of graphs using spreadsheet software, double click in the inside of the graph.) Explain what you did to cause the differences.

_____

_____

Name _____   Date _____

MODULE 3 QUIZ   MID-MODULE

1. Sketch a Venn diagram that includes two sets: the months of the year that begin with a vowel, and the months whose names have more than 5 letters.

Replace each ___?___ with the number that makes the statement true.

2. 2.6 metric tons = ___?___ kg   **3.** 194 mg = ___?___ g   **4.** 57 m = ___?___ mm

5. 1392 mm = ___?___ cm   **6.** 4840 kg = ___?___ metric tons   **7.** 69 cm = ___?___ m

Replace each ___?___ with > , < , or =.

8. 42 cm ___?___ 0.4 m   **9.** 16 kg ___?___ 1600 g   **10.** 0.39 m ___?___ 40 mm

Use mental math to find each value.

11. $\frac{4}{9}$ of 36   **12.** $\frac{3}{8}$ of 64   **13.** $\frac{3}{16}$ of 80   **14.** $\frac{3}{4}$ of 92

Write each percent as a fraction in lowest terms and as a decimal.

15. 28%   **16.** 37%   **17.** 64%   **18.** 80%

Write each fraction as a decimal and as a percent.

19. $\frac{36}{400}$ **20.** $\frac{10}{200}$ **21.** $\frac{23}{50}$ **22.** $\frac{18}{25}$

Replace each ___?___ with > , < , or =.

23. 49% ___?___ 0.051   **24.** $\frac{19}{25}$ ___?___ 80%

25. $\frac{140}{200}$ ___?___ 70%   **26.** $\frac{11}{400}$ ___?___ 3%

27. What is the range of the following set of numbers?
8.1, 9.8, 6.2, 14.5, 9.4, 17.1, 11.3

28. Draw a bar graph and line plot for the data below. What is the greatest length, the shortest length, and the range of the lengths of the birds selected?

Lengths of Selected Birds (From Bill to Tail)			
Bird	Length (inches)	Bird	Length (inches)
great egret	38	pintail duck	27
flamingo	48	loon	32
blue faced booby	32	screech owl	10
puffin	12	blue jay	12

Name _____ Date _____

Use the Venn diagram to answer Exercises 1–3.

1. What green vegetables are shown in the Venn diagram? How do you know where to look for them in the diagram?

2. Name all the vegetables shown in the Venn diagram that are not green.

3. Name two foods that could be placed outside of the two sets shown.

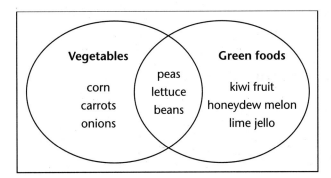

Replace each __?__ with the value that makes the statement true.

4. 3.94 m = __?__ mm

5. 10,000 kg = __?__ metric tons

6. 17.3 g = __?__ mg

7. 2500 cm = __?__ km

8. 0.2 m = __?__ cm

9. 4.2 kg = __?__ g

Find each value.

10. $\frac{2}{3}$ of 90

11. $\frac{7}{8}$ of 64

12. $\frac{1}{5}$ of 75

Write each fraction as a decimal and as a percent.

13. $\frac{20}{400}$

14. $\frac{12}{25}$

15. $\frac{3}{1000}$

16. Make a bar graph and a line plot for the data in the table.

Speed of Selected Land Mammals			
Animal	**Speed (mi/h)**	**Animal**	**Speed (mi/h)**
snake	2	greyhound	40
human	20	jack rabbit	45
elephant	25	gazelle	50
house cat	30	cheetah	65

17. Find the mean, median, and mode for the data in Exercise 16, rounded to the nearest mi/h.

Name _____ Date _____

Find the quotient. Round to the nearest thousandth if necessary.

18. $3\overline{)28.56}$

19. $12\overline{)1024.8}$

20. $\dfrac{76}{16}$

Use front-end estimation to estimate each sum.

21. $\$12.89 + \$46.05$

22. $211 + 754 + 438$

Use trading off to find each sum.

23. $68 + 143$

24. $7.94 + 4.09$

Use the stem-and-leaf plot below to answer Exercises 25–27.

Gray Wolf Lengths (Inches)

```
4 | 1 5 5 8
5 | 0 5 7 7 9
6 | 3 5 6 6 6
7 | 6 9
```

4 | 5 means 45 in.

25. What is the length of the shortest gray wolf in the stem-and-leaf plot?

26. What is the range of the wolf lengths?

27. Find the mean, median, and mode of the wolf lengths.

Find each quotient.

28. $0.036\overline{)3.3156}$

29. $2.7\overline{)2.268}$

30. $8.45\overline{)29.575}$

Name _____ Date _____

Use the Venn diagram to answer Exercises 1–3.

1. Which sports shown in the Venn diagram are indoor sports played with a ball? How do you find them on the Venn diagram?

2. Which sports shown on the Venn diagram are outdoor sports played with a ball?

3. How would you characterize the sports that belong outside of the two sets? Which of the following sports could you place in that area: sailing, bowling, football, pool, boxing, mountain climbing, weightlifting, skydiving, croquet?

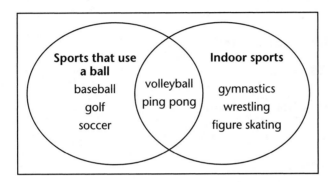

Replace each ___?___ with the value that makes the statement true.

4. 8000 kg = ___?___ metric tons   5. 2.81 m = ___?___ mm

6. 4700 cm = ___?___ km   7. 34.5 g = ___?___ mg

8. 6.2 kg = ___?___ g   9. 0.08 m = ___?___ cm

Find each value.

10. $\frac{5}{8}$ of 72   11. $\frac{1}{3}$ of 108   12. $\frac{2}{5}$ of 220

Write each fraction as a decimal and as a percent.

13. $\frac{22}{25}$ 14. $\frac{420}{1000}$ 15. $\frac{38}{200}$

MODULE 3 TEST   FORM **B**

16. Make a bar graph and a line plot for the data in the table.

Gestation Period for Selected Mammals			
Animal	**Gestation period (months)**	**Animal**	**Gestation period (months)**
antelope	9	giraffe	15
bear	7	horse	11
cow	9	kangaroo	11
donkey	12	human	9

17. Find the mean, median, and mode for the data in Exercise 16, rounded to the nearest tenth of a month.

Find the quotient. Round to the nearest thousandth.

18. $5\overline{)16.46}$ 　　　　　**19.** $12\overline{)297.43}$ 　　　　　**20.** $\dfrac{94}{6}$

Use front-end estimation to estimate each sum.

21. $209 + 543 + 651$ 　　　　　**22.** $12.32 + 2.06 + 3.57$

Use trading off to find each sum.

23. $4.89 + 13.21$ 　　　　　**24.** $4.03 + 8.92 + 5.14$

Use the stem-and-leaf plot below to answer Exercises 25–27.

Bobcat Lengths (inches)

```
2 | 8 9
3 | 0 2 5 5 6
4 | 0 3 3 3 6 8 9
5 | 0
```

3 | 2 means 32 in.

25. What is the length of the longest gray bobcat in the stem-and-leaf plot?

26. What is the range of the bobcat lengths?

27. Find the mean, median, and mode of the bobcat lengths.

Find each quotient.

28. $4.3\overline{)7.224}$ 　　　　　**29.** $0.056\overline{)4.6704}$ 　　　　　**30.** $6.12\overline{)33.66}$

Name _____   Date _____

1. Which of the following animals belong in the shaded area in the Venn diagram?

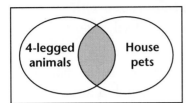

a. elephant   **b.** penguin
c. canary   **d.** dog

2. Use the stem-and-leaf plot to find the range of the data.

**Zoo Population of
Selected Monkey Species**

```
0 | 2 4 4 7
1 | 0 2 6
2 | 3 5
3 | 2
```

1 | 2 means 12 monkeys

a. 28   **b.** 30
c. 32   **d.** 36

3. Which of the following is the greatest mass?

a. 0.023 metric tons   **b.** 200 kg
c. 23,001 g   **d.** 0.21 metric tons

4. Find $\frac{5}{9}$ of 72.

a. 36   **b.** 40
c. 42   **d.** 45

5. Write $\frac{48}{600}$ as a percent.

a. 48%   **b.** 24%
c. 8%   **d.** 6%

6. Find the mean of the following data.
6.2, 4.5, 3.1, 5.8, 7.3, 6.1

a. 5.5   **b.** 5.2
c. 4.7   **d.** 6.1

7. Find the median of the following data.
30, 45, 51, 52, 55, 55, 67

a. 40   **b.** 49.3
c. 52   **d.** 95

8. What is the mode of the data in the line plot below?

Height of Selected 12-Year Olds

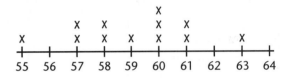

a. 55   **b.** 59
c. 60   **d.** 63

9. How much does each person get if $128.52 is divided evenly among 7 people?

a. $18.14   **b.** $18.29
c. $18.36   **d.** $18.53

10. Which pair of measurements represents equal lengths?

a. 120 mm, 1.2 cm   **b.** 8 km, 800 m
c. 47 cm, 0.47 m   **d.** 6000 mm, 6 km

11. Using the stem-and-leaf plot in Question 2, find the mean.

a. 16   **b.** 14.5
c. 13.5   **d.** 12

12. What is the quotient?
$$32.4\overline{)14.58}$$

a. 4.5   **b.** 0.45
c. 5.4   **d.** 0.49

MODULE 3   MODULE PERFORMANCE ASSESSMENT

To identify an unknown butterfly, it is important to estimate the butterfly's size relative to other butterflies. Butterflies like the swallowtails and Monarch are relatively large. The Clouded Sulfur and Painted Lady are medium sized. Others, like skippers, are small in comparison with the whole range of butterfly sizes.

The table below lists the maximum wingspan of selected butterflies. Use the data to create two different data displays. Then find the mean, median, and mode. How would you categorize a large, medium, and small butterfly?

Butterfly	Maximum wingspan (cm)	Butterfly	Maximum wingspan (cm)
Pipevine Swallowtail	8.6	Pearl Cresent	3.8
Anise Swallowtail	7.6	Question Mark	6.7
Western Tiger Swallowtail	9.8	Mourning Cloak	8.6
Veined White	4.1	American Painted Lady	5.4
Clouded Sulfur	5.1	Buckeye	6.4
Cloudless Sulfur	7.0	Viceroy	7.6
Little Copper	2.9	Hackberry Butterfly	5.7
Banded Hairstreak	3.2	Little Wood Satyr	4.8
Gray Hairstreak	3.2	Monarch	10.2
Silvery Blue	3.2	Long Tailed Skipper	5.1
Gulf Fritillary	7.3	Common Checked Skipper	3.2
Meadow Fritillary	4.8	European Skipper	2.5
Tawny-edged Skipper	2.5	Broad-winged Skipper	4.5

Answers

PRACTICE AND APPLICATIONS

Module 3, Section 1

1.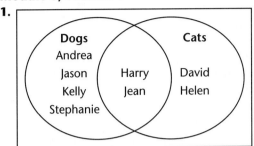

2. **a.** 6 names; Mary, Susan, Jane, Dana, Taylor, Leslie **b.** 7 names; Dana, Taylor, Leslie, Frank, Herb, Ralph, Bob **c.** The names are both girl and boy names. **d.** It is not the name of a girl or a boy; a dog might have such a name.

3. **a.** meter **b.** centimeter **c.** millimeter

4. **a.** 37 mm **b.** 3.7 cm

5. **a.** gram **b.** milligram **c.** metric ton

6. **a.** Sample Response: eagle or ostrich **b.** Sample Response: hummingbird

7. **a.** 2000; 10,000 **b.** 0.002; 0.058 **c.** 2000; 6200

8. **a.** 0.08 **b.** 0.073 **c.** 0.0009 **d.** 0.03 **e.** 29 **f.** 0.001 **g.** 0.0047 **h.** 0.93 **i.** 0.0005

9. **a.** 4000 **b.** 710 **c.** 0.325 **d.** 6.310 **e.** 400 **f.** 520

10. **a.** < **b.** = **c.** > **d.** > **e.** < **f.** >

11. evergreen tree; 1182 cm or 11.82 m

Module 3, Section 2

1. **a.** 6 **b.** 16 **c.** 6 **d.** 21 **e.** 8 **f.** 12

2. **a.** 15 marbles **b.** 14 marbles

3. **a.** $\frac{35}{100}$ or $\frac{7}{20}$, 35% **b.** $\frac{2}{10}$ or $\frac{1}{5}$, 20% **c.** $\frac{17}{100}$, 17% **d.** $\frac{8}{100}$ or $\frac{2}{25}$, 8% **e.** $\frac{24}{100}$ or $\frac{6}{25}$, 24% **f.** $\frac{75}{100}$ or $\frac{3}{4}$, 75%

4. **a.** 0.07, 7% **b.** 0.16, 16% **c.** 0.6, 60% **d.** 0.4, 40% **e.** 0.45, 45% **f.** 0.7, 70%

5. **a.** > **b.** > **c.** = **d.** < **e.** < **f.** =

6. **a.** 1500 **b.** $\frac{1800}{2500}$ or $\frac{18}{25}$, 72%

Module 3, Section 3

1. **a.** 7 **b.** 6.3

2. 1997; 1995

3. Sample Response: about 70

4. 40 participants

5. Sample Response: about 340 participants

6. **a.** 90

b.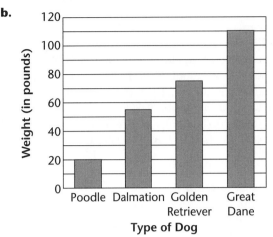

7. 40 min

8. 8 students

9. 16 students

10. Sample Response: Most students exercise 30 or 35 minutes.

11. **a.** 10

b. **Heights of Students in Ms. Samuel's Class**

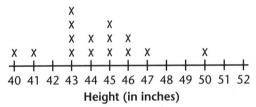

c. Yes; 43 in. **d.** No. **e.** Sample Response: Most students in the class are from 43 to 45 in. tall.

Module 3, Section 4

1. **a.** 3, 3, 2 **b.** 16, 15, 16 **c.** 23, 22, 34 **d.** 15, 15, no mode

2. 24, 23, 22

3. Sample Response: Either the mean of 5 in. or the median of 3 in. would be appropriate. The mode is 0 in. and would not be appropriate since some snow did fall during the 7-day period.

4. **a.** 0.38 **b.** 0.6 **c.** 0.78 **d.** 1.67 **e.** 1.17 **f.** 0.29 **g.** 0.42 **h.** 1.8 **i.** 0.62

5. **a.** 0.5 **b.** 0.156 **c.** 2.80 **d.** 3.8 **e.** 12 **f.** 2.701 **g.** 24.5 **h.** 59

Module 3, Section 5

1. **a.** 32 ÷ 8 = 4; 4.06 **b.** 48 ÷ 4 = 12; 12.35 **c.** 80 ÷ 20 = 4

2. **a.** 2.83; 12 ÷ 4 = 3 **b.** 3.15; 15 ÷ 5 = 3 **c.** 5.225; 30 ÷ 6 = 5 **d.** 7.25; 56 ÷ 8 = 7 **e.** 2.475; 16 ÷ 8 = 2 **f.** 1.05; 12 ÷ 12 = 1

g. 3.235; 12 ÷ 4 = 3 **h.** 5.025; 30 ÷ 6 = 5
i. 4.19; 28 ÷ 7 = 4 **j.** 3.42; 15 ÷ 5 = 3
k. 2.95; 12 ÷ 4 = 3 **l.** 9.315; 18 ÷ 2 = 9
3. a. correct **b.** not correct; 23.45 **c.** not correct;
2.65
4. 3.42 m
5. 122.6 mi
6. a. about 9000 **b.** about 60 **c.** about 1000
d. about 230 **e.** about 7000 **f.** about 18
g. about 12 **h.** about 210 **i.** about 800 **j.** about
7000 **k.** about 32 **l.** about 200
7. a. 103 **b.** 0.78 **c.** 115 **d.** 9.2 **e.** 77 **f.** $4.77
g. 96 **h.** 1.09 **i.** 382 **j.** 8.4 **k.** 177 **l.** 7.6
8. $5.85

Module 3, Section 6
1. 68; 100
2. 5 students
3. 17 students
4. 2 students
5. No students scored 85.
6. 87.1 (to the nearest tenth), 90, 91
7. a. 70 **b.** 0.03 **c.** 2.4 **d.** 0.714 **e.** 16.25 **f.** 4.125
g. 6.9 **h.** 3.7 **i.** 7.6 **8.** $.68
9. 24 pieces

Module 3, Sections 1–6
1. a. April, August, October **b.** October **c.** 4 months
d. They are the months that neither begin with a
vowel nor end with "r."
2. a. 6000 **b.** 580 **c.** 0.418 **d.** 5.27 **e.** 300 **f.** 750
3. a. 18 **b.** 35 **c.** 28
4. a. 0.28, 28% **b.** 0.4, 40% **c.** 0.55, 55%
5. a. 6
b. Cans Collected at Audy School

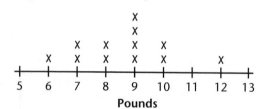

Pounds

6. 10.75, 10, 10
7. a. 0.44 **b.** 0.88 **c.** 0.17
8. a. 3.98 **b.** 4.36 **c.** 2.325
9. a. about 8000 **b.** about 50 **c.** about 900
d. about 170
10. a. 76; 100 **b.** 89.5 (to the nearest tenth), 89, 89
11. a. 3.6 **b.** 18 **c.** 6.55

STUDY GUIDE

Module 3, Section 1
1. a. 175 **b.** 100 **c.** 50 **d.** 275
2. 600

3. meter
4. kilometer
5. millimeter
6. centimeter
7. kilogram
8. metric ton
9. milligram
10. gram
11. 456,130
12. 7.64
13. 0.009245
14. Mrs. Kumar
15. B and D

Module 3, Section 2
1. 14
2. 18
3. 15
4. 700
5. about 10
6. about 20
7. about 40
8. about 6000
9. a. $\frac{1}{10}$

b. $\frac{2}{5}$

c. $\frac{1}{5}$

d. $\frac{3}{10}$

10. almonds: about 5 kg; peanuts: about 20 kg;
pecans: about 10 kg; walnuts: about 15 kg
11. $\frac{70}{100}$ or $\frac{7}{10}$; 0.70 or 0.7
12. $\frac{38}{100}$ or $\frac{19}{50}$; 0.38
13. $\frac{8}{100}$ or $\frac{2}{25}$; 0.08
14. $\frac{15}{100}$ or $\frac{3}{20}$; 0.15
15. 0.07; 7%
16. 0.44; 44%
17. 0.25; 25%
18. 0.12; 12%
19.

20. Sample Response: 3; The terms were used correctly
but the description would not require that this exact
diagram be drawn. More needs to be said about the
segment joining the two bases. "This is a trapezoid
with a segment that connects the left endpoint of the
top base to the bottom base. The segment meets the
lower base at a right angle, dividing the trapezoid into
a right triangle and another trapezoid."

Module 3, Section 3

1. 40

2.

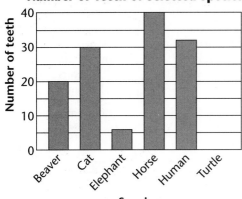

Number of Teeth of Selected Species

Species

3. a. about 1,250,000 metric tons **b.** about 1,725,000 metric tons

4. barite and lead

5. barite

6. diatomite, magnesium

7. zinc

8. U.S. Production of Selected Nonfuel Minerals in 1987

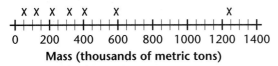

Mass (thousands of metric tons)

9. U.S. Production of Selected Nonfuel Minerals in 1992

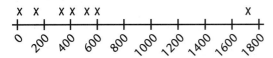

Mass (thousands of metric tons)

10. c

11. Yes; On food and decorations, they spent $195.91. With $4.09 remaining, there is enough for the invitations.

Module 3, Section 4

1. 6; 6; no mode

2. 14; 12; 12

3. 8.3; 8.5; 8 and 10

4. median

5. mean

6. mode

7. Sample Response: The median, $700, or the mode, $600, would be a fair representation since 4 of the 5 incomes are clustered together near these numbers, while the other number is much greater. The mean, $2140, would not be a fair representation since it is significantly greater than 4 of the 5 incomes.

8. 80%; Sample Response: Use guess and check.

9. 0.22

10. 2.25

11. 1.38

12. 0.67

13. 9.3

14. 0.39

15. 154.240

16. 0.078, 0.807, 7.08, 7.8

17. reflection

Module 3, Section 5

1. 1.45; $7 \div 5 = 1.4$

2. 0.895; $20 \div 25 = 0.8$

3. 0.205; $3 \div 15 = 0.2$

4. 12.4 cm

5. $3.15; Sample Response: Divide the given price by 5 to find the cost of one orange, and then multiply the result by 7.

6. about 7000

7. about 35

8. about 250

9. $26 + 40 = 66$

10. $0.14 + 0.80 = 0.94$

11. $700 + 900 + 202 = 1802$

12. about 231,000 male commissioned officers

13. Sample Response: The number of female commissioned officers during each year of the 3-year period clusters around 12,000. Multiply this cluster value by 3, the number of years. So there was a total of about 36,000 female commissioned officers on active duty in the U.S. Army during the 3-year period.

14. 24

15. 18

16. 64

17. No; the sum of the lengths of the two shorter sides is not greater than the length of the longest side.

Module 3, Section 6

1. 25 people

2. 3 people

3. 10 people

4. 9 people

5. 38

6. 39.32

7. 39

8. 23, 28, and 29

9. Heights of Tulips

```
1 | 9
2 | 4  5  7  8
3 | 1  5  6  7  8  9
4 | 0  1  2  3  9
```

1 | 9 means 19 cm

10. a. 7 **b.** 10

11. 25%

12. Germany; the bar graph; The stem-and-leaf plot does not identify the teams.

13. 112; stem-and-leaf plot; The number would have to be estimated from the bar graph.

14. South Korea and France, and Spain and Japan; bar graph; The stem-and-leaf plot does not identify the teams.

15. 566; stem-and-leaf plot; The numbers for a total would have to be estimated from the bar graph.

16. 40.2

17. 93.6

18. 305

19. 903

20. 127 times the blueprint measure

21. a. $\frac{1}{11} = 0.090909...$, $\frac{2}{11} = 0.181818...$, $\frac{3}{11} = 0.272727...$, $\frac{4}{11} = 0.363636...$, $\frac{5}{11} = 0.454545...$

b. Sample Response: Each decimal repeats two digits. The first repeated digit is 1 less than the numerator of the fraction and the sum of the two digits is 9.

22. $\frac{9}{11} = 0.818181...$

TECHNOLOGY

Module 3

1. Check students' work.

2. a. Graph A **b.** The scale for the vertical axis is different in the two graphs. In one graph, the values range from 2 to 20 by twos. In the other graph, the values range from 0 to 100 by twenties.

3. Sample Response:

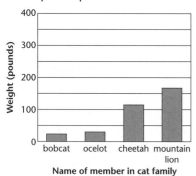

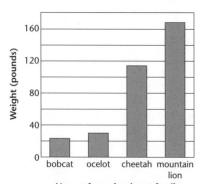

To change the appearance of the graphs, I changed the scale on the vertical axis.

ASSESSMENT

Mid-Module 3 Quiz

1.

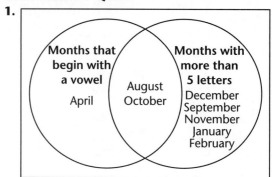

2. 2600

3. 0.194

4. 57,000

5. 139.2

6. 4.84

7. 0.69

8. >

9. >

10. >

11. 16

12. 24

13. 15

14. 69

15. $\frac{7}{25}$, 0.28

16. $\frac{37}{100}$, 0.37

17. $\frac{16}{25}$, 0.64

18. $\frac{4}{5}$, 0.8

19. 0.09, 9%

20. 0.05, 5%

21. 0.46, 46%

22. 0.72, 72%

23. >

24. <

25. =

26. <

27. 10.9

28.

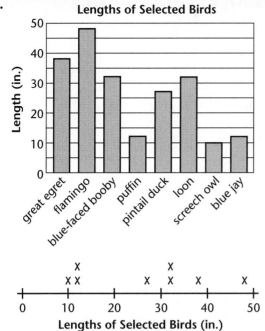

Lengths of Selected Birds

Lengths of Selected Birds (in.)

48 in., 10 in., 38 in.

Module 3 Test (Form A)

1. peas, beans, lettuce; They are found in the area where the two sets overlap.

2. corn, carrots, onions

3. Sample Response: peanut butter, milk

4. 3940

5. 10

6. 17,300

7. 0.025

8. 20

9. 4200

10. 60

11. 56

12. 15

13. 0.05, 5%

14. 0.48, 48%

15. 0.003, 0.3%

16.

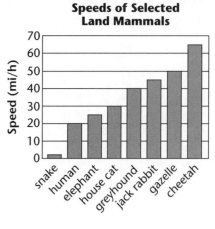

Speeds of Selected Land Mammals

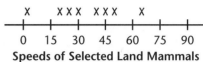

Speeds of Selected Land Mammals (in mi/h)

17. mean = about 35 mi/h, median = 35 mi/h, no mode

18. 9.52

19. 85.4

20. 4.75

21. about $60

22. about 1400

23. 211

24. 12.03

25. 41 in.

26. 38 in.

27. mean = about 58.6 in., median = 58 in., mode = 66 in.

28. 92.1

29. 0.84

30. 3.5

Module 3 Test (Form B)

1. volleyball and pingpong; They are found in the region where the two sets overlap.

2. soccer, baseball, golf

3. outdoor sports played without a ball; sailing, mountain climbing, skydiving

4. 8

5. 2810

6. 0.047

7. 34,500

8. 6200

9. 8

10. 45

11. 36

12. 88

13. 0.88, 88%

14. 0.42, 42%

15. 0.19, 19%

16.

Gestation Periods for Selected Mammals

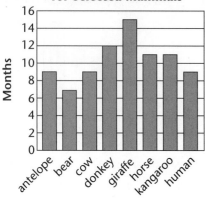

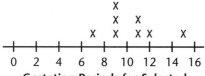

Gestation Periods for Selected Mammals (in months)

17. mean ≈ 10.3 months, median = 10 months, mode = 9 months

18. 3.292

19. 24.786

20. 15.667

21. about 1400

22. about 18

23. 18.1

24. 18.09

25. 50 in.

26. 22 in.

27. mean ≈ 39.1 in., median = 40 in., mode = 43 in.

28. 1.68

29. 83.4

30. 5.5

STANDARDIZED ASSESSMENT

Module 3

1. d

2. b

3. d

4. b

5. c

6. a

7. c

8. c

9. c

10. c

11. c

12. b

MODULE PERFORMANCE ASSESSMENT

Module 3

You can use a stem-and-leaf plot to organize and display the data.

Maximum Butterfly Wingspans

```
 2 | 5 5 9
 3 | 2 2 2 2 8
 4 | 1 5 8 8
 5 | 1 1 4 7
 6 | 4 7
 7 | 0 3 6 6
 8 | 6 6
 9 | 8
10 | 2
```

3 | 2 means 3.2 cm

A line plot is difficult since the numbers are so spread out. Students may first categorize the data and then use a line plot for one category, such as the following one.

Maximum Wingspans of the Smallest Butterflies

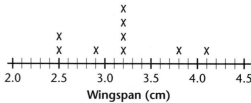

Wingspan (cm)

A bar graph can be constructed with a few of the butterflies. Students may pick any butterflies.

Selected Butterflies of North America

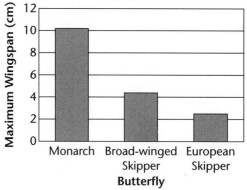

The mean is about 5.5 cm, the median is 5.1 cm, and the mode is 3.2 cm. None of the averages give a good indication for the size categories. Students may classify the butterflies in different ways. One possibility is as follows: large: 7.0 cm or greater; medium: 4.5 to 7.0 cm; small: less than 4.5 cm.

Setting up the animal cards

Make 3 copies of Labsheets 1A and 1B. Make 2 copies of Labsheets 1C and 1D. Cut out the animal cards. There will be a total of 50 cards.

Sort the cards into the following 5 groups of 10 cards:

Group 1	Group 2	Group 3	Group 4	Group 5
Winter Flounder	Royal Albatross	Winter Flounder	European Starling	European Starling
European Starling	Jaguar	Domestic Guinea Pig	Domestic Guinea Pig	California Grunion
California Grunion	Bottlenose Dolphin	Striped Skunk	African Elephant	Striped Skunk
Domestic Guinea Pig	Winter Flounder	Snow Hare	Blue Whale	African Elephant
Striped Skunk	Giant Panda	Blue Whale	English Sole	Rock Crab
African Elephant	Black Widow Spider	Bottlenose Dolphin	Royal Albatross	English Sole
Snow Hare	Monarch Butterfly	Black Widow Spider	Jaguar	Jaguar
Blue Whale	Gila Monster	Monarch Butterfly	Japanese Flying Squid	Japanese Flying Squid
Rock Crab	Northern Copperhead	Northern Copperhead	Giant Panda	Black Widow Spider
English Sole	Muskrat	Muskrat	Gila Monster	Northern Copperhead

Color code or label each group of cards to make sorting them after they get shuffled around a littler easier.

Section 1.1

Divide the class into 5 groups. Give each group a set of animal cards.

Section 2.1

Divide the class into 5 groups. Give each group a set of animal cards.

For Question 9, combine Groups 1 and 3, and Groups 2, 4, and 5.

Section 3.1

Divide the class into 5 groups. Give each group a set of animal cards.

For Question 6:

Group 1 can make a bar graph using grams or centimeters.
Group 2 can make a bar graph using meters or centimeters.
Group 3 can make a bar graph using centimeters only.
Group 4 can make a bar graph using meters or centimeters.
Group 5 can make a bar graph using grams or centimeters.

BOOK 1

TEACHER'S RESOURCES FOR MODULE 4

MIDDLE GRADES

MATH*Thematics*

MODULE 4 — Mind Games

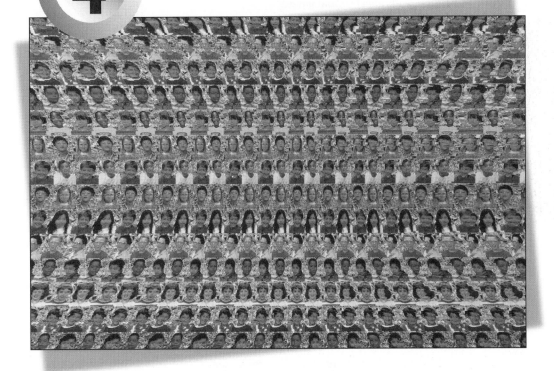

- **Planning and Teaching Suggestions, p. 4-8**
- **Labsheets, p. 4-50**
- **Extended Explorations, p. 4-61**
- **Blackline Masters, p. 4-64**

MODULE 4

MIND GAMES

Module Overview

Students explore mathematical content by playing and analyzing strategy games. Topics studied include number theory, probability, an introduction to algebra, coordinate graphing, and hands-on work with mixed numbers. Winning strategies are developed through the use of tables, Venn diagrams, factor trees, and number sense.

Module Objectives

Section	Objectives	NCTM Standards
1	◆ Find experimental probabilities in fraction, decimal, and percent forms. ◆ Use dividing and rounding to write a fraction as a whole percent. ◆ List the set of outcomes that make up an event. ◆ Find theoretical probabilities. ◆ Identify impossible and certain events. ◆ Understand that probabilities fall between 0 and 1, and plot them on a number line.	**1, 2, 3, 4, 7, 11**
2	◆ Use the divisibility tests for 2, 3, 5, 9, and 10. ◆ List all the factors of a number; find the GCF of two or more numbers. ◆ Identify prime and composite numbers. ◆ Use a factor tree to find the prime factorization of a number. ◆ Convert between standard form and exponential form. ◆ Write the prime factorization of a number using exponents.	**1, 2, 3, 4, 6**
3	◆ Model and find fraction products. ◆ Use common factors to write a fraction in lowest terms.	**1, 2, 3, 4, 6, 7**
4	◆ Find and estimate decimal products.	**1, 2, 3, 4, 7**
5	◆ Write and use a verbal rule for an input/output table. ◆ Graph ordered pairs on a coordinate grid (first quadrant only). ◆ Display input/output values on a coordinate grid to make predictions. ◆ Write and evaluate expressions. ◆ Find the area and perimeter of a rectangle. ◆ Use drawings, tables, verbal rules, and equations for relationships.	**1, 2, 3, 4, 9, 12**
6	◆ List several multiples of a number; find the LCM of two or more numbers. ◆ Write a fraction greater than one as a mixed number, and vice versa. ◆ Write a quotient as a mixed number, and decide when a mixed number quotient is appropriate to solve a problem.	**1, 2, 3, 4, 6, 7**

Topic Spiraling

Section	Connections to Prior and Future Concepts
1	Section 1 is on theoretical and experimental probability. Fraction/decimal/percent relationships are applied and students cut short a division and round to write a fraction as a whole percent. Module 6 continues probability and percent. Book 2 Module 4 introduces repeating decimals.
2	Section 2 applies Venn diagrams as divisibility rules, factors, primes, and powers are explored. Powers are used in Module 8 for scientific notation. Book 2 Module 3 revisits number theory.
3	Section 3 uses paper folding to explore fraction multiplication. Ideas about common factors are applied to write products in lowest terms. Module 5 teaches multiplication of mixed numbers.
4	Section 4 develops decimal multiplication using fraction multiplication and a 10×10 grid. Estimation is a major focus. Decimals are applied throughout the book, especially for ratio and measurement in Modules 6 and 7, and reviewed in the Toolbox and Modules 3–4 of Book 2.
5	Section 5 introduces coordinate graphing, expressions, and equations. Students write and solve equations in Modules 6 and 7 and extend graphing to four quadrants in Module 8. Area of a rectangle is developed in this section and applied to find area of a parallelogram in Module 7.
6	Section 6 introduces multiples. Mixed numbers, first seen in Module 2, are written as fractions and vice versa. These skills are applied in Module 5. In this section students also write an algebraic rule for a sequence of multiples and find the mixed number form of a quotient.

Integration

Mathematical Connections	1	2	3	4	5	6
algebra (including patterns and functions)	245	**248–263**	267	**273–281**	**282–293**	295, 302, 304
geometry	245	260	265–266, 270	280	287–288, 290, 293	297–299, 303
data analysis, probability, discrete math	**234–246***	258, 260	264, 272	276		295, 302
Interdisciplinary Connections and Applications						
social studies and geography	234				285–286	
reading and language arts						
science		258		279		
consumer math		263		279	301	
arts			272		301	303
health, physical education, and sports	234, 244					
computers, energy, farming, parking, twins		259	269	279	289, 291	

Bold page numbers indicate that a topic is used throughout the section.

Guide for Assigning Homework

Regular Scheduling (45 min class period)

Section/ P&A Pages	Core Assignment	Extended Assignment	exercises to note Additional Practice/Review	Open-ended Problems	Special Problems
1 pp. 243–246	**Day 1:** 1–3, 4a–b, SR 12–16	1–4, SR 12–16, *Ext 19	Sec 1 Ex Prac, p. 246	Ext 19	
	Day 2: 4c, 5–10, ROS 11, SR 17–18	5–10, ROS 11, SR 17–18		P&A 9, St Sk, p. 246	
2 pp. 258–263	**Day 1:** 2–14 (even),18, SR 50	2–14 (even), 18, Chal 19, SR 50	Sec 2 Ex Prac, p. 262; TB, p. 603; P&A 1–13 (odd), 15–17		Mod Proj 1–2
	Day 2: 20–32, SR 51	20–32, Chal 33, SR 51			
	Day 3: 34–42, 47, ROS 49, SR 52–55	34–42, 47, ROS 49, Ext 56, SR 52–55	P&A 43, 48	E², p. 263	P&A 44–46; E², p. 263
3 pp. 269–272	**Day 1:** 1, 2–14 (even), ROS 17, SR 18–26	1, 2–14 (even), Chal 16, ROS 17, Ext 27, SR 18–26	Sec 3 Ex Prac, p. 272; TB, p. 595; P&A 3–15 (odd)		Mod Proj 3
4 pp. 278–281	**Day 1:** 1–12, SR 26–30	1–12, 26–30	Sec 4 Ex Prac, p. 281; TB, p. 599		
	Day 2: 13–16, 20, 22, ROS 25, SR 31–33	13–16, 20, 22, Chal 24, ROS 25, SR 31–33	P&A 17–19, 21, 23	P&A 23; Std Test, p. 281	
5 pp. 289–293	**Day 1:** 1–13, SR 38–41	1–13, 15, Chal 16, SR 38–41	Sec 5 Ex Prac, p. 293; P&A 14, 15		
	Day 2: 17–30, 32, 36, ROS 37, SR 42	17–30, 32, 36, ROS 37, SR 42	TB, p. 600; P&A 17, 31, 33–35	P&A 33	Mod Proj 4–5
6 pp. 301–305	**Day 1:** 1–5, 6, 8, 10, 12, Career 43, SR 35–39	1–5, 6, 8, 10, 12, Career 43, SR 35–39	Sec 6 Ex Prac, p. 304; P&A 7–11 (odd)		
	Day 2: 14–28 (even), 29–31, 33, SR 40–42, ROS 34	14–28 (even), 29–31, 33, SR 40–42, ROS 34	P&A 13–27 (odd), 32		Mod Proj 6–9
Review/ Assess	Review and Assess (PE), Quick Quizzes (TRB), Mid-Module Quiz (TRB), Module Tests— Forms A and B (TRB), Standardized Assessment (TRB) Cumulative Test (TRB)				Allow 6 days
Enrich/ Assess	E² (PE) and Alternate E² (TRB), Module Project (PE), Module Performance Assessment (TRB)				
Yearly Pacing	**Mod 4:** 18 days	**Mods 1–4:** 73 days	**Remaining:** 67 days		**Total:** 140 days

Key: P&A = Practice & Application; ROS = Reflecting on the Section; SR = Spiral Rev; TB = Toolbox; Ex Prac= Extra Skill Practice; Ext = Extension; * more time

Block Scheduling (90 min class period)

	Day 1	Day 2	Day 3	Day 4	Day 5	Day 6	
Teach	Sec 1	Sec 2 Expl 1–2	Sec 2 Expl 3; Sec 3 Expl 1	Sec 4	Sec 5	Sec 6	**Allow 3 days** review/assess/projects
Apply/ Assess (P&A)	Sec 1: 1–10, ROS 11, SR 12–18	Sec 2: 2–32 (even), SR 50–55	Sec 2: 34–48 ROS 49, Sec 3: 1, 2–14 (even), ROS 17, SR 18–26	Sec 4: 1–16, 18, 20, 22, ROS 25, SR 26–33	Sec 5: 2–14 (even), 18–32 (even), 34–36, *ROS 37, SR 38–42	Sec 6: 2–4, 5, 6–28 (even), 29–31, 33, ROS 34, SR 35–42	
Yearly Pacing	**Mod 4:** 9 days		**Mods 1–4:** 36 days		**Remaining:** 34 days		**Total:** 70 days

Materials List

Section	Materials
1	a coin, Labsheet 1A, die or numbered cube, probability software (optional), bag, 10 pennies (some shiny, some dull)
2	Labsheets 2A–2C, 2 paper clips, different colored chips, paper for folding, calculator
3	paper for folding, colored pencils
4	Labsheets 4A–4B, calculator
5	Labsheets 5A and 5B, centimeter graph paper, graph paper
6	Labsheet 6A, pattern blocks, die or numbered cube

Support Materials in this Resource Book

Section	Practice	Study Guide	Assessment	Enrichment
1	Section 1	Section 1	Quick Quiz	Technology Activity
2	Section 2	Section 2	Quick Quiz	Alternate Extended Exploration
3	Section 3	Section 3	Quick Quiz, Mid-Module Quiz	
4	Section 4	Section 4	Quick Quiz	
5	Section 5	Section 5	Quick Quiz	
6	Section 6	Section 6	Quick Quiz	
Review/ Assess	Sections 1–6		Module Tests Forms A and B Standardized Assessment Module Performance Assessment Cumulative Test Modules 3–4	

Classroom Ideas

Bulletin Boards:
- 3-D images that are hidden in 2-D pictures
- "function machine" showing input, rule, and output
- coordinate grid system
- examples of puzzles and brain teasers

Student Work Displays:
- student-made puzzles
- *Class Puzzle Book* from the Module Project
- summaries from the E^2

Interest Centers:
- rules and materials for playing the games in the module
- a coin that students can flip and a tally chart to record the results
- index cards for students to write their own rules for *Guess My Rule*

Visitors/Field Trips:
- programmer, choreographer, game inventor

Technology:
- Module 4 Technology Activity in TRB for PE, p. 238
- probability software

The Math Gazette
Mind Games

Sneak Preview!

Over the next four weeks in our mathematics class, we will be finding probabilities, testing numbers for divisibility, learning about prime numbers, multiplying fractions, multiplying decimals, and writing expressions and equations, while completing a thematic unit on Mind Games. Some of the topics we will be discussing are:

✗ strategies for playing games

✗ creating mathematical puzzles

✗ comparing the sizes of oceans

Ask Your Student

What is the probability of an impossible event? of a certain event? (Sec. 1)

What is $\frac{2}{3}$ of $\frac{1}{2}$ cup of flour? (Sec. 3)

What is an expression for how old you will be in x years? (Sec. 5)

How can you write $4\frac{1}{5}$ as a fraction? (Sec. 6)

Connections

Science:
Students will learn how to write numbers in exponential form. They may be interested in finding out how exponents are used to describe large numbers in sciences such as astronomy and biology. Possible sources include science textbooks and encyclopedias.

Language Arts:
Students will read a story about some unevenly divided treasure. They may be interested in writing their own stories about a similar situation. Discuss how fractions might be used in their stories.

Students will learn the rules of a game from a flow chart. They may be interested in rewriting the rules of a board game or card game that they know in flow chart form. Have them use the flow chart on page 276 as a guide.

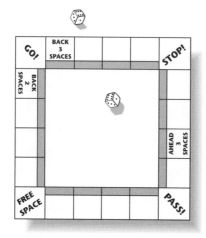

E² Project

Following Section 2, students will have about one week to complete the E² project, *The Cleaning Crew*. Students will analyze two different methods of payment for cleaning community parks and choose the better method for the payee.

Mind Games

Section Title	Mathematics Your Student Will Be Learning	Activities
1: Outcomes in Games	◆ finding experimental and theoretical probabilities ◆ plotting probabilities on a number line	◆ collect and analyze the results of tossing a coin ◆ play the game *Never a Six*
2: Paper Clip Products	◆ using divisibility tests ◆ identifying prime and composite numbers ◆ finding the prime factorization of a number ◆ evaluating and writing powers of numbers	◆ play the game *Paper Clip Products* ◆ make factor trees ◆ model powers of numbers with paper folding ◆ begin Module Project, *Puzzle Making* ◆ choose method of payment for park cleaning
3: A Fair Share	◆ multiplying fractions ◆ writing fractions in lowest terms	◆ solve a puzzle involving fractions ◆ model fractions with paper folding ◆ continue work on Module Project
4: Target Games	◆ multiplying decimals ◆ estimating decimal products	◆ play the game *Target Number* ◆ use 10 x 10 grid to model multiplication of decimals
5: Guess My Rule	◆ graphing points on a coordinate grid ◆ using variables to write and evaluate expressions and to write equations	◆ play the game *Guess My Rule* ◆ solve a geography puzzle ◆ continue work on Module Project
6: Pattern Play	◆ finding the least common multiple of two numbers ◆ writing fractions as mixed numbers and vice versa	◆ play the game *Pattern Tick-Tock* ◆ play the game *Flex Your Hex* ◆ complete the Module Project

Activities to do at Home

◆ Investigate probabilities related to games and puzzles you have at home. Compare theoretical and experimental probabilities for rolling dice, spinning spinners, drawing cards, and so on. (After Sec. 1)

◆ Estimate the cost of several grocery items. For example, estimate the total cost of 5 boxes of rice that are $.89 each. Look for other decimal products to estimate, such as hourly wages, telephone bills, and so on. (After Sec. 4)

◆ Make a map of your neighborhood on a coordinate grid. Choose several ordered pairs on the grid and identify what is at each location. (After Sec. 5)

Related Topics

You may want to discuss these related topics with your student:

 Games and puzzles

 Geography

 Music and dance

a+b=c **Logic**

Section ① Probability

Section Planner

DAYS FOR MODULE 4

1	2	3	4	5	6	7	8	9	10	11	12

SECTION 1

First Day
Setting the Stage, p. 234
Exploration 1, pp. 235–237

Second Day
Exploration 2, pp. 239–241
Key Concepts, p. 242

Block Schedule

Day 1
Setting the Stage, Exploration 1,
Exploration 2, Key Concepts

RESOURCE ORGANIZER

Teaching Resources
• Practice and Applications, Sec. 1
• Study Guide, Sec. 1
• Technology Activity, Sec. 1
• Warm-Up, Sec. 1
• Quick Quiz, Sec. 1

Section Overview

Students will perform coin toss and die rolling experiments in Section 1 so they can learn about experimental and theoretical probabilities. The key terms experiment, outcome, probability, experimental probability, equally likely outcomes, event, theoretical probability, impossible and certain events are all defined. The explorations will suggest that over the long run, an experimental probability will approach the theoretical probability of an experiment. The technology page shows students how they can use probability software to quickly and easily simulate an experiment with a large number of trials. When impossible and certain events are defined, the students learn how to use a number line to display probabilities.

Students will express their experimental probabilities first as fractions, then as decimals and percents. It is expected that students will be able to write fractions as decimals and percents, since those skills were presented in Module 3. Refer students who need to review these skills to page 176.

SECTION OBJECTIVES

Exploration 1
• find experimental probabilities and write them in fraction, decimal, and percent forms
• use dividing and rounding to write a fraction as a whole percent

Exploration 2
• list the set of outcomes that make up an event
• find theoretical probabilities
• identify impossible and certain events
• understand that probabilities fall between 0 and 1, and plot them on a number line

ASSESSMENT OPTIONS

Checkpoint Questions
• Question 7 on p. 236
• Question 19 on p. 241

Embedded Assessment
• For a list of embedded assessment exercises see p. 4-13.

Performance Task/Portfolio
• Exercise 9 on p. 244 (open ended)
• Exercise 10 on p. 244 (writing)
★ Exercise 11 on p. 245 (journal)
• Exercise 19 on p. 245 (extension)

★ = a problem solving task that can be assessed using the Assessment Scales

SECTION 1 MATERIALS

Exploration 1	**Exploration 2**
◆ a coin	◆ Labsheet 1A
	◆ die or numbered cube

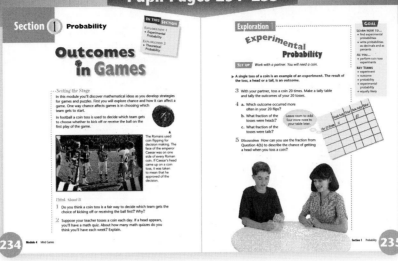

Setting the Stage

MOTIVATE

Discuss with the class how various sports teams choose which side will go first in a game. Most games use a flip of a coin. Consider other ways that board games or events may begin, for example, by picking a number between 1 and 10 or getting the highest roll on a die. As students work through Module 4, you can discuss whether these methods of deciding which side goes first are fair or not fair.

Exploration 1

PLAN

Classroom Management

Exploration 1 is best performed by students working with a partner. If time permits, for *Question 3* you can have students do more than twenty tosses. Some students may find it difficult to flip a coin and then catch it. Provide a small paper cup that they can use to shake the coin and then roll it out. Calculators should be available for students to use with *Question 11*. For *Question 12*, prepare beforehand an area on the board or overhead sheet that can be used to record the results of students' coin tosses.

GUIDE

Developing Math Concepts

Exploration 1 deals with experimental probability. Some students may be inclined to anticipate the concept of *theoretical probability*, which is addressed in Exploration 2. Try to keep their attention on the point that, for the moment, they are performing *experiments* in probability. For that reason they should keep an open mind concerning how an experiment turns out. After students have reviewed the results compiled by the whole class in *Question 12*, they should begin to notice that the greater the number of coin toss experiments, the closer the experimental probability tends to approach down to a value of 0.50.

Classroom Examples

Suppose tails occurred on 17 out of 40 tosses of a coin. What is the experimental probability of tails?

Answer:
Experimental probability of tails

$$= \frac{\text{number of times tails occurred}}{\text{number of times the coin was tossed}}$$

$$= \frac{17}{40}$$

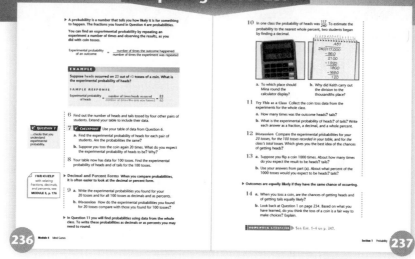

Exploration 1 continued

Checkpoint *Question 7* focuses on how well students understand experimental probability. Intuitively, they should see that the probability of tossing a head is approximately equal to a fraction in which the denominator is twice as great as the numerator. Students should also understand that even though they all were doing the same experiment, they have no reason to be surprised or disappointed by the fact that individual results vary greatly. In fact, it *would* be surprising if the results of the four groups were to agree exactly.

Developing Math Concepts
Before having students do *Question 9*, conduct a quick review of how a fraction can be converted to a decimal or percent. After students answer *Question 10*, discuss with the class the degree of precision you expect in the decimal calculation if the percent form of the answer is to be rounded to the nearest whole percent. (the nearest thousandth) What degree of precision would you expect in the decimal calculation if the percent form of the answer is to be rounded to the nearest tenth of a percent? (the nearest ten thousandth)

HOMEWORK EXERCISES

See the Suggested Assignment for Day 1 on page 4-3. For Exercise Notes, see page 4-13.

Customizing Instruction

Alternative Approach 1 Students enjoy doing experiments. If time permits, have students roll two dice and record the sum of the dots on the two upper faces. To get a good statistical result, have each group of two students do fifty rolls and record its results. Combine the data compiled by all groups and draw conclusions on the probability of rolling a 2, 3, 4, 5, 6, 7, 8, 9, 10, 11, or 12.

Alternative Approach 2 Have students work with various spinners to determine the probability of landing on any one of the spinner's sectors.

Technology If probability software is available, have students use it for the probability simulations.

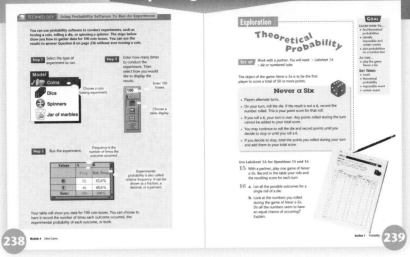

Exploration 2

PLAN	GUIDE

Classroom Management
Exploration 2 is best performed by students working with a partner. As they play *Never a Six*, make sure that students fully understand that they may stop their turn at any time. They are taking a chance on rolling a six, which ends their turn and eliminates the points they have earned during that turn. Before students begin *Question 17*, briefly review the definitions of even and odd numbers.

Managing Time Each group of partners will need a copy of Labsheet 1A for *Questions 15* and *16*.

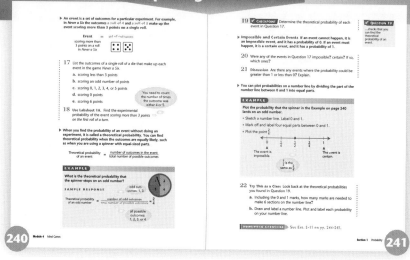

Exploration 2 continued

Checkpoint *Question 19* has students find the theoretical probability of the outcomes of *Question 17*. Encourage them to list *all six* possible outcomes and then refer to the list in answering parts *17(a)–(e)*. Make sure students understand why scoring six points in *Question 17(e)* is not possible. By the rules of the game, no points are awarded for a 6, so the probability of getting 6 points has a probability of zero.

Developing Math Concepts
After students have completed *Question 21*, they should begin to realize that probabilities range from 0 to 1 inclusive. Help students understand that a probability of 1 corresponds to an event that happens 100% of the time a probability experiment is performed. Similarly, a probability of 0 corresponds to an event that happens 0% of the time a probability experiment is performed. All other probabilities fall within the range of 0 to 1.

Classroom Examples
What is the theoretical probability that the spinner stops on a letter?

Answer:
Theoretical probability of a letter

$$= \frac{\text{number of letter outcomes}}{\text{total number of possible outcomes}}$$

$$= \frac{4}{8}$$

Common Error For *Question 22*, students divide a number line into equal segments. Because it is being divided into sixths, some students may think that they need to make only six marks rather than seven. Remind them that the number of marks must always be one greater than the number of sections. Point out the simplest case: for *one* segment, *two* marks are required to indicate the beginning and end of the segment.

Writing As preparation for Exploration 2, have students write a few paragraphs describing each of the following situations: (a) something that is certain to happen, (b) something that might happen, (c) something that is impossible to happen. After finishing Exploration 2, discuss with the class how these situations are related to the probability concepts that were presented.

HOMEWORK EXERCISES

See the Suggested Assignment for Day 2 on page 4-13. For Exercise Notes, see page 4-13.

CLOSE

Closure Question In a probability written as a fraction, what does the numerator tell you? What does the denominator tell you? How can you write the fractional probability as a percent?
Answer: numerator: the number of outcomes in an event; denominator: the total number of possible outcomes in an event; *Sample Response:* First divide the numerator by the denominator and write your answer as a decimal. Then change the decimal to a percent.

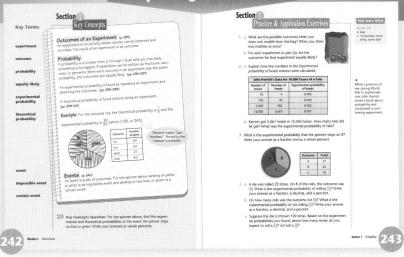

SUGGESTED ASSIGNMENT

Core Course
Day 1: Exs. 1–3, 4a, 4b, 12–16
Day 2: Exs. 4c, 5–11, 17, 18

Extended Course
Day 1: Exs. 1–4, 12–16, 19
Day 2: Exs. 5–11, 17, 18

Block Schedule
Day 1: Exs. 1–18

EMBEDDED ASSESSMENT

These section objectives are
tested by the exercises listed.

**Find experimental proba-
bilities and write them in
fraction, decimal, and percent forms.**

Exercises 2, 4

**Use dividing and rounding
to write a fraction as a
whole percent.**

Exercise 3

**List the set of outcomes
that make up an event.**

Exercises 7, 8a

**Find theoretical probabili-
ties.**

Exercises 8b, 8c, 10

**Identify impossible and
certain events.**

Exercise 9

**Understand that probabili-
ties fall between 0 and 1,
and plot them on a num-
ber line.**

Exercises 8b, 8c, 8d

Practice & Application

EXERCISE NOTES

Technology For *Ex. 2*, it may
be possible to find computer
software that rapidly duplicates
the tossing of 10,000 coins
through the use of a program
that generates random numbers.

Developing Math Concepts In
Exs. 2(b) and *4(b)*, students are
informally presented with a
basic fact concerning any particular outcome of a probability
experiment: *The sum of the probability that the outcome occurs and
the probability that it does not
occur is 1*. Help students to
understand this concept by providing additional examples such
as the probability of rolling a
three or a four and the probability of not rolling a three or a
four.

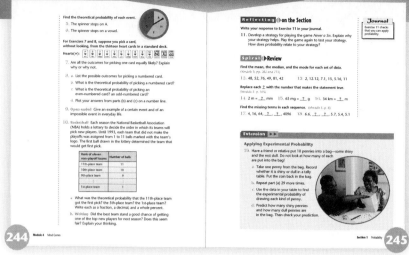

Practice & Application

Developing Math Concepts In *Exs. 7* and *8*, students are asked to apply the concept of theoretical probability to a set of 13 playing cards. The 13 cards are the 13 *elements* of a *sample space* and drawing exactly one of the cards is an example of a *simple event*. Underlying the solutions to *Exs. 8(b)* and *(c)* are the concepts that each simple event is *equally likely* and that you can add the probabilities of simple events in order to get the probability of an event that is not simple.

Closing the Section

With the aid of materials such as spinners, coins, and dice, students have expanded their knowledge of probability. First, they have carried out probability experiments and then proceeded to the concept of theoretical probability. Students have discussed careers in which probability is used and have become aware of how probability affects their lives. In the Reflecting on the Section exercise on page 245, they have applied their knowledge of probability to the development of a strategy for playing the game *Never a Six*.

QUICK QUIZ ON THIS SECTION

1. The table below shows the outcomes of an experiment involving a four-color spinner. What is the experimental probability that the spinner stops on green? Write your answer as a fraction and as a whole percent.

   red   12   green   6
   yellow   10   blue   8

   Write your answers as fractions.

2. What is the theoretical probability of drawing an ace from a standard deck of cards?

3. Kerry got 38 tails in 82 tosses of a coin. What is her experimental probability of heads?

For answers, see Quick Quiz blackline on p. 4-64.

Customizing Instruction

Home Involvement Those helping students at home will find the Key Concepts on page 242 a handy reference to the key ideas, terms, and skills of Section 1.

Absent Students For students who have been absent for all or part of this section, the blackline Study Guide for Section 1 may be used to present the ideas. The Key Concepts on page 242 also provide a good overview of the key ideas, terms, and skills of Section 1.

Extra Help For students who need additional practice, the blackline Practice and Applications for Section 1 provides additional exercises that may be used to confirm the skills of Section 1. The Extra Skill Practice on page 246 also provides additional exercises.

Section ② Factors and Divisibility

Section Planner

DAYS FOR MODULE 4

1	2	3	4	5	6	7	8	9	10	11	12

SECTION 2

First Day
Setting the Stage, *p. 247*
Exploration 1, *pp. 248–250*

Second Day
Exploration 2, *pp. 251–253*

Third Day
Exploration 3, *pp. 254–256*
Key Concepts, *p. 256*

Block Schedule

Day 2
Setting the Stage, Exploration 1,
Exploration 2 through Question 27

Day 3
Exploration 3 (starting at
Question 28), Key Concepts
(Day 3 continues in Sec. 3.)

RESOURCE ORGANIZER

Teaching Resources
• Practice and Applications, Sec. 2
• Study Guide, Sec. 2
• Warm-Up, Sec. 2
• Quick Quiz, Sec. 2

Section Overview

The *Paper Clip Products* game, the *Prime Time* game, and a paper-folding puzzle in Section 2 prepare students for their study of divisibility tests, factors, and powers of a number. Using Venn diagrams to sort numbers, students will identify numbers divisible by 2, 3, 5, 9, and 10 and will develop divisibility rules for these factors. Key concepts include factors and common factors and prime and composite numbers. Students will use lists of factors and prime factorizations to find common factors and a greatest common factor of two numbers. The uniqueness of a number's prime factorization is discussed.

Students will explore the meaning of the expression n^x. Key terms include power, exponent, base, standard form, and exponential form. A procedure for using the power key on a scientific calculator to evaluate powers is given. Students will also learn a shorthand notation for writing prime factorizations using exponents.

SECTION OBJECTIVES

Exploration 1
• use the divisibility tests for 2, 3, 5, 9, and 10
• list all the factors of a number; find the greatest common factor of two or more numbers

Exploration 2
• identify prime and composite numbers
• use a factor tree to find the prime factorization of a number

Exploration 3
• convert between standard form and exponential form
• write the prime factorization of a number using exponents

ASSESSMENT OPTIONS

Checkpoint Questions
• Question 5 on p. 248
• Question 9 on p. 249
• Questions 11, 14 on p. 250
• Question 18 on p. 252
• Question 24 on p. 253
• Question 34 on p. 255

Embedded Assessment
• Embedded assessment exercises see p. 4-22.

Performance Task/Portfolio
• Exercise 49 on p. 260
• Exercise 56 on p. 261
★ Module Project of p. 261
★ Extended Exploration on p. 263
• Standardized Testing on p. 263

★ = a problem solving task that can be assessed using the Assessment Scales

SECTION 2 MATERIALS

Setting the Stage
◆ Labsheet 2A
◆ 2 paper clips
◆ colored chips, 10 each of two different colors

Exploration 1
◆ Labsheets 2A and 2B

Exploration 2
◆ Labsheet 2C
◆ paper clips
◆ colored chips, 15 each of two different colors

Exploration 3
◆ paper for folding
◆ calculator

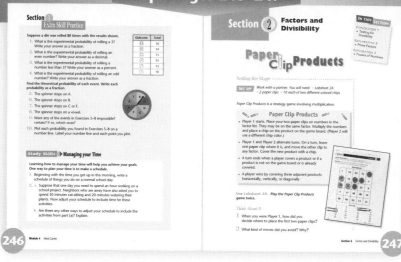

Setting the Stage

MOTIVATE

The game on p. 247 is played in pairs. It is used to develop intuitive notions of factors, common factors, divisibility and multiples. Playing and discussing strategies for *Paper Clip Products* lays the groundwork for material in Explorations 1 and 2 on divisibility tests, greatest common factors, and prime and composite numbers.

You may wish to take an extra day for students to play additional rounds of the game and to revisit it as they work on Exploration 1.

Alternatively, you may wish to take some time to familiarize students with whole-number factors of a number, having them play the following game, called *Factor Bingo*. The rules are similar to those for regular BINGO. Each student prepares his own BINGO card by filling in a 5 × 5 grid (one inch graph paper works well). Have the students head each of the five columns on his card with the letters B, I, N, G, O and then find a number for each of the 25 squares on their BINGO cards by rolling a pair of dice, multiplying the two numbers on the up faces and inserting the result in the square. Students should continue in this fashion until all 25 squares are covered. There are two restrictions on the numbers that they may enter on their cards: no number may be used more than twice and the same number may not appear more than once in the same column.

Have a student lead the class in one game, or lead the game yourself. To determine each square to be covered, the leader rolls the two dice and a third cube that has five of its six faces showing the letters, B, I, N, G, and O. When the leader reads a number (for example "B 30," generated by three faces showing B, 5, and 6) any students with a "30" in the B column may cover that square with a disk. The first student to cover five squares in a row (horizontally, vertically, or diagonally) calls BINGO and wins the game. After the class has played a game, have students discuss the strategies they used to make their cards.

Each group will need a copy of Labsheet 2A, two paper clips, and ten each of two different colored chips. Display a visual of Labsheet 2A on the overhead projector in order to explain and demonstrate to the entire class how the game of *Paper Clip Products* is played. Allow students time to ask questions, making sure that they understand the game rules before beginning play.

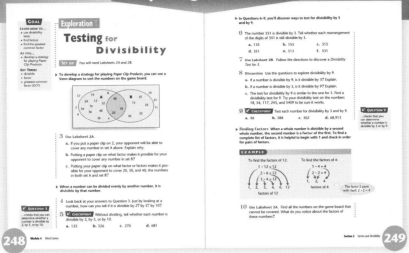

Exploration 1

PLAN

Classroom Management
Exploration 1 is best performed working in pairs. If time permits, initiate a class discussion for *Questions 1* and *2*.

GUIDE

Managing Time
Each pair of students will need a copy of Labsheet 2B. Students will need to use Labsheet 2A for *Question 10*, unless you prepare to display the labsheet on the overhead projector. For *Questions 6–9*, allow students to use a calculator to check divisibility by three and nine.

Developing Math Concepts
Make sure students understand that Exploration 1 deals with whole-number factors only. Relate the concept of *factors* back to the basic multiplication facts that students learned in elementary school. In *Question 10*, students informally begin their investigation of prime and

composite numbers, which will be more fully discussed in Exploration 2. Students should be able to conclude that the numbers that cannot be covered in the *Paper Clip Products* game have only the number one and themselves as factors.

Classroom Examples
Find the factors of 18.

Answer:

$$1 \cdot 18 = 18$$
$$2 \cdot 9 = 18$$
$$3 \cdot 6 = 18$$

1, 2, 3, 6, 9, 18

factors of 18

Customizing Instruction

Alternative Approach Instead of doing *Questions 6–9*, make two columns on the board with the headings *Divisible by 3* and *Not divisible by 3*, respectively. In the appropriate columns, write several numbers, some divisible by three and some not divisible by three. Have students place numbers of their own in both columns. After several numbers have been placed, have students work in groups of three or four to attempt to arrive at a divisibility rule for three. As a class, discuss the rules generated and formalize the correct rule if it has been developed by the class. If it

has not, you will have to guide the class by giving hints such as "Examine the digits in each number." If this activity turns out to be successful in developing the rule, consider having the class use the same process for determining the divisibility rule for nine.

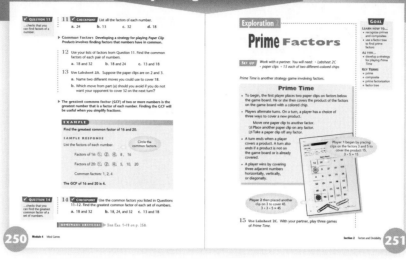

Exploration 1 continued

Writing Before having students do *Questions 10–14*, have them write in their own words the meaning of *greatest*, *common*, and *factor*. After they have done this, ask them to describe and give an example of what they think a *greatest common factor* would be. After the class has covered *Questions 10–14*, have the students return to their definitions and make any changes they feel are necessary.

Classroom Examples
Find the greatest common factor of 28 and 42.

Answer:
List the factors of each number. Then circle the common factors.

Factors of 28: ①, ②, 4, ⑦, ⑭, 28

Factors of 42: ①, ②, 3, 6, ⑦, ⑭, 21, 42

Common factors: 1, 2, 7, 14
The GCF of 28 and 42 is 14.

Checkpoint *Question 9* checks whether students understand the divisibility rules for three and nine. Students should be able to find the sum of the digits of any number and mentally determine whether that number is a multiple of three or nine. Ask students to give an example of a number divisible by three but not by nine. Discuss with students whether there is a number that is divisible by nine, but not by three. (No.) *Question 11* checks whether students can list all of the factors of a number. After it is determined that they can, *Question 14* checks whether they can compare lists of the factors of two or more numbers to find their greatest common factor.

HOMEWORK EXERCISES

See the Suggested Assignment for Day 1 on page 4-22. For Exercise Notes, see page 4-22.

Exploration 2

PLAN

Classroom Management
Exploration 2 is best performed by students working in pairs. Each pair will need a copy of Labsheet 2C, paper clips, and fifteen each of two different colored chips. Display Labsheet 2C on the overhead projector in order to explain and demonstrate to the class how the *Prime Time* game is played. Allow students time to ask questions, making sure that they understand the game rules before beginning to play. When demonstrating *Prime Time*, explain that there is no limit to the number of paper clips that may be placed on top of a factor at any time during the game. Explain also that if a student makes a mistake, he or she must redo the problem and not leave an incorrectly placed chip on the board.

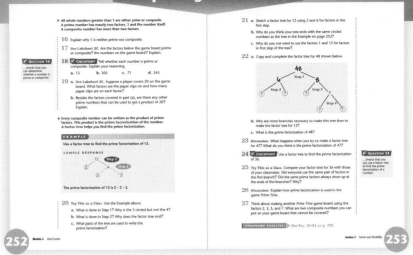

Exploration 2 continued

GUIDE

Developing Math Concepts

Question 16 asks students to explain why the number 1 is neither prime nor composite. In answering this question, students should focus on the introductory sentence: "All whole numbers greater than 1 are either prime or composite." Thus, 1 is purposely omitted from inclusion in the definition. Why is this so? It is done as a matter of simple convenience. Although 1 behaves in some respects like a prime number, mathematicians prefer not to allow it to be so labeled. Many important theorems that have been discovered about prime numbers would not be true for *all* prime numbers if 1 were accepted as a prime. So, rather than having to exclude 1 as a special case each time a new prime-number theorem is stated and discussed, mathematical writers find it much simpler to reject 1 as a prime number in the first instance.

Classroom Examples
Find the prime factorization of 18.

Answer:

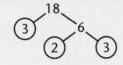

The prime factorization of 18 is 2 • 3 • 3.

Common Error Students may stop too soon when trying to find a prime factorization. In *Question 23* they may wonder how long they have to work until they can be sure that 47 is prime. Have them divide 47 by every prime number starting with 2. None of the quotients is a whole number but students should keep track of these numbers anyway.

$47 \div 2 = 23.5$ $47 \div 3 = 15.67$
$47 \div 5 = 9.4$ $47 \div 7 = 6.71$

Tell students that they no longer have to keep testing; 47 must be prime. To help them see why, have them look for a pattern in the divisors and quotients as shown below.

2	3	5	7
23.5	15.67	9.4	6.71

Ask them why it is not necessary to test 11 or any higher prime. (The quotients already obtained are getting smaller and smaller, so the new quotients clearly will all be less than 6.71. None of them will be prime since all the primes less than 6.71 (2, 3, and 5) have already been tested and proven not to be factors of 47. So, 47 must be a prime number.)

Checkpoint *Question 24* checks to see whether students can use a factor tree to find the prime factorization of a number. Have several students put their work on the board in order to illustrate that numbers can be factored into prime numbers using various factor trees, but the final prime factorization of the number will always be the same. If students are having difficulty, encourage them to always start the prime factorization process by systematically dividing by the least prime number and proceeding through greater and greater primes, as shown earlier for the prime number 47.

HOMEWORK EXERCISES

See the Suggested Assignment for Day 2 on page 4-22. For Exercise Notes, see page 4-22.

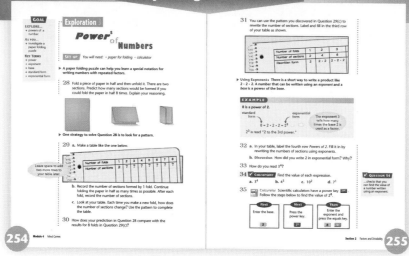

Exploration 3

PLAN

Classroom Management

Exploration 3 is best performed by having students work individually. For *Question 28*, make sure students have a prediction before they begin. List the students' predictions on the board. Students may be surprised to find that when they try to fold the paper in half eight times, they can't do it. However, have them fold the paper in half as many times as they can and then use the pattern that they observe to complete the table in *Question 29*.

GUIDE

Developing Math Concepts

In *Question 31* as students are filling in the third row of their table, point out that the rewritten form is the prime factorization of the number of sections. Students should realize that an exponent tells how many times the base number (in this case 2) is used as a factor. After students have completed *Question 33*, discuss with them the meaning of a number that is *squared* (the exponent is two) and a number that is *cubed* (the exponent is three).

Classroom Examples

Write 81 in exponential form.

Answer:
$$81 = 3 \cdot 3 \cdot 3 \cdot 3$$
$$= 3^4 \leftarrow \text{exponential form}$$

Common Error A common error that students make is to evaluate an exponential expression by multiplying the base by the exponent. For example, 3 to the 4th power might be incorrectly evaluated as 12 instead of 81. If students continually do this, have them write the expression out in factored form and then multiply.

Checkpoint *Question 34* asks students to find the value of a number written in exponential form. Some students may need to write the numbers in factored form in order to understand that the base is used as a factor the number of times indicated by the exponent.

Customizing Instruction

Technology *Question 35* has students using the exponent key of the calculator. Some calculators may have a sequence for finding powers that is different from that explained on page 255. Help students experiment with their own calculators in order to find how they handle exponents. As students do this, they may obtain a number that is too large for their calculators to display. If this happens, the calculators will probably display the number in scientific notation. If you wish, you can use the occasion as an opportunity to teach scientific notation.

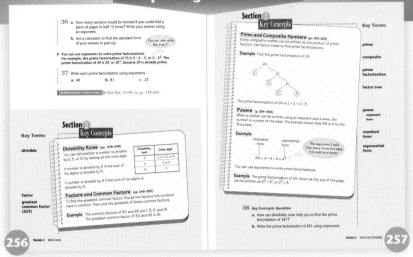

Exploration 3 continued

HOMEWORK EXERCISES

See the Suggested Assignment for Day 2 on page 4-22. For Exercise Notes, see page 4-22.

CLOSE

Closure Question Explain how you can use divisibility rules, a factor tree, and powers to factor a number and write it in factored form.

Sample Response: Use divisibility rules to see if the number is divisible by 2, 3, 5, 9, or 10. If it is divisible by one or more of these numbers, begin a factor tree using a possible combination of two factors. If not, check to see if there are any other possible factors in the number, or if it is prime. Continue this process for the factors written on the factor tree until all the factors written at the ends of the tree are prime numbers. Write a multiplication expression using all the "prime ends" to write the number in factored form. Then, if any of the numbers in the factored form are the same, write them using exponents.

Customizing Instruction

Home Involvement Those helping students at home will find the Key Concepts on pages 256 and 257 a handy reference to the key ideas, terms, and skills of Section 2.

Absent Students For students who have been absent for all or part of this section, the blackline Study Guide for Section 2 may be used to present the ideas. The Key Concepts on pages 256 and 257 also provide a good overview of the key ideas, terms, and skills of Section 2.

Extra Help For students who need additional practice, the blackline Practice and Applications for Section 2 provides additional exercises that may be used to confirm the skills of Section 2. The Extra Skill Practice on page 262 also provides additional exercises.

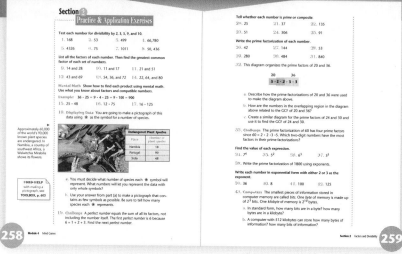

SUGGESTED ASSIGNMENT

Core Course
Day 1: Exs. 2–14 even, 18, 50
Day 2: Exs. 20–32, 51
Day 3: Exs. 34–42, 47, 49, 52–55

Extended Course
Day 1: Exs. 2–14 even, 18, 19, 50
Day 2: Exs. 20–33, 51
Day 3: Exs. 34–42, 47–49, 52–56

Block Schedule
Day 2: Exs. 2–32 even, 50–55
Day 3: Exs. 34–49; Sec. 3, Exs. 1, 2–14 even, 17–26

EMBEDDED ASSESSMENT

These section objectives are tested by the exercises listed.

Use the divisibility tests for 2, 3, 5, 9, and 10.

Exercises 2, 4, 6, 8

List all the factors of a number and find the greatest common factor of two or more numbers.

Exercises 10, 12, 14, 18

Identify prime and composite numbers.

Exercises 20, 22, 24

Use a factor tree to find the prime factorization of a number.

Exercises 26, 28, 30, 32

Convert between standard form and exponential form

Exercises 34, 36, 40, 42, 47

Write the prime factorization of a number using exponents.

Exercise 38

Practice & Application

EXERCISE NOTES

Background Information *Ex. 19* asks students to find a perfect number. Perfect numbers can be traced back over 2,500 years to the Pythagoreans, a society of Greek mathematicians. The Pythagoreans studied not only perfect numbers but also *deficient numbers* and *abundant numbers,* numbers that were, respectively, less than and greater than the sum of all their factors.

Developing Math Concepts
A later development in Pythagorean thought (see earlier note) was the concept of *amicable numbers.* Two numbers are said to be *amicable* if the sum of the factors of the first is equal to the second number and the sum of the factors of the second number is equal to the first number. The first such pair of numbers is 220 and 284 since $1 + 2 + 5 + 11 + 4 + 10 + 22 + 55 + 20 + 44 + 110 = 284$ and $1 + 2 + 71 + 4 + 142 = 220$.

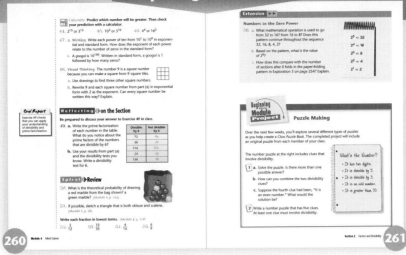

Practice & Application

Visual Learners *Ex. 48* has students drawing a visual representation of square numbers. Discuss with students what they think the meaning of *cube number* might be and ask them to display a visual representation of a cube number. (Examples: 1^3 = 1 cube; 2^3 = 8, which can be visualized as eight $1 \times 1 \times 1$ cubes packed into one $2 \times 2 \times 2$ cube, and so on)

Beginning the Module Project

During this module students will enjoy exploring solve several different types of puzzles. Students will then use the mathematics they have learned in the module to create their own puzzle. After students have created their puzzles, have them exchange the puzzles with one another student and try to solve them. At the end of the module students will combine their puzzles to form a *Class Puzzle Book*. During this module encourage students to bring in their favorite puzzles for the class to try to solve. After students have solved some puzzles, initiate a class discussion about the mathematics that was used in the puzzle.

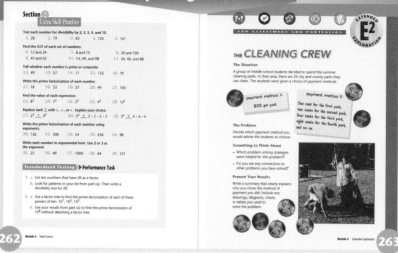

Closing the Section

While exploring various games, students have learned about divisibility tests, factors, greatest common factors, prime factorization, and powers of numbers. They have expanded their knowledge of factors by using exponential notation and prime factorization. They have reinforced and formalized concepts while developing strategies for playing factor and product games. The Reflecting on the Section exercise on page 260 allows students to apply their knowledge of divisibility rules and prime factorization in order to develop a divisibility rule for 6.

QUICK QUIZ ON THIS SECTION

1. Test 123,450 for divisibility by 2, 3, 5, 9, and 10.

2. Use a factor tree to find the prime factorization of 108.

3. What is the greatest common factor of 48 and 120?

4. Write the prime factorization of 400 using exponents.

5. What is the theoretical probability of getting a prime number if you pick a number at random between 20 and 39?

For answers, see Quick Quiz blackline on p. 4-65.

Section ③ Fraction Multiplication

Section Planner

DAYS FOR MODULE 4

1 2 3 4 5 **6** 7 8 9 10 11 12

SECTION 3

First Day
Setting the Stage, *p. 264*
Exploration 1, *pp. 265–268*
Key Concepts, *p. 268*

Block Schedule

Day 3 continued
Setting the Stage, Exploration 1,
Key Concepts

RESOURCE ORGANIZER

Teaching Resources
• Practice and Applications, Sec. 3
• Study Guide, Sec. 3
• Mid-Module Quiz
• Warm-Up, Sec. 3
• Quick Quiz, Sec. 3

Section Overview

In Section 3, solving a puzzle will lead students to develop a rule for finding a fractional part of a part. Using visual aids that involve a vertical fold and a horizontal fold of a piece of paper to model two fractions, students will find the product of two fractions. Students will record the results of several paper foldings in a table. Using a problem solving strategy, they will generalize their table results so they can write a rule for multiplying two fractions.

In Module 2, students learned to write fractions in lowest terms. Because students will use this skill in this section, those who need to can refer to page 114 to review the skill. After multiplying the fractions in the exploration, and recognizing that some of their products are not in lowest terms, students will use both common factors and greatest common factors to write fractions in lowest terms. Students will discuss the advantages to using the greatest common factor to write a fraction in lowest terms.

SECTION OBJECTIVES

Exploration 1
• model and find fraction products
• use common factors to write a fraction in lowest terms

ASSESSMENT OPTIONS

Checkpoint Questions
• Question 11 on p. 267
• Question 14 on p. 268

Embedded Assessment
• For a list of embedded assessment exercises see p. 4-28.

Performance Task/Portfolio
• Exercise 15 on p. 268
• Module Project on page 271

SECTION 3 MATERIALS

Exploration 1
◆ paper for folding
◆ colored pencils

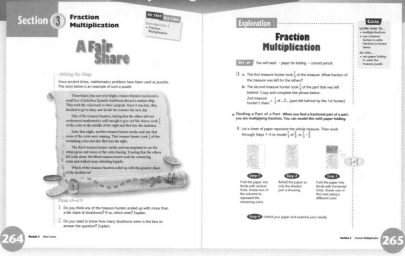

Setting the Stage

MOTIVATE

Hand each student a card with a fraction written on it. Then have them order themselves from least to greatest using the fraction card they were given. This will provide a quick review of fractions, equivalent fractions, and the ordering of fractions and in general get students to thinking about fraction concepts.

Exploration I

PLAN

Classroom Management The Exploration can best be performed by students working in groups of three or four. In answering *Questions 1* and *2*, students will naturally want to solve the puzzle. Allow them enough time to answer the questions based on how they solved the problem. If time permits, have different groups present the strategies they used to solve the puzzle. A variety of approaches will probably surface.

GUIDE

Managing Time Although students are working in groups of three or four, each student will need paper and colored pencils in order to do his or her own paper folding. It will be helpful to students if you also do the paper folding to provide a visual model for them for each step in *Question 4*.

266   Module 4   Mind Games

Section 3   Fraction Multiplication   267

Exploration 1 continued

Developing Math Concepts As you discuss *Question 10* with the students, they should notice that the products can be found by multiplying the numerators and the denominators. As students work on this question, they should be making the connection between the paper folding they did and the paper-and-pencil computation.

Classroom Examples

Find the product $\frac{5}{6} \cdot \frac{9}{20}$. Write the answer in lowest terms.

Answer:
$$\frac{5}{6} \cdot \frac{9}{20} = \frac{45 \div 5}{120 \div 5}$$
$$= \frac{9 \div 3}{24 \div 3}$$
$$= \frac{3}{8}$$

Common Error In *Question 7*, some students may erroneously conclude that the third treasure hunter walked away with as much as the other two treasure hunters, since "all three took away a third." One way for students to see that this is not so without doing multiplication or knowing the original number of doubloons in the treasure box is to reason as follows: The first person takes $\frac{1}{3}$ of the whole and the second person takes $\frac{1}{3}$ of *something less than a whole.* Therefore, there is more than $\frac{1}{3}$ of the whole left for the third person.

Checkpoint *Questions 11* and *14* both check to see whether students can multiply fractions. If students are having trouble with *Question 11*, encourage them to find the product using paper folding. *Question 14* also checks whether students can write a fraction in lowest terms.

HOMEWORK EXERCISES

See the Suggested Assignment for the day on page 4-28. For Exercise Notes, see page 4-28.

CLOSE

Closure Question Describe how to multiply fractions and check that the answer is in lowest terms.

Sample Response: Multiply the numerators of the fractions to find the numerator of the product, and multiply the denominators of the fractions to find the denominator of the product. If the numerator and denominator of the product have any factors in common, it is not in lowest terms. Divide both the numerator and denominator by their GCF (greatest common factor) to put the answer in lowest terms.

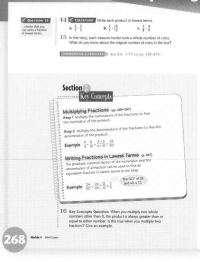

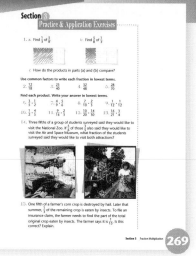

SUGGESTED ASSIGNMENT

Core Course
Day 1: Exs. 1, 2–14 even, 17–26

Extended Course
Day 1: Exs. 1, 2–14 even, 16–27

Block Schedule
Day 3: Sec. 2, Exs. 34–49; Exs.
1, 2–14 even, 17–26

EMBEDDED ASSESSMENT

These section objectives are
tested by the exercises listed.

**Model and find fraction
products.**
Exercises 1, 8, 10, 14

**Use common factors to
write a fraction in lowest
terms.**
Exercises 2, 4, 12

Practice & Application

EXERCISE NOTES

Writing For *Ex. 1*, consider
having students use the paper-
folding activities that were used
in the Exploration.

Developing Math Concepts In
Ex. 1, the mathematical idea
that is illustrated is that the
commutative property of multiplication applies to fractions as
well as to whole numbers. In
symbols, if a and b are fractions
then $a \cdot b = b \cdot a$.

Customizing Instruction

Visual Learners If students are having difficulty
understanding the concept of multiplying fractions,
encourage them to continue to use paper folding or
the drawing of models.

Home Involvement Those helping students at home
will find the Key Concepts on page 268 a handy reference to the key ideas, terms, and skills of Section 3.

Absent Students For students who have been absent
for all or part of this section, the blackline Study Guide
for Section 3 may be used to present the ideas. The
Key Concepts on page 268 also provide a good
overview of the key ideas, terms, and skills of Section 3.

Extra Help For students who need additional practice, the blackline Practice and Applications for Section
3 provides additional exercises that may be used to
confirm the skills of Section 3. The Extra Skill Practice
on page 272 also provides additional exercises.

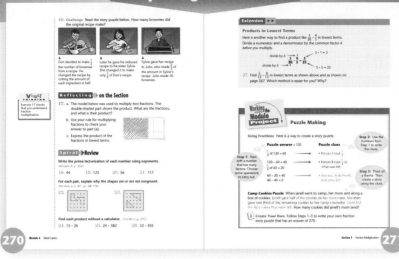

Practice & Application

Using Shortcuts In the example preceding *Ex. 27*, students are shown a shortcut that may reduce the time needed to simplify a product of two or more fractions. Caution students that care must be used when using shortcuts. This particular shortcut happens to work but students should be made to understand that they will encounter situations that superficially resemble the one shown in which a "shortcut" may result in a wrong answer. An example of such a situation is the *addition* of fractions.

With the class, discuss the Camp Cookies Puzzle. It may be necessary to give students another example in order to check for understanding. As students create their own puzzles, encourage them to be imaginative in choosing their puzzle theme. Have them exchange puzzles with one another in order to check solutions. You may wish to have part of the class use 270 as the puzzle answer and assign other puzzle answers to other groups of class members.

Closing the Section

Students have used paper folding to explore the concept of multiplying fractions. They have had the opportunity to have a visual model of what occurs when fractions are multiplied, and used that knowledge to develop an algorithm for multiplying fractions using paper and pencil. The Reflecting on the Section exercise on page 270 ties the visual representation to the paper-and-pencil approach to the multiplication of fractions. Students have extended their knowledge of simplifying fractions to lowest terms by finding the greatest common factor of the numerator and denominator. On the practical side, Exercise 16 addressed recipes and cooking as an everyday application of the multiplication of fractions.

QUICK QUIZ ON THIS SECTION

Use common factors to write each fraction in lowest terms.

1. $\dfrac{60}{105}$ 2. $\dfrac{42}{48}$

Write each product in lowest terms.

3. $\dfrac{2}{9} \cdot \dfrac{3}{4}$ 4. $\dfrac{5}{16} \cdot \dfrac{8}{9}$

5. Two-thirds of the students at Apple Valley Middle School participate in after-school sports. One-quarter of these play basketball. What fraction of the school plays basketball after school?

6. Your mother has a 15-ounce package of roast beef. You and your friends use $\dfrac{2}{3}$ of the package to make yourself an afternoon snack. How many pounds are left in the refrigerator? $\left(15 \text{ ounces} = \dfrac{15}{16} \text{ lb.}\right)$

For answers, see Quick Quiz blackline on p. 4-66.

Section ④ Decimal Multiplication

Section Planner

DAYS FOR MODULE 4

1 2 3 4 5 6 **7** 8 9 10 11 12

SECTION 4

First Day
Setting the Stage, p. 273
Exploration 1, pp. 274–275

Second Day
Exploration 2, pp. 276–277
Key Concepts, p. 278

Block Schedule

Day 4
Setting the Stage, Exploration 1,
Exploration 2, Key Concepts

RESOURCE ORGANIZER

Teaching Resources
• Practice and Applications, Sec. 4
• Study Guide, Sec. 4
• Warm-Up, Sec. 4
• Quick Quiz, Sec. 4

Section Overview

In Section 4, students will play a game using a calculator that will help them find a factor of a given whole number. Students will discover that a decimal may better approximate the factor. Ten by ten grids will help students model decimal multiplication. They will relate decimal multiplication to multiplication of fractions using the shading techniques they applied in Section 3.

After students have discovered how to use the sum of the number of decimal places in the factors to place the decimal point in the product, they will learn how to use estimation to place the decimal point in the product.

In Exploration 2, students will use mental math to multiply a whole number by 0.1 and 0.01.

SECTION OBJECTIVES

Exploration 1
• multiply decimals, including recognizing when a product is reasonable

Exploration 2
• estimate decimal products

ASSESSMENT OPTIONS

Checkpoint Questions
• Question 8 on p. 275

Embedded Assessment
• For a list of embedded assessment exercises see p. 4-34.

Performance Task/Portfolio
• Exercise 11 on p. 279 (writing)
★ Exercise 24 on p. 280 (challenge)
• Exercise 25 on p. 279 (visual thinking)
• Standardized Testing 1 on p. 281

★ = a problem solving task that can be assessed using the Assessment Scales

SECTION 4 MATERIALS

Setting the Stage
◆ Labsheet 4A
◆ calculator

Exploration 1
◆ Labsheet 4B

Exploration 2
◆ one calculator for each group

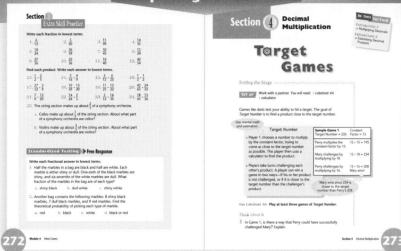

Setting the Stage

MOTIVATE

As students enter the classroom, have an overhead visual of a dart board on display. Ask which students have played darts either at home or in competition. Display several scores and have students determine how they could arrive at the scores if they were throwing three darts at the board. Have students assume that all three darts hit the board and are scored. Then mention that they will be playing a similar game that does not involve darts.

An overhead copy of Labsheet 4A can be used on an overhead projector instead of providing each group with its own copy. When playing *Target Number*, each group will need paper and pencil to record answers and keep score.

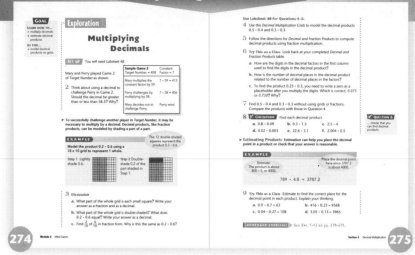

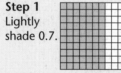

Exploration 1

PLAN

Classroom Management
Exploration 1 is best performed by students working with a partner. Each group will need a calculator and a copy of Labsheet 4B. After students have answered *Question 2*, have students return to the *Target Number* games they played earlier and determine whether they could have come closer to the target number by using decimal numbers.

GUIDE

Developing Math Concepts
To develop the concept of multiplying decimals, students will use the same procedure of shading a grid model that they used when they multiplied fractions. As you discuss with students the 10×10 grid that is used to model multiplication of decimals, you can refer to the 10×10 flat that students used when they were adding and subtracting decimals. This will help

students to see that, just as in the case of multiplying two fractions that are each less than 1, multiplying two decimals that are each less than 1 results in a product that has a lesser value than either of the two factors.

Classroom Examples
Model the product 0.3 · 0.7 using a 10 × 10 grid to represent 1 whole.

Answer:

Step 1
Lightly shade 0.7.

Step 2
Double-shade 0.3 of the part shaded in Step 1.

The 21 double-shaded squares represent the product 0.3 · 0.7.

Ongoing Assessment
Have students do *Question 7* in their journal. Have students explain in their own words why the decimal and fraction answers are equivalent.

Checkpoint *Question 8* checks to see whether students can find a decimal product. If students have difficulty placing the decimal point in the product, have graph paper available for them to model the product as they did in *Question 4*. Stress to students that they should always estimate the product of two decimals before doing the multiplication in order to position the decimal point accurately in the answer.

Classroom Examples
Use estimation to help you place the decimal point when multiplying 412 · 9.08.

Answer:
Estimate:
The product is about
400 · 9, or 3600.

$$412 \cdot 9.08 = 3740.96$$

Place the decimal point between the "0" and the "9" since 3740.96 is about 3600.

HOMEWORK EXERCISES

See the Suggested Assignment for Day 1 on page 4-34. For Exercise Notes, see page 4-34.

MODULE 4 ♦ SECTION 4

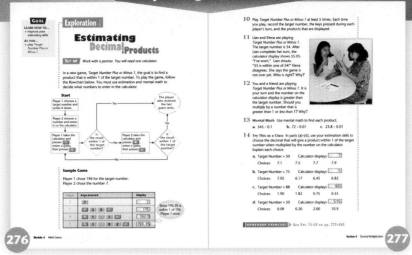

Exploration 2

PLAN

Classroom Management
Exploration 2 is best performed by students working as partners. Each group of partners will need one calculator. Before beginning the new game of *Target Number Plus or Minus 1*, go through the flowchart with the whole class. Make sure that students understand how to follow the chart.

GUIDE

Developing Math Concepts
Before beginning Exploration 2, have students use estimation to find the approximate products of several pairs of whole numbers. Go over the estimated products with the class and have students explain how they arrived at their estimates.

Classroom Examples
Use estimation to find a decimal that will give a product within 1 of 45 when it is multiplied by 7.

Possible answers: 6.3, 6.4, or 6.5

HOMEWORK EXERCISES

See the Suggested Assignment for Day 2 on page 4-34. For Exercise Notes, see page 4-34.

CLOSE

Closure Question How are multiplication of decimals and multiplication of whole numbers alike? How are they different?

Sample Response: Decimal multiplication begins by multiplying the numbers as whole numbers, but for decimal multiplication only, the decimal point must be placed in the product by adding the number of decimal places in the factors.

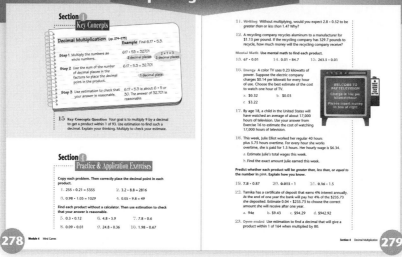

MODULE 4 ♦ SECTION 4

SUGGESTED ASSIGNMENT

Core Course
Day 1: Exs. 1–12, 26–30
Day 2: Exs. 13–16, 20, 22, 25, 31–33

Extended Course
Day 1: Exs. 1–12, 26–30
Day 2: Exs. 13–16, 20, 22, 24, 25, 31–33

Block Schedule
Day 4: Exs. 1–16, 18, 20, 22, 25–33

EMBEDDED ASSESSMENT

These section objectives are tested by the exercises listed.

Multiply decimals including recognizing when a product is reasonable.
Exercises 4, 6, 10, 11, 12

Estimate decimal products.
Exercises 20, 22

Practice & Application

EXERCISE NOTES

Writing In *Ex. 11*, students are asked to predict the approximate result of a multiplication of two decimals. Students who have difficulty with this may be excessively focused on the steps involved in finding the exact answer. Help them to see that since 0.52 is slightly greater than 0.5, the product must be slightly greater than half of 2.8, or 1.4, Then help them to write these ideas in their journals.

Background Information
Ex. 16 is a good example of an everyday use of decimals. It also provides an opportunity to discuss the cost of energy in your local area.

Customizing Instruction

Home Involvement Those helping students at home will find the Key Concepts on page 278 a handy reference to the key ideas, terms, and skills of Section 4.

Absent Students For students who have been absent for all or part of this section, the blackline Study Guide for Section 4 may be used to present the ideas. The Key Concepts on page 278 also provide a good overview of the key ideas, terms, and skills of Section 4.

Extra Help For students who need additional practice, the blackline Practice and Applications for Section 4 provides additional exercises that may be used to confirm the skills of Section 4. The Extra Skill Practice on page 281 also provides additional exercises.

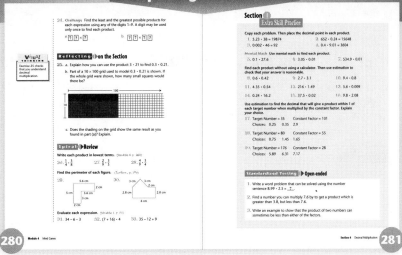

Closing the Section

While playing the *Target Number* games in this section , students have had the opportunity to improve their estimation skills. Using a visual model, students are able to formalize the concept of multiplying decimal numbers. In multiplying decimals, they use their estimation skills to determine whether an answer is reasonable, thereby ensuring the proper placement of the decimal point in the product. In the Reflecting on the Section exercise on page 280, students are asked to visualize the entirety of a partially shown grid model of a decimal multiplication statement. This exercise helps them to check their understanding of multiplication of two decimal numbers.

QUICK QUIZ ON THIS SECTION

Estimate to find the correct place for the decimal point in each product.

1. 0.018 • 245.3 = 44154

2. 0.6 • 1214.7 = 72882

Find each product without using a calculator. Then use estimation to check that your answer is reasonable.

3. 32.7 • 0.052   **4.** 408.9 • 1.06

5. How much does 2.23 lb of hamburger cost at $2.89/lb?

6. A woman works 52.3 h in a week. She is paid $9.84 per hour for the first 40 h, and for each hour over 40 h she is paid for 1.5 h. How much does she make that week?

For answers, see Quick Quiz blackline on p. 4-67.

MODULE 4 ◆ SECTION 4

4-35

Section ⑤ Equations and Graphs

Section Planner

DAYS FOR MODULE 4

| 1 | 2 | 3 | 4 | 5 | 6 | 7 | 8 | 9 | 10 | 11 | 12 |

SECTION 5

First Day
Setting the Stage, *p. 282*
Exploration 1, *pp. 283–284*

Second Day
Exploration 2, *pp. 285–287*
Key Concepts, *p. 288*

Block Schedule

Day 5
Setting the Stage, Exploration 1, Exploration 2, Key Concepts

RESOURCE ORGANIZER

Teaching Resources
• Practice and Applications, Sec. 5
• Study Guide, Sec. 5
• Warm-Up, Sec. 5
• Quick Quiz, Sec. 5

Section Overview

Students will learn how to graph ordered pairs on a coordinate grid, evaluate algebraic expressions, and write equations for finding the perimeter and area of a rectangle in Section 5. From a table of input and output values, students will graph ordered pairs of numbers, examine the graph, and use the graph to predict other output values for given input values. The terms ordered pair, coordinate grid, axes, and origin will be presented as the students graph their tables of values in Exploration 1.

Before students begin Exploration 2, which discusses writing and evaluating variable expressions, they may need to review page 51 in Module 1, where they first worked with numerical expressions. In this section, they will learn how equations for perimeter and area involve variable expressions. Area can also be reviewed, if necessary, in the Toolbox on page 600. Key terms introduced in this exploration are variable, evaluate an expression, and equation.

Practice and Application Exercises 15 and 16 provide a geometry connection.

SECTION OBJECTIVES

Exploration 1
• write a verbal rule for an input/output table and use a rule to find input and output values
• graph ordered pairs on a coordinate grid (first quadrant only)
• display input/output values on a coordinate grid to make predictions

Exploration 2
• write and evaluate expressions
• find the area and perimeter of a rectangle
• use drawings, tables, verbal rules, and equations to discover and represent relationships

ASSESSMENT OPTIONS

Checkpoint Questions
• Question 7 on p. 284
• Question 13 on p. 286
• Question 17 on p. 287

Embedded Assessment
• For a list of embedded assessment exercises see p. 4-41.

Performance Task/Portfolio
• Exercise 13 on p. 289
• Exercise 33 on p. 290 (open-ended)
• Exercise 36 on p. 291
• Exercise 37 on p. 291 (journal)
• Module Project on p. 292

SECTION 5 MATERIALS

Setting the Stage
♦ Labsheet 5A

Exploration 1
♦ Labsheet 5B

Exploration 2
♦ Centimeter graph paper

Practice & Application Exercises
♦ graph paper

Module Project on page 292
♦ grid paper

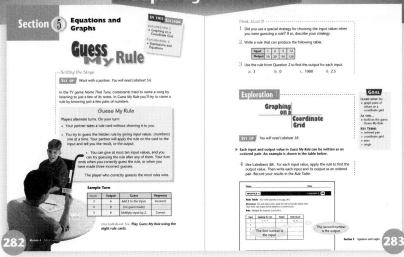

Setting the Stage

MOTIVATE

Play a quick classroom version of *Name That Tune*. Ask a student who would be willing to play the first few notes of several familiar songs using a keyboard, harmonica, or guitar. Another option is to play the beginnings of several songs that have been recorded on tape or compact disk.

Next, have students read the rules for *Guess My Rule* and answer *Questions 1–3*. Tell the students that in this section they will be learning about various ways of representing the rule that relates an input number to an output number.

Exploration I

PLAN

Classroom Management
Exploration 1 can best be performed by students working individually. Each student will need a copy of Labsheet 5B. After students complete *Question 4*, have them check their results with another student in order to be sure that they have the correct ordered pairs listed. For *Questions 6–9*, you may need to have extra copies of the *Empty Coordinate Grid* on Labsheet B for students who need more than one try at correctly graphing the ordered pairs or correctly drawing the line segments.

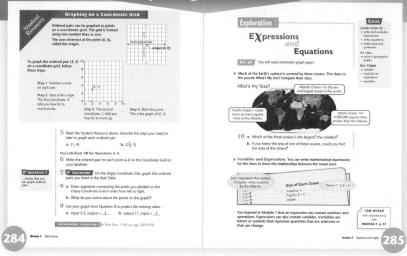

Exploration 1 continued

GUIDE

Developing Math Concepts
As students write ordered pairs, remind them that the number pairs are called *ordered* because the order of the numbers is important. Thus, (3, 4) is not the same ordered pair as (4, 3). In *Question 6*, two of the points, *C* and *D*, are not located at the intersection of two grid lines. Assure students that they may make the reasonable assumption that the points are halfway between two grid points.

Classroom Examples
Graph the ordered pair (6, 8) on a coordinate grid.

Answer: Number a scale on each axis. Start at the origin and move 6 units across. From there, move 8 units up. Mark and label the point.

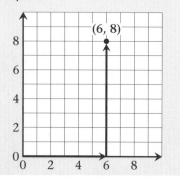

Common Error Students may confuse the order of the input number and the output number of an ordered pair. Point out that since they have to begin with an input number in order to obtain an output number, it is reasonable to write the input number first and the output number second.

Checkpoint In *Question 7*, students are asked to graph ordered pairs. Check students work to make sure that the points are graphed correctly. If they are, you will notice that the points are in a straight line. The rule "multiply the input by 2 and add 1" corresponds to the algebraic rule $y = 2 \cdot x + 1$, which is the equation of a straight line.

HOMEWORK EXERCISES

See the Suggested Assignment for Day 1 on page 4-40. For Exercise Notes, see page 4-40.

Exploration 2

PLAN

Classroom Management
Exploration 2 is best performed by students working individually. If graph paper with centimeter squares is not available, other grid paper can be used for *Questions 15–17*.

Managing Time You may wish to spread the material in Exploration 2 over two days. On the first day you could cover expressions, completing *Question 10–14*. In addition, you could have students practice writing expressions for word phrases in a variety of situations.

On the second day you could spend more time on the introduction of equations. As a class or in small groups, students can devise situations for which equations are helpful, such as the following:

- ticket money collected = number of tickets sold · price per ticket

- number of days remaining in the month = total days of month – the number for today's date

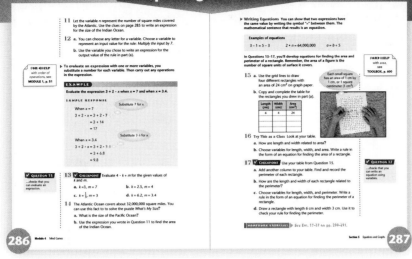

Exploration 2 continued

Classroom Examples
**Evaluate 3 · x – 6 when x = 9
and when x = 4.2.**

Answer:
When x = 9:
$$3 · x – 6 = 3 · 9 – 6$$
$$= 27 – 6$$
$$= 21$$

When x = 4.2:
$$3 · x – 6 = 3 · 4.2 – 6$$
$$= 12.6 – 6$$
$$= 6.6$$

Developing Math Concepts
Examples of three kinds of equations appear at the top of page 287. The first of these is a true equation with no variable; the other two equations are true for some values of their variables and false for others. Mention that in the third equation, $a = b + 5$, the variables a and b are different, so the numbers that are allowed to replace them may be different also.

Checkpoint *Question 17* checks to see whether students can devise an equation that describes a relationship among three geometric measures concerning rectangles: length, width, and perimeter. Students may use any letters that they wish, but if they have not already used the initial letters of the words *length*, *width*, *area*, and *perimeter* in *Question 16*, you can suggest that they do so now.

Visual Learners Many students will already be familiar with the relationships among area, perimeter, length and width. Students having difficulty with these relationships may need to see how the rule works by drawing several different rectangles and testing the rules that they devised in *Questions 16* and *17*.

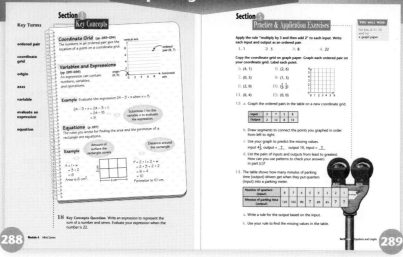

Exploration 2 continued

HOMEWORK EXERCISES

See the Suggested Assignment for Day 2 on page 4-40. For Exercise Notes, see page 4-40.

CLOSE

Closure Question How are expressions and equations alike? How are they different? Explain how you can graph expressions or equations on a coordinate grid.

Sample Response: Expressions and equations both contain numbers, variables, and operations, but equations also contain an equal sign and expressions do not. You can use expressions or equations to find output values for selected input values, write these values as ordered pairs, and then plot the ordered pairs as points on a coordinate grid.

SUGGESTED ASSIGNMENT

Core Course
Day 1: Exs. 1–13, 38–41
Day 2: Exs. 17–30, 32, 36, 37, 42

Extended Course
Day 1: Exs. 1–13, 15, 16, 38–41
Day 2: Exs. 17–30, 32, 36, 37, 42

Block Schedule
Day 5: Exs. 2–14 even, 18–32 even, 34–42

Customizing Instruction

Home Involvement Those helping students at home will find the Key Concepts on page 288 a handy reference to the key ideas, terms, and skills of Section 5.

Absent Students For students who have been absent for all or part of this section, the blackline Study Guide for Section 5 may be used to present the ideas. The Key Concepts on page 288 also provide a good overview of the key ideas, terms, and skills of Section 5.

Extra Help For students who need additional practice, the blackline Practice and Applications for Section 5 provides additional exercises that may be used to confirm the skills of Section 5. The Extra Skill Practice on page 293 also provides additional exercises.

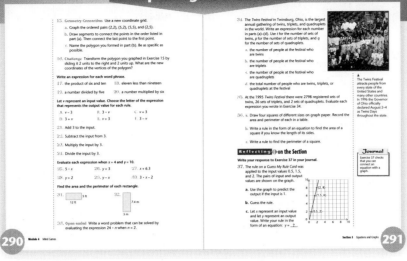

EMBEDDED ASSESSMENT

These section objectives are tested by the exercises listed.

Write a verbal rule for an input/output table and use a rule to find input and output values.

Exercises 2, 4, 14

Graph ordered pairs on a coordinate grid. (first quadrant only)

Exercises 6, 8, 10

Display input/output values on a coordinate grid to make predictions.

Exercise 13

Write and evaluate expressions.

Exercises 18, 24, 28, 30, 34

Find the area and perimeter of a rectangle.

Exercises 32, 36

Use drawings, tables, verbal rules, and equations to discover and represent relationships.

Exercise 36

Practice & Application

EXERCISE NOTES

Challenge In *Ex. 16*, remind students that *sliding* a figure is a *translation* that moves it to a new location without rotating it at the same time.

Writing For *Exs. 31* and *32*, have students write in their Journal a paragraph describing the difference between the area and perimeter of a polygon.

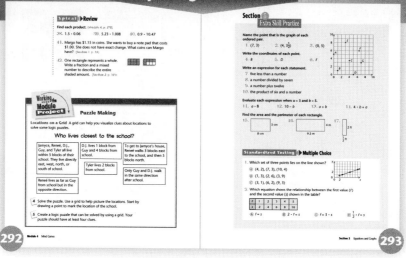

Working on the Module Project

Have one inch graph paper available for students to use to solve the puzzle on page 292 and to design their own puzzle. It is likely that many students will make some false starts and thus need several pieces of graph paper. Students may more easily solve the puzzle if they create a chart with four columns labeled west, north, south, and east and with five rows labeled with the names of the five boys. Positions in the chart can then be filled with circles to indicate confirmed locations and crosses to indicate firmly eliminated possibilities.

Closing the Section

While playing *Guess My Rule*, students learned about ordered pairs and how to graph them on a coordinate grid. Students also became more familiar with algebraic tools such as expressions and equations. They also applied their knowledge by writing equations for the area and perimeter of a rectangle. In the Reflecting on the Section exercise on page 291, students used their knowledge of ordered pairs and equations to write an equation that describes the graph of a straight line.

QUICK QUIZ ON THIS SECTION

Apply the rule "multiply by 12, then subtract from 100" to each input. Write each input and output as an ordered pair.

1. $\frac{1}{3}$ 2. 2   3. $\frac{15}{4}$

4. Graph the ordered pairs on a coordinate grid. Label each point.

(0, 0) (2, 4) (6, 6) (8,7)

5. Write an expression for the word phrase. Let *x* represent the input value. 200 minus six times the input value

6. Evaluate $6 \cdot b - a$ when $a = 3$ and $b = 1.2$.

For answers, see Quick Quiz blackline on p. 4-68.

Section 6 · Multiples and Mixed Numbers

Section Planner

DAYS FOR MODULE 4

1 2 3 4 5 6 7 8 9 10 **11 12**

SECTION 6

First Day
Setting the Stage, *p. 294*
Exploration 1, *pp. 295–296*

Second Day
Exploration 2, *pp. 297–299*
Key Concepts, *p. 300*

Block Schedule

Day 6
Setting the Stage, Exploration 1, Exploration 2, Key Concepts

RESOURCE ORGANIZER

Teaching Resources
- Practice and Applications, Sec. 6
- Study Guide, Sec. 6
- Module Tests Forms A and B
- Standardized Assessment
- Module Performance Assessment
- Cumulative Test Modules 3–4
- Warm-Up, Sec. 6
- Quick Quiz, Sec. 6

Section Overview

In Section 6 students will work with multiples, least common multiples, and fractions greater than 1. They will examine the sequences formed by multiples of numbers and will use lists of multiples to identify the least common multiple of two numbers.

At this point in the course, students have already examined how a fraction greater than a whole can be written as a mixed number. Because writing a fraction as a mixed number is a necessary skill for this section, any students needing to review this topic should do so by referring back to Module 2. In Section 6, students will use physical models to find rules for expressing fractions greater than 1 as mixed numbers, then will reverse the process to express mixed numbers as fractions greater than 1. Students will also see how a quotient with a remainder can be expressed as a mixed number.

SECTION OBJECTIVES

Exploration 1
- list several multiples of a number
- find the least common multiple of two or more numbers

Exploration 2
- rewrite a fraction greater than one as a mixed number and vice versa
- write a quotient as a mixed number and decide when a mixed number quotient is appropriate to solve a problem

ASSESSMENT OPTIONS

Checkpoint Questions
- Question 6 on p. 295
- Question 8 on p. 296
- Question 15 on p. 298
- Question 19 on p. 299

Embedded Assessment
- For a list of embedded assessment exercises see p. 4-47.

Performance Task/Portfolio
- Exercise 34 on p. 302 (discussion)
- Exercise 43 on p. 303 (career connection)
- Module Project on p. 305

- ★ = a problem solving task that can be assessed using the Assessment Scales

SECTION 6 MATERIALS

Exploration 1
- ◆ Labsheet 6A

Exploration 2
- ◆ pattern blocks
- ◆ die or numbered scale

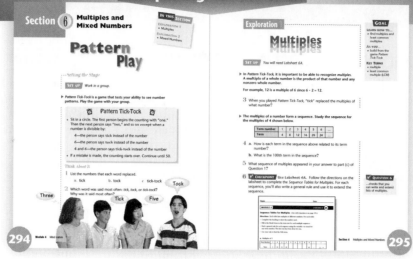

Setting the Stage

MOTIVATE

Have the class play *Pattern Tick-Tock*. After students have played one round, have them play another round, perhaps picking up the tempo or having students start with 100 and count to 150. *Questions 1* and *2* can be answered by the whole class after playing the game. Play a third round using different numbers such as 3 and 4.

Exploration 1

PLAN

Classroom Management
Exploration 1 can best be performed by students working individually. Each student will need a copy of Labsheet 6A.

GUIDE

Developing Math Concepts
Mention to students that the number of multiples of a number is infinite. It is also the case that any pair of numbers has an infinite number of common multiples. However, any such pair has only one *least* common multiple.

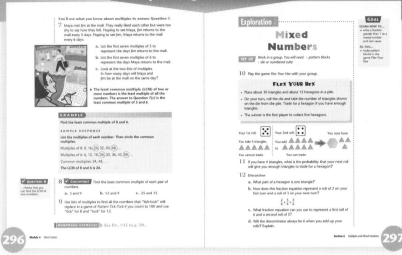

Exploration 1 continued

Developing Math Concepts

Question 7 connects the ideas of GCF and LCM. If the GCF of two numbers is 1, then their LCM is the product of the numbers. Since the GCF of 5 and 6 is 1, their LCM is 5 • 6, or 30. *Question 8(a)* illustrates that if one number is a factor of the other, then their LCM is the larger number: 3 is a factor of 9, so the LCM of 3 and 9 is 9.

Classroom Examples
Find the least common multiple of 9 and 12.

Answer:
List the multiples of each number. Then circle the common multiples.

Multiples of 9: 9, 18, 27, (36), 45, 54, 63, (72) ...

Multiple of 12: 12, 24, (36), 48, 60, (72) ...

Common multiples: 36, 72 ...

The least common multiple of 9 and 12 is 36.

Checkpoint
After students have completed *Questions 6* and *7* and the Example on page 296 , ask them the following questions about the numbers 5, 8, 9, and 13 that are the basis for the four tables on Labsheet 6A.

What is the GCF of 5 and 8?
What is their LCM?
What is the GCF of 5 and 9?
What is their LCM?
What is the GCF of 5 and 13?
What is their LCM?
What is the GCF of 8 and 9?
What is their LCM?
What is the GCF of 8 and 13?
What is their LCM?
What is the GCF of 9 and 13?
What is their LCM?
Have students first refer to their completed tables. After they notice that none of the LCMs are in the tables, they may begin to realize that if two numbers have no common factor (except 1) then their LCM is the product of the two numbers.

Common Error
Some students may confuse *least common multiple* with *greatest common factor*. Even though the words *least*, *greatest multiple*, and *factor* seem clear, some students will benefit from seeing an example of both concepts based on the same pair of numbers. You can use 4 and 6 to illustrate the two ideas: The GCF of 4 and 6 is 2, since no number greater than 2 is a common factor of 4 and 6.
The LCM of 4 and 6 is 12, since no number less than 12 is a common multiple of 4 and 6.

Writing
In their journals, have students define the terms *least*, *common*, and *multiple*. Then have them use their definitions to define *least common multiple* in their own words.

▌ HOMEWORK EXERCISES ▶

See the Suggested Assignment for Day 1 on page 4-47. For Exercise Notes, see page 4-47.

Exploration 2

PLAN

Classroom Management
Exploration 2 is best performed by students working in groups of three to five. Each group will need more than 30 equilateral triangles and approximately 15 regular hexagons each of whose sides has the same length as that of one of the triangles. Have students play two rounds of *Flex Your Hex*. If students trade incorrectly, they should do their turn again. Have students answer *Questions 12, 13, 14, 16,* and *17* within their groups, sharing solutions as a whole class if time allows.

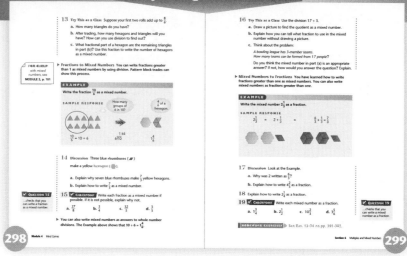

Exploration 2 continued

GUIDE

Classroom Examples

Write $\frac{15}{6}$ as a mixed number.

Answer:

How many groups of 6 in 15?

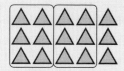

$$\frac{15}{6} = 15 \div 6$$

Trade:

$$6\overline{)15} \quad \begin{array}{c} 2\ R3 \end{array} \qquad 2\frac{3}{6}$$

Write $4\frac{2}{3}$ as a fraction.

Answer:
$$4\frac{2}{3} = 4 + \frac{2}{3}$$

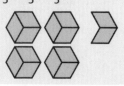

$$4\frac{2}{3} = \frac{12}{3} + \frac{2}{3} = \frac{14}{3}$$

Technology A fraction calculator can be used throughout Exploration 2 to rewrite fractions greater than one as mixed numbers and mixed numbers to fractions greater than one.

Checkpoint *Question 15* checks to see that students can write a fraction as a mixed number and *Question 19* checks to see that students can write a mixed number as a fraction. Students will often face situations where they have to decide which of the two forms is more useful for solving a particular problem that faces them.

HOMEWORK EXERCISES

See the Suggested Assignment for Day 2 on page 4-47. For Exercise Notes, see page 4-47.

CLOSE

Closure Question Explain how you can use the least common multiple (LCM) to add or subtract two fractions with unlike denominators. Then explain how you can tell if your answer can be written as a mixed number and, if it can, how to write it as a mixed number.

Sample Response: Find the LCM of the two denominators and rewrite both fractions with the LCM as the denominator. Then add or subtract the numerators and write the resulting fraction. If the result is a fraction greater than 1, then it can be rewritten as a mixed number. Divide the numerator by the denominator. The quotient is the whole number part of the mixed number, and the remainder over the divisor is the fractional part of the mixed number.

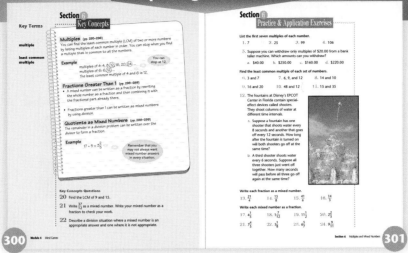

SUGGESTED ASSIGNMENT

Core Course

Day 1: Exs. 1–6, 8, 10, 12, 35–39, 43

Day 2: Exs. 14–28 even, 29–31, 33, 34, 40–42

Extended Course

Day 1: Exs. 1–6, 8, 10, 12, 35–39 43,

Day 2: Exs. 14–28 even, 29–31, 33, 34, 40–42

Block Schedule

Day 6: Exs. 2–5 even, 6, 28, 29–31, 33–42

EMBEDDED ASSESSMENT

These section objectives are tested by the exercises listed.

List several multiples of a number.

Exercises 2, 4, 5

Find the least common multiple of two or more numbers.

Exercises 6, 8, 10, 12

Write a fraction greater than one as a mixed number and vice versa.

Exercises 14, 16, 22, 24

Write a quotient as a mixed number, and decide when a mixed number quotient is appropriate to solve a problem.

Exercises 29, 30, 33

Practice & Application

EXERCISE NOTES

Writing After students have completed *Exs. 6–11*, have them write in their journals an explanation of the difference between a least common multiple and a greatest common factor. Encourage them to use examples and models of these two concepts.

Customizing Instruction

Home Involvement Those helping students at home will find the Key Concepts on page 300 a handy reference to the key ideas, terms, and skills of Section 6.

Absent Students For students who have been absent for all or part of this section, the blackline Study Guide for Section 6 may be used to present the ideas. The Key Concepts on page 300 also provide a good overview of the key ideas, terms, and skills of Section 6.

Extra Help For students who need additional practice, the blackline Practice and Applications for Section 6 provides additional exercises that may be used to confirm the skills of Section 6. The Extra Skill Practice on page 304 also provides additional exercises.

MODULE 4 ◆ SECTION 6

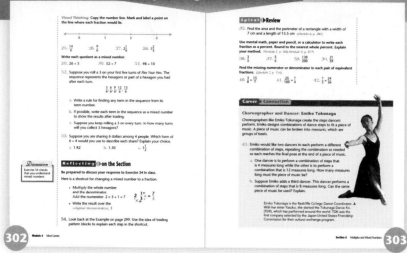

Practice & Application

Developing Math Concepts

Ex. 34 is based on the Example on page 299. To change $2\frac{1}{3}$ to a mixed number, proceed as shown below:

$$2\overset{+}{\underset{\times}{\rlap{\raise2pt{\hbox{$\nearrow$}}}\lower2pt{\hbox{$\swarrow$}}}}\frac{1}{3} = \frac{7}{3} \qquad \frac{2 \times 3}{3} + \frac{1}{3} = \frac{6}{3} + \frac{1}{3} = \frac{7}{3}$$

Shortcut   **Full Version**

Here, you multiply the denominator (3) of the fractional part of the mixed number by the whole number part (2) and add the result (6) to the numerator (1) to get 7; this is the numerator of the desired fraction. For the denominator, use the same denominator as the fractional part of the mixed number. The full version of the process (see above) relies on the fact that $\frac{2 \times 3}{3}$ and 2 are symbols that represent the same number. So, but less obviously, does the shortcut.

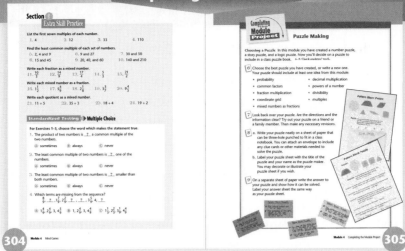

Closing the Section

While playing *Pattern Tick-Tock* and *Flex Your Hex*, students have developed an understanding of least common multiples of numbers and of mixed numbers. They have expanded their knowledge of fractions by converting mixed numbers into improper fractions. Students have completed the module by creating a puzzle for their classmates to solve.

QUICK QUIZ ON THIS SECTION

1. Find the least common multiple of 4, 6, and 7.

2. Write as a mixed number: $\dfrac{32}{6}$

3. Write as a fraction: $2\dfrac{4}{13}$

4. Write as a mixed number: $16 \div 3$

5. Suppose you were sharing 5 small pizzas among 3 hungry 6th graders. Which form of $5 \div 3$ would be best to describe each share?

   a. 1 R2   **b.** 1.67   **c.** $1\dfrac{2}{3}$

For answers, see Quick Quiz blackline on p. 4-69.

Completing the Module Project

During this module students have created a number puzzle, a story puzzle, and a logic puzzle. Each student is now required to submit a puzzle for a class puzzle book. Encourage students to use more than one idea. Better students should be encouraged to create more challenging puzzles.

MODULE 4 | **LABSHEET** **1A**

Never a Six (Use with Questions 15 and 16 on page 239.)

Directions You'll need a die or a numbered cube. Work with a partner. Follow the game rules in your book to play one game of *Never a Six*. To keep track of your score, record the results of each of your turns in the table.

	Player 1			Player 2		
Turn	Numbers rolled	Total points rolled	Total score	Numbers rolled	Total points rolled	Total score
1						
2						
3						
4						
5						
6						
7						
8						
9						
10						
11						
12						
13						
14						
15						

Paper Clip Products (Use with Setting the Stage on page 247, Question 3 on page 248, Question 10 on page 249, and Question 13 on page 250.)

Directions You'll need 2 paper clips and 10 each of two different colored chips. Follow the game rules in your book to play *Paper Clip Products*.

Game Board

7	14	24	16	40
20	15	55	28	9
35	8	12	25	19
4	17	30	48	45
36	18	32	11	21

Factor List

2	3	4	5
6	7	8	9
10	11	12	13
14	15	16	17
18	19	20	21
22	23	24	25

MODULE 4 | **LABSHEET 2B**

Divisibility Test for 3 (Use with Question 7 on page 249.)

Directions Follow the steps below to fill in the table. Then use the completed table to answer parts (a)–(d).

Step 1 Multiply the number in the first row by 3. Write the product in the second row.

Step 2 Add the digits of the product in the second row. Write the sum in the third row.

$3 \cdot 4 = 12$

Number	1	2	3	4	5	6	13	27	55	456	659	2260
Multiply by 3	3			12								
Sum of the digits	3			3								

The sum of the digits 1 and 2 is 3.
$1 + 2 = 3$

a. Are all the numbers in the second row divisible by 3? How do you know?

b. What do all the numbers in the third row have in common?

c. Use the pattern from part (b) to develop a test for divisibility by 3.

d. Choose several three-digit and four-digit numbers and use your test to check them for divisibility by 3. Does your divisibility test seem to work?

MODULE 4   LABSHEET **2C**

Prime Time

(Use with Question 15 on page 251, and Questions 17 and 19 on page 252.)

Directions You'll need a supply of paper clips and 15 each of two different colored chips. Work with a partner. Follow the game rules in your book to play *Prime Time*.

Game Board

12	50	49	6	18
15	9	27	30	105
4	8	10	35	20
32	25	14	28	42
40	21	75	54	63
45	98	60	125	81

Factor List

2	3	5	7

Math Thematics, Book 1 **4-53**

MODULE 4

Target Number   (Use with Setting the Stage on page 273.)

Directions Work with a partner. Follow the game rules in your book to play *Target Number*. Place a sheet of paper over the table. To begin a game, slide the paper down to reveal the target number and the constant factor. Record the numbers you chose to multiply by and the resulting products. Start with Game 2, since a sample game is shown on page 273 for Game 1.

Game 1	Target Number = 226	Constant Factor = 13
Game 2	Target Number = 408	Constant Factor = 7
Game 3	Target Number = 845	Constant Factor = 38
Game 4	Target Number = 256	Constant Factor = 6
Game 5	Target Number = 942	Constant Factor = 64
Game 6	Target Number = 537	Constant Factor = 27
Game 7	Target Number = 351	Constant Factor = 19
Game 8	Target Number = 1031	Constant Factor = 8

Name _____   Date _____

Decimal Multiplication Grids (Use with Question 4 on page 275.)

Directions Shade each grid to model the given product. Then write each product in both fraction and decimal form.

Find 0.5 • 0.4.   Find 0.3 • 0.3.

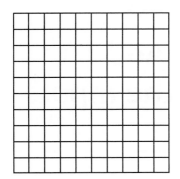   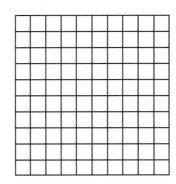

$\frac{5}{10} \cdot \frac{4}{10} =$ _____   0.5 • 0.4 = _____ $\frac{3}{10} \cdot \frac{3}{10} =$ _____   0.3 • 0.3 = _____

Decimal and Fraction Products

(Use with Questions 5 and 6 on page 275.)

Directions Write each decimal multiplication problem as a fraction multiplication problem. Then find the fraction product and write it in decimal form.

The whole number 4 written in fraction form is $\frac{4}{1}$.

Decimal multiplication problem	Equivalent fraction problem	Fraction product	Decimal product
4 • 0.6	$\frac{4}{1} \cdot \frac{6}{10}$	$\frac{24}{10}$	2.4
0.3 • 0.2			
0.8 • 0.09			
0.05 • 0.7			
6 • 0.03			
0.03 • 0.07			

Guess My Rule   (Use with Setting the Stage on page 282.)

Directions Cut out the rule cards, shuffle the cards, and place them in a pile face down. Follow the game rules in your book to play *Guess My Rule*.

Multiply the input by 7.	**Add 5 to the input.**
Multiply the input by 3 and add 5.	**Multiply the input by 8 and subtract 2.**
Divide the input by 2.	**Multiply the input by 11.**
Multiply the input by 3 and divide by 2.	**Multiply the input by itself.**

MODULE 4   **LABSHEET 5B**

Rule Table (Use with Question 4 on page 283.)

Directions For each input value, apply the rule to find the output value. Then write each input and its output as an ordered pair.

Rule: Multiply the input by 2 and add 1.

Input	Applying the rule	Output	Ordered pair
3	$3 \cdot 2 + 1$	7	(3, 7)
4			
0			
2			
1			

Coordinate Grid

(Use with Question 6 on page 284.)

Directions Write the ordered pair for each point *A–D*.

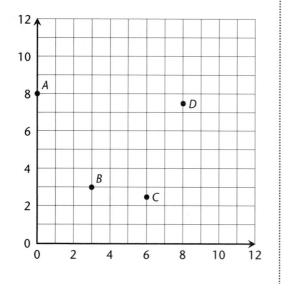

Empty Coordinate Grid

(Use with Questions 7–9 on page 284.)

Directions Follow the directions in your book to plot points.

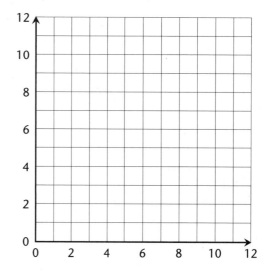

MODULE 4   **LABSHEET** (6A)

Sequence Tables for Multiples   (Use with Question 6 on page 295.)

Directions Each table lists multiples of different numbers. For each table:

- Complete the heading to show the number used.

- Fill in the blank boxes in the term row for each multiple sequence.

- Find a general rule for each sequence using the variable n to stand for any term number. The first one has been done for you.

- Use your rule to find the 50th term.

a. Multiples of 5

Term Number	1	2	3	4	5	6	7	8	9	...	n
Term	5	10	15	20					45	...	$\underline{5} \cdot n$

50th term = _____

b. Multiples of _____

Term Number	1	2	3	4	5	6	7	8	9	10	...	n
Term	13	26	39							130	...	____ $\cdot n$

50th term = _____

c. Multiples of _____

Term Number	1	2	3	4	5	6	7	...	n
Term		16	24		40	48	56	...	____ $\cdot n$

50th term = _____

d. Multiples of 9

Term Number	1	2	3	4	5	6	7	...	n
Term							63	...	____ $\cdot n$

50th term = _____

Name _____ Problem _____

☆ *The star indicates*
that you excelled
in some way.

 Problem Solving

❶   ❷   ❸   ❹   ❺

You did not understand
the problem well enough
to get started or you did
not show any work.

You understood the problem
well enough to make a plan
and to work toward a solution.

You made a plan, you used it to
solve the problem, and you verified
your solution.

 Mathematical Language

❶   ❷   ❸   ❹   ❺

You did not use any mathematical
vocabulary or symbols, or you did
not use them correctly, or your
use was not appropriate.

You used appropriate mathematical
language, but the way it was used
was not always correct or other
terms and symbols were needed.

You used mathematical language
that was correct and appropriate
to make your meaning clear.

 Representations

❶   ❷   ❸   ❹   ❺

You did not use any representations
such as equations, tables, graphs,
or diagrams to help solve the
problem or explain your solution.

You made appropriate representations to help solve the problem or
help you explain your solution, but
they were not always correct or
other representations were needed.

You used appropriate and correct
representations to solve the problem
or explain your solution.

 Connections

❶   ❷   ❸   ❹   ❺

You attempted or solved the
problem and then stopped.

You found patterns and used them to
extend the solution to other cases,
or you recognized that this problem
relates to other problems, mathematical ideas, or applications.

You extended the ideas in the
solutionto the general case, or you
showed how this problem relates
to other problems, mathematical
ideas, or applications.

 Presentation

❶   ❷   ❸   ❹   ❺

The presentation of your
solution and reasoning is
unclear to others.

The presentation of your solution
and reasoning is clear in most
places, but others may have
trouble understanding parts of it.

The presentation of your solution
and reasoning is clear and can
be understood by others.

Content Used: _____ **Computational Errors:**   Yes ☐ No ☐

Notes on Errors: _____

_____

Name _____   Problem _____

 STUDENT   **SELF-ASSESSMENT SCALES**

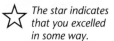 *If your score is in the shaded area, explain why on the back of this sheet and stop.*   *The star indicates that you excelled in some way.*

Problem Solving

❶   ❷   ❸   ❹   ❺   ☆

I did not understand the problem well enough to get started or I did not show any work.

I understood the problem well enough to make a plan and to work toward a solution.

I made a plan, I used it to solve the problem, and I verified my solution.

Mathematical Language

❶   ❷   ❸   ❹   ❺   ☆

I did not use any mathematical vocabulary or symbols, or I did not use them correctly, or my use was not appropriate.

I used appropriate mathematical language, but the way it was used was not always correct or other terms and symbols were needed.

I used mathematical language that was correct and appropriate to make my meaning clear.

Representations

❶   ❷   ❸   ❹   ❺   ☆

I did not use any representations such as equations, tables, graphs, or diagrams to help solve the problem or explain my solution.

I made appropriate representations to help solve the problem or help me explain my solution, but they were not always correct or other representations were needed.

I used appropriate and correct representations to solve the problem or explain my solution.

Connections

❶   ❷   ❸   ❹   ❺   ☆

I attempted or solved the problem and then stopped.

I found patterns and used them to extend the solution to other cases, or I recognized that this problem relates to other problems, mathematical ideas, or applications.

I extended the ideas in the solution to the general case, or I showed how this problem relates to other problems, mathematical ideas, or applications.

Presentation

❶   ❷   ❸   ❹   ❺   ☆

The presentation of my solution and reasoning is unclear to others.

The presentation of my solution and reasoning is clear in most places, but others may have trouble understanding parts of it.

The presentation of my solution and reasoning is clear and can be understood by others.

The Cleaning Crew (E² on textbook page 263)

All of the *Math Thematics* Assessment Scales should be used to assess students' solutions to this problem. Students will need a calculator and may want to use a computer spreadsheet to determine the amount of money made for cleaning each park and the total payment.

The first sample response shows the results for the first 19 parks cleaned using both payment methods. Students will realize that Payment Method B is the best by this point. Students should look for some other way to determine the final total for Payment Method B. An alternate representation is used in the second partial sample response.

Partial Solution

Since Payment Method A pays $100 per park, I multiplied to find the total for 25 parks. $100 per park • 25 parks = $2500. I used a table to figure out how much could be made with Payment Method B.

Number of parks cleaned	1	2	3	4	5	6	7	8	9	10
Payment in cents	1	2	4	8	16	32	64	128	256	512
Payment in dollars	.01	.02	.04	.08	.16	.32	.64	1.28	2.56	5.12
Total payment in dollars	.01	.03	.07	.15	.31	.63	1.27	2.55	5.11	10.23

Number of parks cleaned	11	12	13	14	15	16	17	18	19
Payment in cents	1024	2048	4096	8192	16384	32768	65536	131072	262144
Payment in dollars	10.24	20.48	40.96	81.92	163.84	327.68	655.36	1310.72	2621.44
Total payment in dollars	20.47	40.95	81.91	163.83	327.67	655.35	1310.71	2621.43	5242.87

I noticed that the payments in cents for Payment Method B form a pattern of powers of 2. After the first park is cleaned, the cleaning crew gets 2^0 cents. After the second park, they get 2^1 cents. So the payment for a park is 2^{n-1} cents, where n is the nth park cleaned. After the 25th park, the cleaning crew would get 2^{24} cents or $167,772.16!
I noticed that the total payment in cents is 2 times the payment minus 1 cent. The expression $2^{n-1} \cdot 2 - 1$ describes the total payment after n parks. The total amount the cleaning crew would earn after cleaning the 25th park is $2^{24} \cdot 2 - 1 = 33,554,431$ cents or $335,544.31.

Partial Solution

After I figured out how much would be made with each method, I wanted to see how quickly you could make money with the two methods. I graphed the results and connected the points. I could see that Payment Method A is best for 17 parks or less and Payment Method B is best for more than 17 parks.

Other Considerations
- **Connections** Students may make a connection to the paper folding activity in Section 2, extend the problem to 100 parks, or write an expression for the general case.

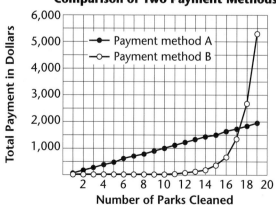

Comparison of Two Payment Methods

MODULE 4   ALTERNATE E²

Domino Sums

The Situation

A standard set of dominoes has 28 pieces. The face of each piece is divided in half, with each half showing a number from zero (blank) to six. The pieces that include a six are shown on the right. The game *Domino Sums* uses a standard set of dominoes. The rules are given below.

> The *value* of a domino is the sum of the two numbers

Domino Sums

* Each player starts with 15 chips and a number line that goes from 0 to 12.
* Each player places the chips above numbers on his or her number line. The players can put as many chips as they want above any number.
* The dominoes are placed in a sack. The first player draws a domino from the sack. If the player has a chip on the number line that corresponds to the value of the domino, the player can remove one chip from that number.
* The domino is put back in the sack, the sack is shaken, and the next player draws a domino.
* The first player to remove all the chips from his or her number line wins.

Value = 12

Value = 11

Value = 10

Value = 9

Value = 8

Value = 7

Value = 6

The Problem

Develop a winning strategy for placing the 15 chips on the number line in *Domino Sums*.

Something to Think About

* Are you just as likely to get a value of 11 as a value of 10?
* How could you test your strategy?

Present Your Results

Along with presenting your strategy, explain why you feel that it is an effective one.

How does probability relate to your strategy? Think about the best way to present your solution.

Domino Sums

The strategies students use in *Domino Sums* will vary, but all students should state which values are most likely to be chosen. All of the *Math Thematics* Assessment Scales should be used to assess student work.

Most students will need to play the game a few times before realizing that some values are chosen more often than others.

Partial Solution

I wasn't sure I could figure out a strategy unless I played the game a few times. I did and I noticed that the person who won usually had more chips on the center numbers (5, 6, 7, 8). I decided to list all the ways to get the values from 0 to 12, and the probability of getting each value. I realized that there is only one domino with a 0–1 and this is the same as a 1–0 domino. From my list I could tell that it is easiest to get a value of 6, since there are four different dominoes that have that value. The most difficult chips to remove from the number line have a value of 0, 1, 11, or 12.

Value	Possible dominoes	Probability as a fraction	Probability as a decimal
0	0–0	$\frac{1}{28}$	0.0357
1	0–1	$\frac{1}{28}$	0.0357
2	0–2, 1–1	$\frac{2}{28}$	0.0714
3	0–3, 1–2	$\frac{2}{28}$	0.0714
4	0–4, 1–3, 2–2	$\frac{3}{28}$	0.1071
5	0–5, 1–4, 2–3	$\frac{3}{28}$	0.1071
6	0–6, 1–5, 2–4, 3–3	$\frac{4}{28}$	0.1429

Value	Possible dominoes	Probability as a fraction	Probability as a decimal
7	1–6, 2–5, 3–4	$\frac{3}{28}$	0.1071
8	2–6, 3–5, 4–4	$\frac{3}{28}$	0.1071
9	3–6, 4–5	$\frac{2}{28}$	0.0714
10	4–6, 5–5	$\frac{2}{28}$	0.0714
11	5–6	$\frac{1}{28}$	0.0357
12	6–6	$\frac{1}{28}$	0.0357

I would not place any chips on the 0, 1, 11, or 12 since the probability of picking one of these dominoes is so low. The 2, 3, 9, and 10 have a higher probability of being chosen, so I would place one chip on each of them. I would put two chips on the 4, 5, 7, and 8 and three chips on the 6 because these have the highest probabilities.

Other Considerations

- **Problem Solving** Students may play the game after determining a strategy and then compare the results with their expectations.
- **Connections** Students might extend the ideas by changing the game to *Domino Differences* or *Domino Products*.

List all of the possibilities for each problem.

1. the digits displayed on a calculator
2. the color of lights on a traffic light
3. the letters on a stop sign
4. the even numbers from 11 to 20
5. the odd numbers from 11 to 20

1. The outcomes of an experiment involving a four-color spinner are given below. What is the experimental probability that the spinner stops on green? Write your answer as a fraction and as a whole percent.

   red   12   yellow   10
   green   6   blue   8

Write your answers as fractions.

2. What is the theoretical probability of drawing an ace from a standard deck of cards?

3. Kerry got 38 tails in 82 tosses of a coin. What is her experimental probability of heads?

ANSWERS

Warm-Ups: 1. 0, 1, 2, 3, 4, 5, 6, 7, 8, 9   **2.** red, green, yellow   **3.** S, T, O, P
4. 12, 14, 16, 18, 20   **5.** 11, 13, 15, 17, 19

Quick-Quiz: 1. $\frac{1}{6}$, 17%   **2.** $\frac{1}{13}$ **3.** $\frac{22}{41}$

Give two possible ways to multiply with whole numbers to get each answer.

1. 16   **2.** 18   **3.** 27

4. 36   **5.** 100   **6.** 26

1. Test 123,450 for divisibility by 2, 3, 5, 9, and 10.

2. Use a factor tree to find the prime factorization of 108.

3. What is the greatest common factor of 48 and 120?

4. Write the prime factorization of 400 using exponents.

5. What is the theoretical probability of getting a prime number if you pick a number at random between 20 and 39?

ANSWERS

Warm-Ups: Sample responses are given. **1.** $2 \cdot 8$ and $4 \cdot 4$ **2.** $2 \cdot 9$ and $6 \cdot 3$
3. $9 \cdot 3$ and $3 \cdot 3 \cdot 3$ **4.** $6 \cdot 6$ and $9 \cdot 4$ **5.** $4 \cdot 25$ and $10 \cdot 10$ **6.** $1 \cdot 26$ and $2 \cdot 13$

Quick-Quiz: 1. divisible by 2, 3, 5, and 10 **2.** $2 \cdot 2 \cdot 3 \cdot 3 \cdot 3$ **3.** 24 **4.** $2^4 \cdot 5^2$ **5.** $\frac{1}{5}$

State the greatest common factor for each group of numbers.

1. 6 and 15

2. 13 and 65

3. 18, 36, and 99

4. 21, 56, and 119

5. 9, 16, and 25

MODULE 4 SECTION 3   **QUICK QUIZ**

Use common factors to write each fraction in lowest terms.

1. $\dfrac{60}{105}$ **2.** $\dfrac{42}{48}$

Write each product in lowest terms.

3. $\dfrac{2}{9} \cdot \dfrac{3}{4}$ **4.** $\dfrac{5}{16} \cdot \dfrac{8}{9}$

5. Two-thirds of the students at Apple Valley Middle School participate in after-school sports. One-quarter of these play basketball. What fraction of the school plays basketball after school?

6. Your mother has a 15-ounce package of roast beef. You and your friends use $\dfrac{2}{3}$ of the package to make yourself an afternoon snack. How many pounds are left in the refrigerator? (15 ounces $= \dfrac{15}{16}$ lb)

ANSWERS

Warm-Ups: 1. 3 **2.** 13 **3.** 9 **4.** 7 **5.** 1

Quick-Quiz: 1. $\dfrac{4}{7}$ **2.** $\dfrac{7}{8}$ **3.** $\dfrac{1}{6}$ **4.** $\dfrac{5}{18}$ **5.** $\dfrac{1}{6}$ **6.** $\dfrac{5}{16}$ lb, or 0.3125 lb

Multiply.

1. $18 \cdot 9$ 2. $44 \cdot 3$

3. $15 \cdot 21$ 4. $13 \cdot 13$

5. $5 \cdot 5 \cdot 5$ 6. $68 \cdot 52$

Estimate to find the correct place for the decimal point in each product.

1. $0.018 \cdot 245.3 = 44154$ 2. $0.6 \cdot 1214.7 = 72882$

Find each product without using a calculator. Then use estimation to check that your answer is reasonable.

3. $32.7 \cdot 0.052$ 4. $408.9 \cdot 1.06$

5. How much does 2.23 lb of hamburger cost at $2.89/lb?

6. A woman works 52.3 h in a week. She is paid $9.84 for the first 40 h, and for each hour over 40 h she is paid for 1.5 h. How much does she make that week?

ANSWERS

Warm-Ups: 1. 162   2. 132   3. 315   4. 169   5. 125   6. 3536

Quick-Quiz: 1. 4.4154   2. 728.82   3. 1.7004   4. 433.434   5. $6.44   6. $575.15

Evaluate each expression

1. $6 \cdot 7 + 4$ **2.** $8 \cdot 3 + 4 \cdot 4$

3. $(9 \cdot 2) + 3$ **4.** $9 \cdot (2 + 3)$

5. $4 + 6 - 9 \div 3$ **6.** $4 \div (7 - 5) \div 2$

Apply the rule "multiply by 12, then subtract from 100" to each input. Write each input and output as an ordered pair.

1. $\dfrac{1}{3}$ **2.** 2 **3.** $\dfrac{15}{4}$

4. Graph the ordered pairs on a coordinate grid. Label each point.

    (0, 0)
    (2, 4)
    (6, 6)
    (8, 7)

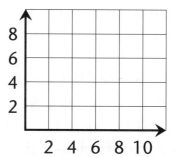

5. Write an expression for the word phrase. Let *x* represent the input value: 200 minus six times the input value

6. Evaluate the expression $6 \cdot b - a$ when $a = 3$ and $b = 1.2$.

ANSWERS

Warm-Ups: 1. 46   **2.** 40   **3.** 21   **4.** 45   **5.** 7   **6.** 1

Quick-Quiz: 1. $\left(\dfrac{1}{3}, 96\right)$ **2.** (2, 76)   **3.** $\left(\dfrac{15}{4}, 55\right)$

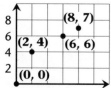

4.   **5.** $200 - 6x$ **6.** 4.2

Find the missing term in each sequence.

1. 4, 7, 10, ___?___, 16, 19

2. 1, 4, 16, ___?___, 256, 1024

3. 96, ___?___, 24, 12, 6, 3

4. ___?___ , 111, 104, 97, 90, 83

5. 2, 4, 7, 11, ___?___, 22, 29

6. 1, 4, 2, 5, 3, 6, ___?___

1. Find the least common multiple of 4, 6, and 7.

2. Write as a mixed number: $\frac{32}{6}$

3. Write as a fraction: $2\frac{4}{13}$

4. Write as a mixed number: $16 \div 3$

5. Suppose you were sharing 5 small pizzas among 3 hungry 6th graders. Which form of $5 \div 3$ would be best to describe each share?

    A. 1 R2   **B.** 1.67   **C.** $1\frac{2}{3}$

ANSWERS

Warm-Ups: 1. 13   **2.** 64   **3.** 48   **4.** 118   **5.** 16   **6.** 4

Quick-Quiz: 1. 84   **2.** $5\frac{1}{3}$ **3.** $\frac{30}{13}$ **4.** $5\frac{1}{3}$ **5.** C

Name _____   Date _____

For use with Exploration 1

1. a. Some students took turns tossing a coin. They recorded their
results in a table. Explain how the numbers in the "Experimental
probability of heads" column were calculated.

Number of tosses	Number of heads	Experimental probability of heads
500	208	0.416
800	424	0.53

b. How many tails did the students get in 800 tosses? What is the
experimental probability of tails?

2.

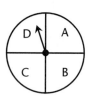

Outcome	Total
A	14
B	11
C	19
D	16

a. What is the experimental probability that the spinner stops on D?
Write your answer as a fraction and as a whole percent.

b. What is the experimental probability that the spinner stops on A,
B, or C? Write your answer as a fraction and as a whole percent.

3. a. A die was rolled 30 times. On 7 of the rolls, the outcome was 2.
What is the experimental probability of rolling 2? Write your
answer as a fraction, a decimal, and a percent.

b. On how many rolls was the outcome not 2? What is the
experimental probability of not rolling 2? Write your answer as a
fraction, a decimal, and a percent.

c. Suppose the die is thrown 100 times. Based on the experimental
probabilities you found, about how many times do you expect to
roll a 2? not roll a 2?

(continued)

MODULE 4 SECTION 1   **PRACTICE AND APPLICATIONS**

For use with Exploration 2

4. Find the theoretical probability of each event.

   a. The spinner stops on 3.

   b. The spinner stops on 1.

   c. The spinner stops on an even number.

   d. The spinner stops on 5.

   e. Were any of the events in parts (a)–(d) impossible? If so, which ones?

5. Suppose you pick a card, without looking, from the number cards numbered 1 through 10.

   a. List the possible outcomes for picking an even numbered card.

   b. What is the theoretical probability of picking an even numbered card?

   c. What is the theoretical probability of picking a card greater than or equal to 5? Less than 5?

   d. Plot your answers from parts (b) and (c) on a number line.

6. Is the event a certain event or an impossible event?

   a. A whale will speak English today.

   b. Water will evaporate today.

7. Ron has a bag of crayons. There are 2 red, 3 green, 4 blue, 1 yellow, 1 black, 2 brown, 1 orange, and 3 purple crayons in the bag. All of the crayons are the same size. Ron selects one crayon without looking. What is the theoretical probability that Ron selects a green crayon? What colors have the same probability of being selected as green?

MODULE 4 SECTION 2   PRACTICE AND APPLICATIONS

For use with Exploration 1

1. Without dividing, tell whether each number is divisible by 2, by 5, or by 10.

   a. 118   **b.** 225   **c.** 350

   d. 420   **e.** 371   **f.** 685

2. Test each number for divisibility by 3 and by 9.

   a. 138   **b.** 279   **c.** 608

   d. 189   **e.** 451   **f.** 342

3. Test each number for divisibility by 2, 3, 5, 9, and 10.

   a. 670   **b.** 240   **c.** 567

   d. 925   **e.** 414   **f.** 168

4. List all the factors of each number.

   a. 36   **b.** 20   **c.** 42

   d. 45   **e.** 29   **f.** 16

5. Find the greatest common factor of each set of numbers.

   a. 16 and 36   **b.** 20 and 45   **c.** 15 and 24

   d. 16, 20, and 30   **e.** 12 and 25   **f.** 9, 18, and 21

6. Mr. Gerald has $13.65. He wants to divide the money equally between his 3 grandchildren. Can he do this so that each child gets the same amount of money? Explain.

(continued)

MODULE 4 SECTION 2 — PRACTICE AND APPLICATIONS

For use with Exploration 2

7. Tell whether each number is *prime* or *composite*.

   a. 33   **b.** 47   **c.** 153

   d. 19   **e.** 366   **f.** 95

8. Use a factor tree to find the prime factorization of 40.

For use with Exploration 3

9. Write the prime factorization of each number.

   a. 30   **b.** 24   **c.** 57

   d. 98   **e.** 180   **f.** 200

10. Find the value of each expression.

   a. 3^4 **b.** 8^2 **c.** 4^4

   d. 8^3 **e.** 5^3 **f.** 2^4

11. Write each number in exponential form with either 2 or 3 as the exponent.

   a. 81   **b.** 27   **c.** 144

   d. 16   **e.** 49   **f.** 216

12. Replace each __?__ with >, <, or =.

   a. 3^3 __?__ 4^2 **b.** 2^5 __?__ $5 \cdot 5$ **c.** 6^3 __?__ $6 \cdot 6 \cdot 6$

13. One byte of memory stored in a computer is made up of 2^3 bits.

   a. In standard form, how many bits are in a byte?

   b. In exponential form, how many bits are in 2 bytes of memory? Explain.

MODULE 4 SECTION 3   **PRACTICE AND APPLICATIONS**

For use with Exploration 1

1. a. Find $\frac{3}{4}$ of 8.   **b.** Find $\frac{3}{8}$ of $\frac{1}{4}$.

2. Use common factors to write each fraction in lowest terms.

a. $\frac{6}{15}$ **b.** $\frac{35}{45}$ **c.** $\frac{24}{36}$

d. $\frac{9}{45}$ **e.** $\frac{14}{24}$ **f.** $\frac{12}{27}$

g. $\frac{9}{18}$ **h.** $\frac{18}{20}$ **i.** $\frac{16}{28}$

j. $\frac{7}{35}$ **k.** $\frac{16}{30}$ **l.** $\frac{33}{55}$

3. Find each product. Write your answer in lowest terms.

a. $\frac{2}{5} \cdot \frac{1}{4}$ **b.** $\frac{4}{5} \cdot \frac{5}{12}$ **c.** $\frac{2}{3} \cdot \frac{9}{10}$

d. $\frac{3}{4} \cdot \frac{5}{6}$ **e.** $\frac{1}{2} \cdot \frac{8}{9}$ **f.** $\frac{1}{8} \cdot \frac{1}{5}$

g. $\frac{3}{8} \cdot \frac{4}{5}$ **h.** $\frac{10}{20} \cdot \frac{6}{8}$ **i.** $\frac{1}{10} \cdot \frac{2}{3}$

j. $\frac{16}{25} \cdot \frac{5}{12}$ **k.** $\frac{7}{8} \cdot \frac{16}{21}$ **l.** $\frac{2}{3} \cdot \frac{4}{9}$

4. Brittany has $\frac{7}{8}$ of a yard of fabric. She uses $\frac{4}{5}$ of the fabric to make a scarf. What fraction of a yard of fabric does Brittany use to make the scarf? Is it more or less than $\frac{1}{2}$ yard?

5. Students who take music lessons make up about $\frac{3}{4}$ of a sixth grade class.

a. About $\frac{1}{2}$ of the students take piano lessons. About what part of the class take piano lessons?

b. About $\frac{5}{12}$ of the students take violin lessons. About what part of the class take violin lessons?

MODULE 4 SECTION 4   **PRACTICE AND APPLICATIONS**

For use with Exploration 1

1. Copy each problem. Then correctly place the decimal point in each product.

   a. $346 \cdot 0.16 = 5536$

   b. $4.8 \cdot 9.3 = 4464$

   c. $59 \cdot 2.15 = 12685$

   d. $2.34 \cdot 0.8 = 1872$

   e. $72 \cdot 1.03 = 7416$

   f. $0.03 \cdot 6.7 = 201$

2. Use mental math to find each product.

   a. $0.1 \cdot 78$

   b. $43.6 \cdot 0.01$

   c. $382.5 \cdot 0.01$

   d. $5.07 \cdot 0.01$

   e. $32.7 \cdot 0.1$

   f. $0.01 \cdot 39.2$

3. Find each product without a calculator. Then use estimation to check that your answer is reasonable.

   a. $0.4 \cdot 0.17$

   b. $3.7 \cdot 6.2$

   c. $4.6 \cdot 0.9$

   d. $0.08 \cdot 0.01$

   e. $32.1 \cdot 0.25$

   f. $1.92 \cdot 0.53$

   g. $412 \cdot 1.18$

   h. $26.3 \cdot 0.02$

   i. $1.8 \cdot 3.02$

4. A dietician orders fruit for cafeteria lunches. Apples cost $0.59 per pound this week. What is the total cost for an order of 215.8 pounds of apples?

For use with Exploration 2

5. Predict whether each product will be *greater than*, *less than*, or *equal to* the number in boldface. Explain how you know.

   a. $\mathbf{6.9} \cdot 1.2$

   b. $\mathbf{0.43} \cdot 0.95$

   c. $\mathbf{0.059} \cdot 1$

6. Isabelle has $184.56 in a savings account that earns 3% interest annually. At the end of one year, the bank will pay her 3% of the $184.56 she has in the account. Estimate $0.03 \cdot \$184.56$ to choose the correct amount she will receive after one year.

   A. $553.68

   B. $55.37

   C. $5.54

   D. $0.55

Name _____ Date _____

For use with Exploration 1

1. Apply the rule "multiply by 2 and then add 5" to each input. Write each input and output as an ordered pair.

  a. 1   **b.** 3   **c.** 5

  d. 9   **e.** 11   **f.** 20

2. Name the point that is the graph of each ordered pair.

  a. $(3, 2)$ **b.** $\left(7, 4\frac{1}{2}\right)$ **c.** $(4, 6)$

  d. $(0, 3)$ **e.** $\left(9, 1\frac{1}{2}\right)$ **f.** $(2, 5)$

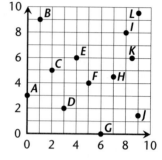

3. Write the coordinates of each point.

  a. B **b.** I **c.** F

  d. G **e.** K **f.** L

4. Copy the coordinate grid on graph paper. Graph each ordered pair on your coordinate grid. Label each point.

  a. $(2, 5)$ **b.** $(0, 0)$ **c.** $(0, 2)$

  d. $(4, 0)$ **e.** $\left(3\frac{1}{2}, 1\right)$ **f.** $(2, 1)$

  g. $\left(2\frac{1}{2}, 4\right)$ **h.** $(3, 3)$ **i.** $(4, 3)$

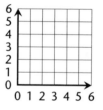

5. Draw a coordinate grid on graph paper.

  a. Graph the ordered pairs in the table on your new coordinate grid.

  b. Draw segments to connect the points you graphed in order from left to right.

  c. Use your graph to predict the missing values.

Input	1	3	6	8
Output	4	6	9	11

  input $2\frac{1}{2}$, output = ___?___   output 10, input = ___?___

(continued)

Name _____   Date _____

For use with Exploration 2

6. Write an expression for each word phrase.

    a. the product of three and nine   **b.** eight less than 20

    c. a number divided by six   **d.** a number plus fifteen

    e. a number multiplied by ten   **f.** the product of four and a number

    g. three less than a number   **h.** a number divided by two

7. Let s represent an input value. Choose the letter of the expression that represents the output value for each rule.

    a. Add 6 to the input.   **A.** $6 \div s$

                                      B. $6 - s$

    b. Subtract the input from 6.

                                        C. $s - 6$

    c. Multiply the input by 6.   **D.** $6 \cdot s$

                                        E. $s + 6$

    d. Divide the input by 6.   **F.** $s \div 6$

8. Evaluate each expression when $x = 3$ and $y = 8$.

    a. $4x$ **b.** $y + 5$ **c.** $x + 7.9$

    d. $y \div 4$ **e.** $y - x$ **f.** $6 \cdot x - 3$

9. Use the equations $A = l \cdot w$ and $P = l + l + w + w$ to find the area and perimeter of each rectangle.

    a. 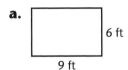   **b.** 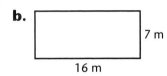   **c.**

10. A rectangular garden is 15 ft long and 8 ft wide. How much fencing will be needed to enclose the garden? How many square feet are enclosed in the garden?

MODULE 4 SECTION 6   **PRACTICE AND APPLICATIONS**

For use with Exploration 1

1. List the first seven multiples of each number.

   a. 8   **b.** 30   **c.** 104

2. Suppose you withdraw only multiples of $10 from a bank teller machine. Which amounts can you not withdraw?

   a. $30.00   **b.** $50.00   **c.** $75.00   **d.** $90.00

3. Find the least common multiple of each set of numbers.

   a. 4 and 5   **b.** 3, 8, and 12   **c.** 18 and 10

   d. 15 and 25   **e.** 64 and 16   **f.** 12 and 20

4. Short tours of the Lone Mine Cave leave every 15 minutes. Long tours of the cave leave every 40 minutes. If both tours start at 8 A.M., at what time will the tours leave together again?

For use with Exploration 2

5. Write each fraction as a mixed number.

   a. $\dfrac{11}{4}$ **b.** $\dfrac{7}{5}$ **c.** $\dfrac{19}{6}$

   d. $\dfrac{13}{8}$ **e.** $\dfrac{11}{3}$ **f.** $\dfrac{35}{8}$

6. Write each mixed number as a fraction.

   a. $1\dfrac{7}{12}$ **b.** $2\dfrac{5}{6}$ **c.** $8\dfrac{1}{2}$

   d. $5\dfrac{1}{3}$ **e.** $2\dfrac{3}{8}$ **f.** $1\dfrac{4}{5}$

7. Write each quotient as a mixed number.

   a. $28 \div 3$ **b.** $39 \div 5$ **c.** $84 \div 10$

8. Suppose you are sharing 9 dollars among 4 people. Which form of $9 \div 4$ would you use to describe each share? Explain your choice.

   a. 2 R1   **b.** 2.25   **c.** $2\dfrac{1}{4}$

| MODULE 4 SECTIONS 1–6 | PRACTICE AND APPLICATIONS |

For use with Section 1

1. a. A die was rolled 60 times. On 8 of the rolls, the outcome was 1. What is the experimental probability of rolling 1? Write your answer as a fraction, a decimal, and a percent.

   b. On how many rolls was the outcome not 1? What is the experimental probability of not rolling 1? Write your answer as a fraction, a decimal, and a percent.

   c. Suppose the die is rolled 100 times. Based on the experimental probabilities you found, about how many times do you expect to roll a 1? not roll a 1?

2. Find the theoretical probability of each event.

   a. The spinner stops on C.

   b. The spinner stops on a vowel.

   c. The spinner stops on K.

For use with Section 2

3. Find the greatest common factor of each set of numbers.

   a. 15 and 21   **b.** 24 and 30   **c.** 14 and 42

4. Write the prime factorization of each number.

   a. 34   **b.** 48   **c.** 120

5. Find the value of each expression.

   a. 6^3 **b.** 11^2 **c.** 3^5

For use with Section 3

6. Find each product. Write your answer in lowest terms.

   a. $\dfrac{3}{5} \cdot \dfrac{1}{6}$ **b.** $\dfrac{2}{7} \cdot \dfrac{5}{8}$ **c.** $\dfrac{5}{12} \cdot \dfrac{2}{9}$

   d. $\dfrac{4}{5} \cdot \dfrac{5}{16}$ **e.** $\dfrac{6}{11} \cdot \dfrac{7}{18}$ **f.** $\dfrac{2}{3} \cdot \dfrac{9}{20}$

(continued)

Name _____   Date _____

For use with Section 4

7. Use mental math to find each product.

 a. $0.1 \cdot 93$ **b.** $72.1 \cdot 0.01$ **c.** $0.01 \cdot 428.6$

8. Find each product without a calculator. Then use estimation to check that your answer is reasonable.

 a. $0.8 \cdot 0.12$ **b.** $6.9 \cdot 5.1$ **c.** $7.26 \cdot 0.9$

For use with Section 5

9. The table shows the total cost for buying different numbers of magazines.

Number of Magazines (Input)	1	2	3	4	5	6	7
Total Cost in Dollars (Output)	2	4	6	?	10	?	?

 a. Write a rule for the output based on the input. Let c = cost and m = number of magazines.

 b. Use your rule to find the missing values in the table.

10. Evaluate each expression when $a = 4$ and $b = 12$.

 a. $a \cdot 7$ **b.** $17 - b$ **c.** $a + b$

 d. $2 \cdot b + a$ **e.** $b - a$ **f.** $4 \cdot a - b$

For use with Section 6

11. Write each fraction as a mixed number.

 a. $\dfrac{19}{15}$ **b.** $\dfrac{23}{8}$ **c.** $\dfrac{31}{6}$

12. Write each mixed number as a fraction.

 a. $2\dfrac{3}{5}$ **b.** $1\dfrac{4}{11}$ **c.** $6\dfrac{7}{9}$

13. Local trains leave the station every 30 minutes. Express trains leave the station every 45 minutes. If a local train and an express train both left the station at 6 A.M., what time will another local and express train leave together?

Name _____ Date _____

Outcomes in Games   Probability

GOAL **LEARN HOW TO:** • find experimental and theoretical probabilities
• write probabilities as decimals and as percents
• identify impossible and certain events
• plot probabilities on a number line

AS YOU: • perform coin toss experiments

Exploration 1: Experimental Probability

Outcomes of an Experiment

An **experiment** is an activity whose results can be observed and recorded.
Each result of an experiment is called an **outcome**.

> **Example**
>
> Kim and Hal conducted an experiment in which there were 10 balls placed in a bag.
> Five of the balls were shaded and five were unshaded.
>
> Without looking, Hal selected a ball from the bag and Kim recorded whether the ball
> was shaded or unshaded. Hal replaced the ball and selected again. They did this 100
> times in all. Their results are shown below.
>
> | Outcome | Number of times |
> |---------|-----------------|
> | shaded | 53 |
> | unshaded | 47 |

Probability

A **probability** is a number from 0 through 1 that tells you how likely it is
for something to happen. A probability can be written as a fraction, a
decimal, or a percent. An **experimental probability** is found by repeating
an experiment a number of times and observing the results.

$$\text{Experimental probability of an outcome} = \frac{\text{number of times the outcome happened}}{\text{number of times the experiment was repeated}}$$

> **Example**
>
> Kim and Hal's table shows that a shaded ball was drawn in 53 of the 100 selections.
> So, $\frac{53}{100}$ (or 0.53 or 53%) is the experimental probability of selecting a shaded ball and
> $\frac{47}{100}$ (or 0.47 or 47%) is the experimental probability of the selecting an unshaded ball.

Outcomes with the same chance of occurring are **equally likely**. The
possible outcomes of the experiment above are equally likely.

MODULE 4 SECTION 1   **STUDY GUIDE**

Exploration 2: Theoretical Probability

Events

An **event** is a set of outcomes for a particular experiment.

Kim and Hal did another experiment using the same 10 balls. When a ball was selected, they recorded the number of the ball before placing it back in the bag. In this experiment, one event is *selecting a ball with an even number*. This event includes the five outcomes *select the 2*, *select the 4*, *select the 6*, *select the 8*, and *select the 10*.

Theoretical Probability

When you can determine the probability of an event without doing an experiment, it is called a **theoretical probability**. You can find a theoretical probability most easily when all the possible outcomes are equally likely.

$$\text{Theoretical probability of an outcome} = \frac{\text{number of outcomes in the event}}{\text{total number of possible outcomes}}$$

Example

For the 10 numbered balls that Kim and Hal are using, what is the theoretical probability that Hal will select a ball with a number that is

a. even?   **b.** less than 11?   **c.** greater than 10?

■ Sample Response ■

a. probability of a ball with an even number: $\dfrac{5}{10}$ ← even outcomes: 2, 4, 6, 8, 10
                                                   ← all possible outcomes: 1, 2, 3, ..., 10

b. probability of a ball with a number $< 11 : \dfrac{10}{10}$ or 1 ← This event is *certain* to happen.

c. probability of a ball with a number $> 10 : \dfrac{0}{10}$ or 0 ← This event is *impossible*.

An event that cannot happen is an **impossible event**. Impossible events have a probability of 0. An event that must happen is a **certain event**. Certain events have a probability of 1. All other events have a probability between 0 and 1.

You can plot probabilities on a number line by labeling two points on the line as 0 and 1, and then dividing the space between these two points into equal parts.

MODULE 4 SECTION 1 | PRACTICE & APPLICATION EXERCISES | STUDY GUIDE

Exploration 1

The 20 slips of paper shown at the right are placed in a bag. Selections are made without looking.

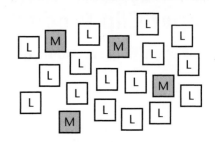

1. What are the possible outcomes when you

   a. draw one slip of paper from the bag?

   b. draw two slips of paper from the bag at the same time?

2. When selecting a slip of paper, are the outcomes equally likely? Explain.

The table shows the results achieved while conducting an experiment with a standard deck of cards four times. In the experiment, one card was drawn from the deck without looking and then replaced before drawing another card. A standard deck of cards contains 26 red cards and 26 black cards.

Number of draws	Number of red cards	Experimental probability of red
25	16	0.64
50	22	0.44
100	47	0.47
200	104	0.52

3. Explain how the numbers in the *Experimental probability of red* column were calculated.

4. In the fourth running of the experiment, 104 red cards were drawn in 200 draws.

   a. How many black cards were drawn?

   b. What is the experimental probability of *black*?

5. **a.** For a standard deck of cards, are the outcomes *red* and *black* equally likely? Explain.

   b. Do the data in the table support your answer to part (a)?

Exploration 2

Each of the days of the week is written on a separate slip of paper and the papers are placed in a box. Without looking, Jessica draws a slip of paper from the box.

6. Determine the theoretical probability that Jessica draws a day that

   a. begins with T   **b.** has 6 letters   **c.** ends in y   **d.** begins with Q

7. Plot your answers for Exercise 6 on a number line.

Spiral Review

For the data set 36, 61, 36, 43, 58, 43, 36, 43, 54, 51, find each measure. (Module 3, pp. 185, 196–198)

8. the range   9. the mean   10. the median   11. the mode

Name _____   Date _____

Paper Clip Products   Factors and Divisibility

GOAL   **LEARN HOW TO:** • use divisibility tests
• find factors, including the greatest common factor
• recognize primes and composites
• use a factor tree to find prime factors
• explore powers of a number

AS YOU: • develop game-playing strategies and investigate puzzles

Exploration 1: Testing for Divisibility

Divisibility Rules

When a number can be divided evenly by another number (no remainder), it is **divisible** by that number. You can tell whether a number is divisible by 2, by 3, by 5, by 9, or by 10 by applying the divisibility tests shown in the table.

A number is divisible by:	if:
2	the ones digit is 0, 2, 4, 6, or 8
3	the sum of the digits is divisible by 3
5	the ones digit is 0 or 5
9	the sum of the digits is divisible by 9
10	the ones digit is 0

Factors and Common Factors

When a whole number is divisible by a second whole number, the second number is a **factor** of the first.

Since 20 is divisible by 2, 2 is a factor of 20.

When two numbers have the same factor, that factor is a **common factor** of both numbers.

Since $20 = \mathbf{2} \cdot 10$ and $12 = \mathbf{2} \cdot 6$, 2 is a common factor of 20 and 12.

Since $20 = \mathbf{4} \cdot 5$ and $12 = \mathbf{4} \cdot 3$, 4 is a common factor of 20 and 12.

The **greatest common factor (GCF)** of two or more numbers is the greatest number that is a factor of each number.

The GCF of 20 and 12 is 4.

Example

Find the greatest common factor of 12 and 64.

Sample Response

List the factors of each number and circle the common factors.

factors of 12: ①, ②, 3, ④, 6, 12   factors of 64: ①, ②, ④, 8, 16, 32, 64

The GCF of 12 and 64 is 4.

MODULE 4 SECTION 2   **STUDY GUIDE**

Exploration 2: Prime Factors

All whole numbers greater than 1 are either *prime* or *composite*. A **prime** number has exactly two factors, 1 and the number itself. A **composite** number has more than two factors.

The number 7 is a prime number.
The number 12 is a composite number.

Every composite number can be written as the product of prime factors. This product is the **prime factorization** of the number. Drawing a **factor tree** can help you find the prime factorization of a number.

Example

Use a factor tree to find the prime factorization of 50.

The prime factorization of 50 is 2 • 5 • 5.

Exploration 3: Powers of Numbers

There is a short way to write an expression that repeats a factor.

$4 \cdot 4 \cdot 4 = 4^3$ The **exponent** 3 tells how many times the **base** 4 is used as a factor.

A number that can be written using an exponent and a base is a **power** of the base.

standard form   **exponential form**
↓   ↓
$64 = 4 \cdot 4 \cdot 4 = 4^3 \rightarrow$ 64 is the 3rd **power** of 4.

You can use exponents to write prime factorizations. The prime factorization of a number is the same, no matter how you begin.

Example

Use a factor tree to write the prime factorization of 36.

The prime factorization of 36 is 2 • 2 • 3 • 3, or $2^2 \cdot 3^2$.

Name _____   Date _____

MODULE 4 SECTION 2 | PRACTICE & APPLICATION EXERCISES | STUDY GUIDE

Exploration 1

Test each number for divisibility by 2, 3, 5, 9, and 10.

1. 90   **2.** 150   **3.** 66   **4.** 225

For Exercises 5–8, list all the factors of each number. Then find the GCF of each set of numbers.

5. 55 and 77   **6.** 19 and 49   **7.** 20, 40, and 90   **8.** 18, 72, and 90

9. Copy and complete the Venn diagram at the right to illustrate all the common factors of 48 and 64.

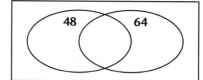

10. Use your completed Venn diagram from Exercise 9 to find the GCF of 48 and 64.

11. The factors of a number other than itself are called the proper divisors of the number. For example, the proper divisors of 12 are 1, 2, 3, 4, and 6. The number 12 can be written as a sum using only its proper divisors (once each) in exactly two ways, $1 + 2 + 3 + 6 = 12$ and $2 + 4 + 6 = 12$. Find the proper divisors of 24. Then find all the ways that 24 can be written as a sum using only its proper divisors.

Exploration 2

Tell whether each number is *prime* or *composite*.

12. 17   **13.** 39   **14.** 11   **15.** 101

Write the prime factorization of each number.

16. 100   **17.** 288   **18.** 360   **19.** 540

Exploration 3

For Exercises 20–23, find the value of each expression.

20. 6^2 **21.** 2^6 **22.** 8^2 **23.** 5^3

24. Write the prime factorization of 2400 using exponents.

25. One number is chosen at random from the set of all the prime factors of 12. What is the probability that the number will be odd? Explain.

Spiral Review

For Exercises 26–28, find each quotient. Show your work.
(Module 3, pp. 221–222)

26. $24\overline{)21.48}$ **27.** $0.2\overline{)86.48}$ **28.** $0.008\overline{)0.968}$

29. Is the following statement *true* or *false*? Explain. **(Module 3, pp. 196–198)**
"For the data set 62, 74, 86, 69, the median is less than the mean."

4-86   Math Thematics, Book 1   Copyright © by McDougal Littell Inc. All rights reserved.

MODULE 4 SECTION 3   STUDY GUIDE

A Fair Share   Fraction Multiplication

GOAL **LEARN HOW TO:** • multiply fractions
                              • use common factors to write fractions in lowest terms
           AS YOU: • use paper folding to solve puzzles

Exploration 1: Fraction Multiplication

Multiplying Fractions

To multiply two fractions, follow these steps:

Step 1 Multiply the numerators of the fractions
to find the numerator of the product.

Step 2 Multiply the denominators of the fractions
to find the denominator of the product.

Multiply $\dfrac{5}{8} \cdot \dfrac{4}{3}$.

$$\frac{5}{8} \cdot \frac{4}{3} = \frac{5 \cdot 4}{} = \frac{20}{}$$

$$\frac{5}{8} \cdot \frac{4}{3} = \frac{5 \cdot 4}{8 \cdot 3} = \frac{20}{24}$$

Writing Fractions in Lowest Terms

Divide both the numerator and the denominator of a
fraction by a common factor to write an equivalent fraction.
At the right, the greatest common factor is used, resulting
in an equivalent fraction in lowest terms. Recall that a
fraction is in lowest terms when 1 is the only whole number
that will divide its numerator and denominator evenly.

$$\frac{20}{24} = \frac{20 \div 4}{24 \div 4} = \frac{5}{6}$$

If you have not used the greatest common factor, you
will have to continue dividing until the fraction is in
lowest terms.

$$\frac{20}{24} = \frac{20 \div 2}{24 \div 2} = \frac{10}{12}$$

$$\frac{10}{12} = \frac{10 \div 2}{12 \div 2} = \frac{5}{6}$$

Reducing Fractions Before Multiplying

When multiplying fractions, you may choose to divide a
numerator and a denominator (not necessarily in the same
fraction) by a common factor *before* you multiply.

Multiply $\dfrac{5}{8} \cdot \dfrac{4}{3}$.

Divide a numerator and a denominator by a
common factor.

Divide 8 by 4. → $\dfrac{5}{\overset{}{\underset{2}{\cancel{8}}}} \cdot \dfrac{\overset{1}{\cancel{4}}}{3}$ ← Divide 4 by 4.

Using the reduced numbers, multiply the numerators
and multiply the denominators.

$$= \frac{5 \cdot 1}{2 \cdot 3} = \frac{5}{6}$$

Name _____   Date _____

Exploration 1

Use common factors to write each fraction in lowest terms.

1. $\dfrac{12}{36}$ **2.** $\dfrac{14}{28}$ **3.** $\dfrac{24}{72}$ **4.** $\dfrac{144}{576}$

For Exercises 5–12, find each product. Write your answer in lowest terms.

5. $\dfrac{3}{4} \cdot \dfrac{1}{2}$ **6.** $\dfrac{5}{7} \cdot \dfrac{2}{3}$ **7.** $\dfrac{3}{8} \cdot \dfrac{7}{11}$ **8.** $\dfrac{2}{5} \cdot \dfrac{3}{13}$

9. $\dfrac{5}{8} \cdot \dfrac{2}{3}$ **10.** $\dfrac{3}{2} \cdot \dfrac{4}{9}$ **11.** $\dfrac{4}{7} \cdot \dfrac{21}{8}$ **12.** $\dfrac{6}{8} \cdot \dfrac{3}{12}$

13. Writing Explain how you would find the product $\dfrac{2}{3} \cdot 12$.

14. Mrs. Simmons has a recipe that makes 24 muffins. To make a smaller batch of muffins, she decides to use $\dfrac{5}{6}$ of each ingredient. After mixing the ingredients, Mrs. Simmons decides to bake only $\dfrac{1}{2}$ of the mixture she has prepared. How many muffins will she bake?

15. For use in a parking lot during the winter, the lot manager ordered $\dfrac{3}{4}$ of a ton of salt. Throughout the winter, $\dfrac{2}{3}$ of the supply was used. How many tons of salt were used?

Spiral Review

For Exercises 16 and 17, use the table at the right which shows the earnings from ten Disney animated movies for 1988–1997.

16. Create a bar graph to display the data.
(Module 3, pp. 183–184)

17. a. Find the mean, the median, and the mode of the data.

b. Which average do you think best describes the data? Explain.
(Module 3, pp. 196–199)

Name of animated movie	Amount earned (millions of dollars)
Aladdin	217
Beauty and the Beast	146
Hercules	97
Hunchback of Notre Dame	100
Lion King	313
Little Mermaid	84
Nightmare Before Xmas	50
Pocahontas	142
Toy Story	192
Who Framed Roger Rabbit?	154

MODULE 4 SECTION 4   **STUDY GUIDE**

Target Games   Decimal Multiplication

GOAL | **LEARN HOW TO:** • multiply decimals
                            • estimate decimal products
                            • improve your estimating skills
        AS YOU: • model decimal products on grids

Exploration 1: Multiplying Decimals

Decimal products can be modeled on a grid by shading a part of a part.

Example

Model the product 0.3 • 0.9 using a 10 × 10 grid.

Step 1 Lightly shade grids modeling 0.9 in a vertical direction.

Step 2 Lightly shade grids modeling 0.3 in a horizontal direction.

Result The region that is shaded twice models the product: 0.3 • 0.9 = 0.27

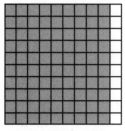   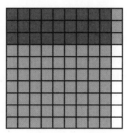   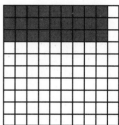

Decimal multiplication is similar to whole number multiplication.

Example

To multiply 55.5 • 1.75, follow these steps:

Step 1 Multiply the numbers as whole numbers.   555 • 175 = 97125

Step 2 Place the decimal point in the product.   55.5 • 1.75 = 97.125

Use the sum of the number of the decimal places in the factors.

1 decimal place + 2 decimal places = 3 decimal places

Exploration 2: Estimating Decimal Products

You can use estimation to check that your answer is reasonable, especially to see if you have placed the decimal point correctly.

The product 55.5 • 1.75 in the Example above is about 55 • 2, or 110. So, the answer 97.125 is reasonable.

MODULE 4 SECTION 4 | PRACTICE & APPLICATION EXERCISES | STUDY GUIDE

Exploration 1

Copy each problem. Then correctly place the decimal point.

1. $4.8 \cdot 5.1 = 2448$ **2.** $2.39 \cdot 7.6 = 18164$ **3.** $5.6 \cdot 0.9 = 504$

For Exercises 4–6, find each product without a calculator. Then use estimation to check that your answer is reasonable.

4. $3.2 \cdot 0.99$ **5.** $12.8 \cdot 5.9$ **6.** $69.84 \cdot 11.9$

7. Use a calculator to multiply 27.8 by each decimal. Record the results and tell whether the product is less than or greater than 27.8.

    a. 0.25   **b.** 0.82   **c.** 1.04   **d.** 2.6

8. Frank types other students' term papers on his word processor. He charges $1.75 per page. A page with a table counts as 1.5 pages. Lillian's term paper turned out to be 52 pages in all, with tables on 8 of the pages. How much does Lillian owe Frank?

Exploration 2

9. Measurement One inch is equivalent to about 2.54 cm. To find out how many centimeters there are in one yard. Carlos used the following key sequence on his calculator.

    [2] [.] [5] [4] [×] [1] [.] [2] [×] [3] [=] [9.144]

Is this answer reasonable? If not, what did Carlos do wrong?

10. Energy Where Jean lives, regular unleaded gasoline costs $1.369 per gallon. The tank in her car holds 14 gallons of gasoline.

    a. Choose the best estimate of the cost to fill the gas tank in Jean's car if the tank is completely empty.

        A. $0.02   **B.** $0.20   **C.** $2.00   **D.** $20.00

    b. For highway driving, Jean's car averages 32 miles per gallon. Use your answer from part (a) to estimate the cost of a trip of 1750 mi.

Spiral Review

11. Copy and complete the table at the right. Write your fractions in lowest terms. (Module 3, pp. 174–175)

12. Find the value of the expression $5 + 3 \times 7$.
(Module 1, pp. 48–49)

Fraction	Decimal	Percent
$\frac{1}{4}$	?	?
?	0.625	?
?	?	80%

MODULE 4 SECTION 5   **STUDY GUIDE**

Guess My Rule   Equations and Graphs

GOAL **LEARN HOW TO:** • graph pairs of values on a coordinate grid
• write and evaluate expressions
• write equations
• relate area and perimeter

AS YOU: • play number games and solve puzzles

Exploration 1: Graphing on a Coordinate Grid

An **ordered pair** consists of two pieces of data that go together. The order
tells which comes first. An ordered pair of numbers, called *coordinates*, is
used to indicate the location of a point on a **coordinate grid**. A coordinate
grid is formed by a pair of number lines called **axes**.

Example

To graph the ordered pair (6, 3), begin at the
origin, the point at which the axes meet.

The first number in the ordered pair tells how
many units to move across the horizontal axis.
In this ordered pair, the first number, 6,
indicates a movement 6 units to the right.

The second number in the ordered pair tells
how many units to move up the vertical axis.
In this ordered pair, the second number, 3,
indicates a movement 3 units up.

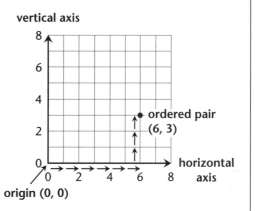

Exploration 2: Expressions and Equations

Variables and Expressions

A **variable** is a letter or symbol used to represent a quantity that is
unknown or can change. An **expression** can contain numbers, variables,
and operations. To **evaluate an expression** with one or more variables,
substitute a number for each variable and then carry out the operations.

Example

To evaluate the expression $15 + 7 \cdot x$ when $x = 6$, substitute the 6 for x and then follow
the order of operations.

$15 + 7 \cdot x = 15 + 7 \cdot 6$ ← Replace x with 6.

$\qquad = 15 + 42 = 57$

Name _____ Date _____

Equations

An **equation** is a mathematical sentence that uses the symbol "=" to show that two expressions have the same value.

$100 \div 25 = 9 - 5$ is an equation.

The rules you wrote for finding the area and perimeter of a rectangle are equations.

Example

Find the area and perimeter of the rectangle.

$w = 3$ cm

$l = 5$ cm

Sample Response

The area of a rectangle is the product of its length and its width.

$A = l \cdot w$ ← Substitute 5 for l →
$\quad = 5 \cdot 3$ and 3 for w.
$\quad = 15$ cm^2

The perimeter of a rectangle is the distance around the rectangle.

$P = 2 \cdot l + 2 \cdot w$
$\quad = 2 \cdot 5 + 2 \cdot 3$
$\quad = 10 + 6$
$\quad = 16$ cm

MODULE 4 SECTION 5 | **PRACTICE & APPLICATION EXERCISES**

Exploration 1

**Apply the rule "divide by 5 and then add 5" to each input.
Write each input and output as an ordered pair.**

1. 10   **2.** 25   **3.** 5   **4.** 0

**Use the diagram shown at the right.
Write the coordinates of each point
as an ordered pair.**

5. M **6.** N

7. O **8.** P

9. Q **10.** R

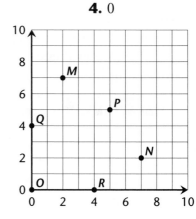

MODULE 4 · SECTION 5 | PRACTICE & APPLICATION EXERCISES | STUDY GUIDE

Graph each ordered pair on a coordinate grid. Label each point.

11. $A(7, 4)$ **12.** $B(1, 9)$ **13.** $C(0, 5)$ **14.** $D(6, 0)$

15. Writing Explain how the graph of $(7, 4)$ differs from that of $(4, 7)$.

16. Geometry Connection Draw a coordinate grid.

   a. Graph the ordered pairs $A(0, 5)$, $B(12, 5)$, $C(9, 8)$, and $D(3, 8)$.

   b. Draw segments to form polygon $ABCD$.

   c. Name polygon $ABCD$. Be as specific as possible.

   d. Transform polygon $ABCD$ by sliding it 4 units right and 4 units down. Label the vertices of the new polygon with their coordinates.

Exploration 2

Write an expression for each word phrase. Use the variable _n_.

17. 2 times a number   **18.** 4 less than a number   **19.** the sum of 12 and a number

Evaluate each expression when _u_ = 5 and _v_ = 20.

20. $u + 3 \cdot v$ **21.** $5 \cdot v - u$ **22.** $10 \cdot u - v$

23. a. On a coordinate grid, graph the values shown in the table as ordered pairs (input, output).

   b. Make an observation about how the points fall on the grid.

   c. Write a rule to describe the relationship between the input and output values.

Input	Output
0	4
1	5
2	6
5	9
10	14

   d. Use your rule to predict the output value if the input value is 7. Write the values as an ordered pair. On your graph for part (a), find the location indicated by the ordered pair. Does this point verify your observation in part (b)? Explain.

Spiral Review

24. Avi draws a card at random from a standard deck of playing cards (excluding the jokers). What is the theoretical probability that the card will be a red 10? Explain. **(Module 4, pp. 239–241)**

25. If the pattern below is extended, what fractional part of the next rectangle will be shaded? **(Module 1, pp. 3–5)**

 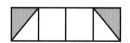 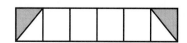

MODULE 4 SECTION 6   **STUDY GUIDE**

Pattern Play   Multiples and Mixed Numbers

GOAL   **LEARN HOW TO:** • find multiples and least common multiples
                                  • write a fraction greater than 1 as a mixed number and vice versa
        AS YOU: • play pattern games

Exploration 1: Multiples

A **multiple** of a whole number is the product of that number and any nonzero whole number.

Since 4 • 3 = 12, 12 is a multiple of 3.

The multiples of a number form a sequence.

multiples of 2: 2, 4, 6, 8, 10, 12, …
multiples of 3: 3, 6, 9, 12, 15, 18, …

Two numbers may have common multiples.

Some common multiples of 2 and 3 are 6, 12, and 18.

The **least common multiple (LCM)** of two or more numbers is the least number of all the common multiples.

The LCM of 2 and 3 is 6.

Example

Find the least common multiple of 8 and 12.

■ Sample Responses ■

List the multiples of each number. Then circle the common multiples.

multiples of 8: 8, 16, (24), 32, 40, (48), …
multiples of 12: 12, (24), 36, (48), …
common multiples: 24, 48, …
The LCM of 8 and 12 is 24.

When you are trying to find the LCM of two numbers, you can stop listing the multiples of the second number as soon as you come upon the *first* common multiple.

multiples of 8: 8, 16, 24, 32, 40, 48, …
                          ↕
multiples of 12: 12, 24, …

| **MODULE 4 SECTION 6** | **STUDY GUIDE** |

Exploration 2: Mixed Numbers

Meaning of a Mixed Number

A *mixed number* consists of a whole-number part and a fraction part.

whole-number part $\nearrow \; 1\frac{5}{8} \; \nwarrow$ fraction part

Quotients as Mixed Numbers

The remainder in a division problem can be written over the divisor to form the fraction part of a mixed number.

$$13 \div 8 \rightarrow \overset{\text{1 R5}}{8\overline{)13}} = 1\frac{5}{8}$$

Fractions Greater Than 1

Fractions to Mixed Numbers

You can write fractions greater than 1 as mixed numbers by using division.

$$\frac{13}{8} = \overset{\text{1 R5}}{8\overline{)13}} = 1\frac{5}{8}$$

Mixed Numbers to Fractions

You can write a mixed number as a fraction greater than 1 by rewriting the whole number as a fraction and then combining it with the fraction part that is already there.

$$1\frac{5}{8} = \frac{8}{8} + \frac{5}{8} = \frac{13}{8}$$

| **MODULE 4 SECTION 6** | **PRACTICE & APPLICATION EXERCISES** |

Exploration 1

List the first seven multiples of each number.

1. 9 **2.** 24 **3.** 75 **4.** 110

For Exercises 5–8, find the least common multiple of each set of numbers.

5. 15 and 25 **6.** 120 and 144 **7.** 12, 24, and 36 **8.** 36, 72, and 120

9. a. Copy and complete the Venn diagram to show all the prime factors of 24 and 30, and those prime factors that are common factors. (Be sure to show each prime factor as many times as it occurs in the prime factorization of each number.)

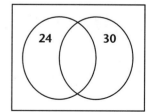

  b. Find the LCM of 24 and 30 by listing multiples.

  c. Explain how you could use your Venn diagram from part (a) to find the LCM of 24 and 30.

MODULE 4 SECTION 6   STUDY GUIDE

10. A traveling entertainment company has two Ferris wheels. One of them makes a complete rotation every 120 seconds, while the other makes a complete rotation every 144 seconds. If they start at the same time, how many *minutes* will it take before the wheels begin a new rotation together?

11. Eastbound trains leave Central Depot every 24 minutes and northbound trains leave every 42 minutes. If both an eastbound and a northbound train left at 6 P.M., when is the next time that two such trains will leave at the same time? Explain your process.

Exploration 2

Write each fraction as a mixed number.

12. $\frac{15}{2}$ **13.** $\frac{23}{4}$ **14.** $\frac{143}{10}$ **15.** $\frac{120}{11}$

Write each mixed number as a fraction.

16. $3\frac{2}{5}$ **17.** $1\frac{7}{16}$ **18.** $30\frac{5}{7}$ **19.** $10\frac{10}{13}$

Visual Thinking Copy the number line. Mark and label a point on the line where each fraction would lie.

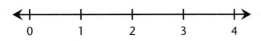

20. $\frac{9}{8}$ **21.** $\frac{27}{8}$ **22.** $\frac{16}{8}$ **23.** $\frac{26}{16}$

Spiral Review

24. Find the area and perimeter of the rectangle at the right. **(Module 4, p. 287)**

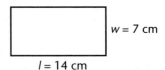

$w = 7$ cm

$l = 14$ cm

Find the value of each expression. (Module 1, pp. 48–49)

25. $12 + 8 \div 4$ **26.** $100 - 3 \cdot (9 + 4)$ **27.** $(63 - 14) \div 7$

MODULE 4   **TECHNOLOGY**

For Use with Section 1

You can use spreadsheet software to simulate rolling a die 100 times. You can also use the software to graph the results.

A random number generator can simulate the rolling of a die. Use the formula =INT(RAND()*6+1) to generate randomly the numbers from 1 through 6. This formula must be put in rows 1 through 10 and columns A through J. A "Fill" command can help you do this.

1. To simulate rolling a die 120 times, what rows and columns must be filled with the formula given above?

_____

You can use the spreadsheet software to count how many times each number turns up. In cell A13, use the formula: =COUNTIF(A1:J10,1). The computer will count how many times the number 1 occurred in the 100 cells from cell A1 in the upper left corner to cell J10 in the lower right corner.

2. How many times would you expect each number to turn up if the die is rolled 100 times? Explain your thinking.

_____

3. What formula can you use in cell G13 to make sure that the 100 rolls are accounted for in row 13?

_____

4. In row 15 have the computer calculate theoretical probability. What formula is entered in cell A15?

_____

MODULE 4   **TECHNOLOGY**

5. Create a bar graph like the one below to display the results.

	A	B	C	D	E	F	G	H	I	J
1	5	4	2	1	5	1	3	4	4	2
2	2	2	5	5	5	3	6	6	6	1
3	1	1	2	3	2	6	1	1	5	2
4	4	2	6	6	1	1	2	2	2	4
5	4	4	6	1	6	5	2	2	6	5
6	5	2	5	3	6	5	6	3	4	1
7	6	6	3	6	3	3	4	3	1	3
8	1	3	2	6	5	5	4	4	3	4
9	2	5	5	5	2	4	2	1	6	5
10	6	2	5	6	5	2	5	4	2	6
11										
12	number 1	number 2	number 3	number 4	number 5	number 6	Total Rolls			
13	14	21	12	14	20	19	100			

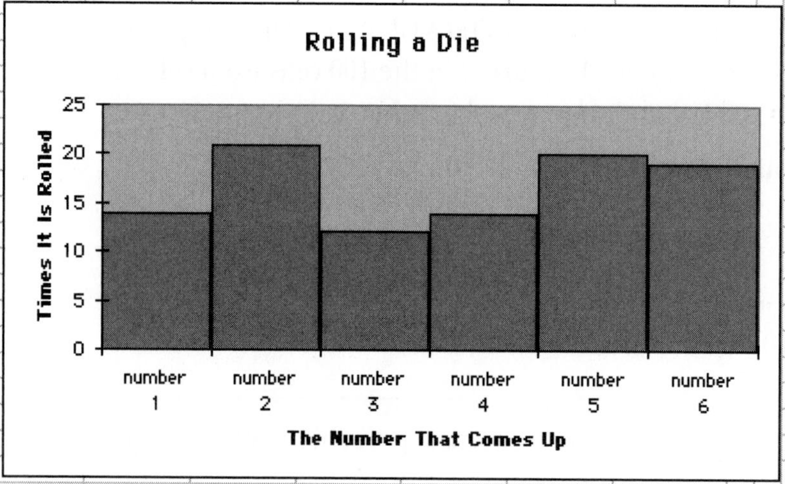

Rolling a Die

(Bar graph — "Times It Is Rolled" on vertical axis, "The Number That Comes Up" on horizontal axis, with bars for number 1 through number 6.)

To have the computer generate a 100 new rolls, press F9.

MODULE 4 QUIZ

A number cube labeled with the even numbers from 2 to 12 was rolled 50 times with the results shown. For Exercises 1–3 find the experimental probability of each event. Write each answer as a whole percent.

Outcome	Total
2	7
4	9
6	12
8	6
10	8
12	8

1. rolling a number that is a multiple of 4

2. rolling a number that is greater than 5

3. rolling a number that is a multiple of 5

4. Find the theoretical probability of each event in Exercises 1–3.

5. Using the die described for Exercises 1–3, give an example of an event that has probability 1. Give an example of an event that has probability 0.

List every digit from 0 through 9 that will complete the number 504,362,16 ? to make each statement true.

6. The number is divisible by 5.

7. The number is divisible by 8.

8. The number is divisible by 3.

9. The number is divisible by 2.

Find the GCF of each set of numbers.

10. 180, 45

11. 1000, 56

12. 42, 70

Tell whether each number is prime or composite. If it is composite, use a factor tree to find the prime factorization.

13. 79

14. 165

15. 280

16. 107

17. What is the theoretical probability of picking a prime number if you choose at random from the whole numbers from 1 to 50? (Remember that the number 1 is neither prime nor composite.)

Replace each ___?___ with > , < , or =.

18. 10^2 ___?___ 2^{10}

19. 2^2 ___?___ 4^5

20. $3 \cdot 3 \cdot 3 \cdot 3 \cdot 3$ ___?___ 5^3

Write the prime factorization of each number using exponents.

21. 1500

22. 64

23. 96

Find each product. Write each answer in lowest terms.

24. $\dfrac{16}{25} \cdot \dfrac{5}{8}$

25. $\dfrac{15}{7} \cdot \dfrac{49}{50}$

26. $\dfrac{25}{27} \cdot \dfrac{3}{10}$

MODULE 4 TEST

FORM **A**

A spinner with five equal sections numbered from 3 to 7 was spun 60 times. The results are shown in the table. For Exercises 1–3, find the experimental probability of each event. Write each answer as a whole percent.

Outcome	Total
3	10
4	12
5	9
6	15
7	14

1. The spinner stops at an odd number.

2. The spinner stops at a number less than 2.

3. The spinner stops at 5.

4. Find the theoretical probability of each event in Exercises 1–3.

The one's digit in the following number is missing.

439,156,82 ?

For Exercises 5–7 list every digit from 0 through 9 that will complete the number to make each statement true.

5. The number is divisible by 5.

6. The number is divisible by 9.

7. The number is divisible by 3.

8. Saul listed 1, 2, 3, 4, 5, 6, 8, 10, 12, 15, 20, 24, 30, 48, 80, and 120 as the factors of 240. Is his list complete? If not, what factors did he omit?

Find the GCF of each set of numbers.

9. 60 and 48   10. 15, 85, and 30   11. 66 and 35

Tell whether each number is *prime* or *composite*.

12. 71   13. 123,123   14. 49

Replace each ___?___ with > , < , or =. Explain your choice.

15. 3^4 ___?___ 9^2 16. 2^7 ___?___ 7^2 17. $7 \cdot 7 \cdot 7$ ___?___ 7^4

18. Write the prime factorization for 242 using exponents.

Find each product. Write each answer in lowest terms.

19. $\dfrac{4}{9} \cdot \dfrac{18}{20}$ 20. $\dfrac{15}{18} \cdot \dfrac{2}{5}$ 21. $\dfrac{2}{3} \cdot \dfrac{4}{9}$

Name _____   Date _____

Find each product without using a calculator. Then use estimation to check that your answer is reasonable.

22. 0.08 • 4.32   **23.** 1.84 • 0.92   **24.** 62.1 • 0.3

25. a. Graph the ordered pairs in the table on a coordinate grid.

Input	1	4	6	8
Output	14	8	4	0

b. Draw segments to connect the points you graphed in order from left to right.

c. Use your graph to predict the missing values.

input = 3, output = __?__ ; input = __?__ , output = 2

26. Let ℓ represent the length of a rectangle whose length is 4 times its width. Write an expression for each.

a. the width of the rectangle   **b.** the perimeter of the rectangle

27. The geyser known as Old Faithful shoots up a stream of water every 65 min. If a tour group sees the eruption at 7 A.M., and groups pass by every 40 min, when will a group next see Old Faithful in action?

Find each missing number.

28. $6\frac{2}{7} = \frac{?}{7}$ **29.** $\frac{41}{3} = ?\frac{2}{3}$ **30.** $\frac{37}{4} = 9\frac{?}{4}$

MODULE 4 TEST   FORM **B**

A spinner with six equal sections numbered from 3 to 8 was spun 60 times. The results are shown in the table. For Exercises 1–3, find the experimental probability of each event. Write each answer as a whole percent.

Outcome	Total
3	8
4	11
5	12
6	10
7	9
8	10

1. The spinner stops at an even number.

2. The spinner stops at a number greater than 9.

3. The spinner stops at 5.

4. Find the theoretical probability of each event in Exercises 1–3.

The one's digit in the following number is missing.

$$612{,}394{,}05\,\underline{?}$$

For Exercises 5–7, list every digit from 0 through 9 that will make each statement true.

5. The number is divisible by 3.

6. The number is divisible by 5.

7. The number is divisible by 9.

8. Paolo listed the numbers 2, 4, 5, 7, 10, 14, 20, 28, 40, 70, 140, and 280 as the factors of 280. Is his list complete? If not, what factors did he omit?

Find the GCF of each set of numbers.

9. 120 and 45   **10.** 21, 28, and 29   **11.** 56 and 88

Tell whether each number is *prime* or *composite*.

12. 97   **13.** 39   **14.** 57

Replace each __?__ with > , < , or =. Explain your choice.

15. 5^2 __?__ $5 \cdot 5 \cdot 5$ **16.** 6^2 __?__ 4^3 **17.** 2^6 __?__ 8^2

18. Write the prime factorization for 288 using exponents.

Find each product. Write each answer in lowest terms.

19. $\dfrac{5}{11} \cdot \dfrac{33}{40}$ **20.** $\dfrac{2}{7} \cdot \dfrac{14}{20}$ **21.** $\dfrac{16}{20} \cdot \dfrac{7}{8}$

MODULE 4 TEST   FORM B

Find each product without using a calculator. Then use estimation to check that your answer is reasonable.

22. $0.07 \cdot 81.4$ **23.** $6.41 \cdot 0.79$ **24.** $0.6 \cdot 2.95$

25. a. Graph the ordered pairs in the table on a coordinate grid.

Input	2	4	6	10
Output	6	7	8	10

b. Draw segments to connect the points you graphed in order from left to right.

c. Use your graph to predict the missing values.

input = 8, output = ___?___ ; input = ___?___ , output = 12

26. Let ℓ represent the length of a rectangle that is 6 in. wider than it is long. Write an expression for each.

a. width of the rectangle   **b.** area of the rectangle

27. Halley's Comet is visible on Earth every 76 years. Suppose another comet is discovered that appears every 12 years. If at some point the two comets are visible in the same year, when will they appear together again?

Find the missing number.

28. $8\dfrac{1}{4} = \dfrac{?}{4}$ **29.** $\dfrac{29}{2} = ?\dfrac{1}{2}$ **30.** $\dfrac{58}{9} = 6\dfrac{?}{9}$

MODULE 4 — **STANDARDIZED ASSESSMENT**

1. A number cube has sides numbered from 1 to 6. You roll the cube 85 times and get 6 a total of 15 times. How does the theoretical probability of rolling 6 compare with the experimental probability?
a. The theoretical probability is greater.
b. The experimental probability is greater.
c. The two probabilities are equal.
d. Cannot tell from the information given.

2. What is the theoretical probability of drawing a red card less than 8 from a standard deck of 52 cards? (Count an ace as a face card.)
a. $\frac{8}{26}$
b. $\frac{10}{26}$
c. $\frac{3}{13}$
d. $\frac{14}{52}$

3. What is the prime factorization of 360?
a. $3 \cdot 120$
b. $2^4 \cdot 3 \cdot 5^2$
c. $2^2 \cdot 3^3 \cdot 5$
d. $2^3 \cdot 3^2 \cdot 5$

4. Use divisibility rules to tell which of the numbers 2, 3, 5, and 9 are divisors of 492,630.
a. 2 and 3 only
b. 5 and 9 only
c. 2, 3, and 5 only
d. 2, 3, and 9 only

5. What is the greatest common factor of 160 and 96?
a. 6
b. 32
c. 40
d. 16

6. What is the theoretical probability of picking a composite number from the whole numbers from 20 to 29?
a. $\frac{4}{5}$
b. $\frac{7}{10}$
c. $\frac{1}{5}$
d. $\frac{3}{10}$

7. Tom spends $\frac{3}{10}$ of his weekly earnings on lunch and $\frac{2}{3}$ of the remaining money on a CD. What fraction of his earnings did he spend on the CD?
a. $\frac{1}{5}$
b. $\frac{7}{15}$
c. $\frac{2}{5}$
d. $\frac{8}{15}$

8. Find the product $\frac{10}{36} \cdot \frac{45}{100}$ and express in simplest terms.
a. $\frac{1}{8}$
b. $\frac{55}{136}$
c. $\frac{450}{360}$
d. $\frac{5}{9}$

9. Evaluate $3y - 2x$ when $x = 14$ and $y = 18$.
a. 6
b. 16
c. 18
d. 26

10. For Mother's Day you want to buy a 2.3 lb box of mixed nuts at $7.29/lb. How much would that cost?
a. $15.56
b. $15.87
c. $16.77
d. $16.92

11. Let w represent the width of a rectangle. What is an expression for the perimeter of the rectangle if the length is 8 inches more than its width?
a. $4w + 8$
b. $w \cdot (w + 8)$
c. $4w - 16$
d. $4w + 16$

12. What is $63 \div 14$ expressed as a mixed number with the fractional part in lowest terms?
a. $4\frac{1}{2}$
b. $4\frac{2}{7}$
c. $4\frac{5}{14}$
d. $4\frac{4}{7}$

Name _____   Date _____

You will need graph paper.

Many patterns found in the factors of numbers can be seen using a coordinate grid.

1. Create a list of the factors of the numbers from 1 to 15 as ordered pairs in the form (number, factor). Examples: (1, 1), (2, 1), (2, 2), (3, 1), (3, 3)

2. Draw a coordinate grid like the one shown below and plot the ordered pairs from Exercise 1.

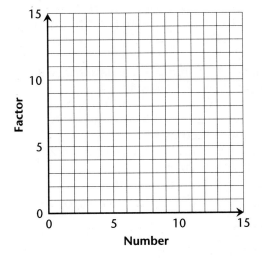

3. Describe two patterns you see in the graph.

4. What is true of the prime numbers in your graph? What can you conclude about composite numbers?

5. Suppose a graphed point was chosen at random. What is the probability that the point would represent a factor of 12?

6. Suppose you extended your graph so that it included numbers up to 25. Which number has more factors than the number 12?

Answers

PRACTICE AND APPLICATIONS

Module 4, Section 1
1. a. The number of heads was divided by the number of tosses.
b. 376 tails; 0.47
2. a. $\frac{16}{60}$ or $\frac{4}{15}$; 27%
b. $\frac{44}{60}$ or $\frac{11}{15}$; 73%
3. a. $\frac{7}{30}$, 0.23, 23% **b.** 23 rolls; $\frac{23}{30}$, 0.77, 77%
c. about 23 times; about 77 times
4. a. $\frac{1}{6}$ **b.** $\frac{3}{6}$ or $\frac{1}{2}$ **c.** $\frac{2}{6}$ or $\frac{1}{3}$ **d.** 0
e. Yes; the event "the spinner stops on 5."
5. a. 2, 4, 6, 8, 10 **b.** $\frac{5}{10}$ or $\frac{1}{2}$ **c.** $\frac{6}{10}$ or $\frac{3}{5}$; $\frac{4}{10}$ or $\frac{2}{5}$
d.

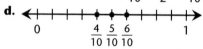

$$0 \qquad \frac{4}{10} \, \frac{5}{10} \, \frac{6}{10} \qquad 1$$

6. a. impossible **b.** certain **7.** $\frac{3}{17}$; purple

Module 4, Section 2
1. a. divisible by 2 **b.** divisible by 5 **c.** divisible by 2, 5, and 10 **d.** divisible by 2, 5, and 10 **e.** not divisible by 2, 5, or 10 **f.** divisible by 5
2. a. divisible by 3 **b.** divisible by 3 and 9
c. not divisible by 3 or 9 **d.** divisible by 3 and 9
e. not divisible by 3 or 9 **f.** divisible by 3 and 9
3. a. divisible by 2, 5, and 10 **b.** divisible by 2, 3, 5, and 10 **c.** divisible by 3 and 9 **d.** divisible by 5
e. divisible by 2, 3, and 9 **f.** divisible by 2 and 3
4. a. 1, 2, 3, 4, 6, 9, 12, 18, 36 **b.** 1, 2, 4, 5, 10, 20
c. 1, 2, 3, 6, 7, 14, 21, 42 **d.** 1, 3, 5, 9, 15, 45
e. 1, 29 **f.** 1, 2, 4, 8, 16
5. a. 4 **b.** 5 **c.** 3 **d.** 2 **e.** 1 **f.** 3
6. Yes; 1365 is divisible by 3.
7. a. composite **b.** prime **c.** composite **d.** prime
e. composite **f.** composite
8. $2 \cdot 2 \cdot 2 \cdot 5$
9. a. $2 \cdot 3 \cdot 5$ **b.** $2^3 \cdot 3$ **c.** $3 \cdot 19$ **d.** $2 \cdot 7^2$
e. $2^2 \cdot 3^2 \cdot 5$ **f.** $2^3 \cdot 5^2$
10. a. 81 **b.** 64 **c.** 256 **d.** 512 **e.** 125 **f.** 16
11. a. 9^2 **b.** 3^3 **c.** 12^2 **d.** 4^2 **e.** 7^2 **f.** 6^3
12. a. > **b.** > **c.** =
13. a. 8 bits **b.** 2^4 bits; $2^3 + 2^3 = 8 + 8 = 16 = 2^4$

Module 4, Section 3
1. a. 6 **b.** $\frac{3}{32}$
2. a. $\frac{2}{5}$ **b.** $\frac{7}{9}$ **c.** $\frac{2}{3}$ **d.** $\frac{1}{5}$ **e.** $\frac{7}{12}$ **f.** $\frac{4}{9}$ **g.** $\frac{1}{2}$ **h.** $\frac{9}{10}$ **i.** $\frac{4}{7}$
j. $\frac{1}{5}$ **k.** $\frac{8}{15}$ **l.** $\frac{3}{5}$

3. a. $\frac{1}{10}$ **b.** $\frac{1}{3}$ **c.** $\frac{3}{5}$ **d.** $\frac{5}{8}$ **e.** $\frac{4}{9}$ **f.** $\frac{1}{40}$ **g.** $\frac{3}{10}$ **h.** $\frac{3}{8}$ **i.** $\frac{1}{15}$
j. $\frac{4}{15}$ **k.** $\frac{2}{3}$ **l.** $\frac{8}{27}$
4. $\frac{7}{10}$ yd; more
5. a. $\frac{3}{8}$ **b.** $\frac{5}{16}$

Module 4, Section 4
1. a. 55.36 **b.** 44.64 **c.** 126.85 **d.** 1.872 **e.** 74.16
f. 0.201
2. a. 7.8 **b.** 0.436 **c.** 3.825 **d.** 0.0507 **e.** 3.27
f. 0.392
3. a. 0.068; $0.4 \cdot 0.2 = 0.08$ **b.** 22.94; $4 \cdot 6 = 24$
c. 4.14; $5 \cdot 0.9 = 4.5$ **d.** 0.0008; $0.1 \cdot 0.01 = 0.001$
e. 8.025; $32 \cdot 0.2 = 6.4$ **f.** 1.0176; $2 \cdot 0.5 = 1$
g. 486.16; $400 \cdot 1.2 = 480$ **h.** 0.526; $26 \cdot 0.02 = 0.52$ **i.** 5.436; $2 \cdot 3 = 6$
4. $127.32
5. a. greater than; $1.2 > 1$ **b.** less than; $0.95 < 1$
c. equal to; multiplied by 1
6. c

Module 4, Section 5
1. a. (1, 7) **b.** (3, 11) **c.** (5, 15) **d.** (9, 23)
e. (11, 27) **f.** (20, 45)
2. a. D **b.** H **c.** E **d.** A **e.** J **f.** C
3. a. (1, 9) **b.** (8, 8) **c.** (5, 4) **d.** (6, 0) **e.** $\left(8\frac{1}{2}, 6\right)$
f. $\left(9, 9\frac{1}{2}\right)$
4.

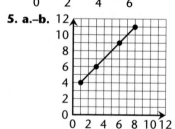

5. a.–b.

c. $5\frac{1}{2}$; 7
6. a. $3 \cdot 9$ **b.** $20 - 8$ **c.** $n \div 6$ or $\frac{n}{6}$ **d.** $n + 15$
e. $10 \cdot n$
f. $4 \cdot n$ **g.** $n - 3$ **h.** $n \div 2$ or $\frac{n}{2}$
7. a. E **b.** B **c.** D **d.** F
8. a. 12 **b.** 13 **c.** 10.9 **d.** 2 **e.** 5 **f.** 15

9. a. 54 ft^2; 30 ft   **b.** 112 m^2; 46 m
c. 7.6 cm^2; 11.6 cm
10. 46 ft; 120 ft^2

Module 4, Section 6
1. a. 8, 16, 24, 32, 40, 48, 56
b. 30, 60, 90, 120, 150, 180, 210
c. 104, 208, 312, 416, 520, 624, 728
2. c
3. a. 20 **b.** 24 **c.** 90 **d.** 75 **e.** 64 **f.** 60
4. 10 A.M. **5. a.** $2\frac{3}{4}$ **b.** $1\frac{2}{5}$ **c.** $3\frac{1}{6}$ **d.** $1\frac{5}{8}$ **e.** $3\frac{2}{3}$ **f.** $4\frac{3}{8}$
6. a. $\frac{19}{12}$ **b.** $\frac{17}{6}$ **c.** $\frac{17}{2}$ **d.** $\frac{16}{3}$ **e.** $\frac{19}{8}$ **f.** $\frac{9}{5}$
7. a. $9\frac{1}{3}$ **b.** $7\frac{4}{5}$ **c.** $8\frac{4}{10}$ or $8\frac{2}{5}$
8. Choices b and c both represent two and a quarter.

Module 4, Sections 1–6
1. a. $\frac{8}{60}$, 0.13, 13% **b.** 52, $\frac{52}{60}$, 0.87, 87%
c. about 13 times; about 87 times
2. a. $\frac{1}{8}$ **b.** $\frac{2}{8}$ or $\frac{1}{4}$ **c.** 0
3. a. 3 **b.** 6 **c.** 14
4. a. 2 • 17 **b.** $2^4 \cdot 3$ **c.** $2^3 \cdot 3 \cdot 5$
5. a. 216 **b.** 121 **c.** 243
6. a. $\frac{1}{10}$ **b.** $\frac{5}{28}$ **c.** $\frac{5}{54}$ **d.** $\frac{1}{4}$ **e.** $\frac{7}{33}$ **f.** $\frac{3}{10}$
7. a. 9.3 **b.** 0.721 **c.** 4.286
8. a. 0.096; 0.8 • 0.1 = 0.08 **b.** 35.19; 7 • 5 = 35
c. 6.534; 7 • 1 = 7
9. a. $c = 2 \cdot m$ **b.** 8, 12, 14
10. a. 28 **b.** 5 **c.** 16 **d.** 28 **e.** 8 **f.** 4
11. a. $1\frac{4}{15}$ **b.** $2\frac{7}{8}$ **c.** $5\frac{1}{6}$
12. a. $\frac{13}{5}$ **b.** $\frac{15}{11}$ **c.** $\frac{61}{9}$
13. 7:30 A.M.

STUDY GUIDE

Module 4, Section 1
1. a. either L or M **b.** both L, both M, or one L and one M
2. No; there are more slips of paper with L on them than slips of paper with M on them.
3. Sample Response: Divide the entry in the *Number of red cards* column by the entry in the *Number of draws* column.
4. a. 96
b. $\frac{96}{200}$ or 0.48
5. a. Yes; there are the same number of red cards and black cards.
b. Yes; Sample Response: The experimental probabilities are all close to 0.50. Also, as the total number of cards drawn increases, the experimental probability gets closer to 0.50.

6. a. $\frac{2}{7}$ **b.** $\frac{3}{7}$ **c.** $\frac{7}{7}$ or 1 **d.** $\frac{0}{7}$ or 0
7.

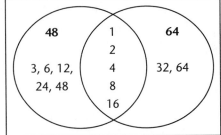

0     $\frac{2}{7}$ $\frac{3}{7}$ 1

8. 25
9. 46.1
10. 43
11. 36 and 43

Module 4, Section 2
1. divisible by 2, 3, 5, 9, and 10
2. divisible by 2, 3, 5, and 10
3. divisible by 2 and 3
4. divisible by 3, 5, and 9
5. 1, 5, 11, 55; 1, 7, 11, 77; 11
6. 1, 19; 1, 7, 49; 1
7. 1, 2, 4, 5, 10, 20; 1, 2, 4, 5, 8, 10, 20, 40; 1, 2, 3, 5, 6, 9, 10, 15, 18, 30, 45, 90; 10
8. 1, 2, 3, 6, 9, 18; 1, 2, 3, 4, 6, 8, 9, 12, 18, 24, 36, 72; 1, 2, 3, 5, 6, 9, 10, 15, 18, 30, 45, 90; 18
9.

48		64
3, 6, 12, 24, 48	1, 2, 4, 8, 16	32, 64

10. 16
11. proper divisors of 24: 1, 2, 3, 4, 6, 8, and 12;
24 = 1 + 2 + 3 + 4 + 6 + 8, 24 = 1 + 2 + 3 + 6 + 12,
24 = 4 + 8 + 12, 24 = 1 + 3 + 8 + 12,
and 24 = 2 + 4 + 6 + 12
12. prime
13. composite
14. prime
15. prime
16. 2 • 2 • 5 • 5, or $2^2 \cdot 5^2$
17. 2 • 2 • 2 • 2 • 2 • 3 • 3, or $2^5 \cdot 3^2$
18. 2 • 2 • 2 • 3 • 3 • 5, or $2^3 \cdot 3^2 \cdot 5$
19. 2 • 2 • 3 • 3 • 3 • 5, or $2^2 \cdot 3^3 \cdot 5$
20. 36
21. 64
22. 64
23. 125
24. $2^5 \cdot 3 \cdot 5^2$
25. The prime factorization of 12 is 2 • 2 • 3. 3 is odd, so the probability is $\frac{1}{3}$.
26. 0.895
27. 432.4
28. 121
29. True; the median is 71.5 and the mean is 72.75.

Module 4, Section 3

1. $\frac{1}{3}$

2. $\frac{1}{2}$

3. $\frac{1}{3}$

4. $\frac{1}{4}$

5. $\frac{3}{8}$

6. $\frac{10}{21}$

7. $\frac{21}{88}$

8. $\frac{6}{65}$

9. $\frac{5}{12}$

10. $\frac{2}{3}$

11. $\frac{3}{2}$ or $1\frac{1}{2}$

12. $\frac{3}{16}$

13. Sample Response: Write the whole number 12 as the fraction $\frac{12}{1}$. Then use the procedure for multiplying fractions: $\frac{2}{3} \cdot \frac{12}{1} = \frac{24}{3} = 8$.

14. 10 muffins

15. $\frac{1}{2}$ ton (or 1000 lb)

16.

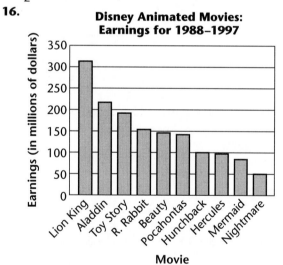

Disney Animated Movies: Earnings for 1988–1997

17. a. 149.5 million dollars; 144 million dollars; no mode **b.** Sample Response: Either the mean or the median since they are relatively close.

Module 4, Section 4

1. 24.48

2. 18.164

3. 5.04

4. 3.168; $3 \cdot 1 = 3$

5. 75.52; $13 \cdot 6 = 78$

6. 831.096; $70 \cdot 12 = 840$

7. a. 6.95; < 27.8 **b.** 22.796; < 27.8
c. 28.912; > 27.8 **d.** 72.28; > 27.8

8. $98.00

9. No; the second number entered should have been 12, not 1.2.

10. a. D **b.** Sample Response: about $80

11.

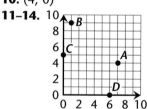

Fraction	Decimal	Percent
$\frac{1}{4}$	0.25	25%
$\frac{5}{8}$	0.625	62.5%
$\frac{4}{5}$	0.8	80%

12. 26

Module 4, Section 5

1. (10, 7)

2. (25, 10)

3. (5, 6)

4. (0, 5)

5. (2, 7)

6. (7, 2)

7. (0, 0)

8. (5, 5)

9. (0, 4)

10. (4, 0)

11–14.

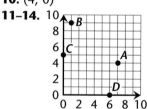

15. Sample Response: The order of the numbers in the pair is reversed. From the origin, (7, 4) is 7 right and 4 up while (4, 7) is 4 right and 7 up.

16. a, b. See figure in part (d).
c. isosceles trapezoid
d.

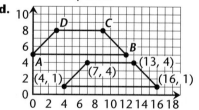

17. $2 \cdot n$

18. $n - 4$

19. $12 + n$

20. 65

21. 95

22. 30

23. a.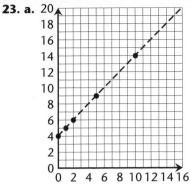

b. Sample Response: The points lie on a straight line.
c. output = input + 4 **d.** 11; (7, 11); Yes, this point falls on the same line as those in part (a).
24. $\frac{2}{52}$ or $\frac{1}{26}$; Sample Response: There are 52 cards in all. Two of them are red 10's, the 10 of hearts and the 10 of diamonds.
25. $\frac{2}{16}$ or $\frac{1}{8}$

Module 4, Section 6
1. 9, 18, 27, 36, 45, 54, 63
2. 24, 48, 72, 96, 120, 144, 168
3. 75, 150, 225, 300, 375, 450, 525
4. 110, 220, 330, 440, 550, 660, 770
5. 75
6. 720
7. 72
8. 360
9. a.

```
 _____
|   _____   _____ |
|  /          / \          \  |
| |  24      | 2 |   30     | |
| | 2        | 3 |   5      | |
| | 2        |   |          | |
|  _____\ _/ _____/   |
|_____|
```

b. multiples of 24: 24, 48, 72, 96, 120, ...; multiples of 30: 30, 60, 90, 120, ...; LCM: 120 **c.** Multiply all the prime factors shown in the diagram, using the common multiples only once; LCM: 120.
10. 12 minutes (720 seconds)
11. 8:48 P.M.; Sample Response: Find the LCM of 24 and 42, which is 168. Since 168 = 2 · 60 + 48, two trains will leave together 2 h 48 min after the last pair of trains left at the same time.
12. $7\frac{1}{2}$
13. $5\frac{3}{4}$
14. $14\frac{3}{10}$
15. $10\frac{10}{11}$
16. $\frac{17}{5}$
17. $\frac{23}{16}$

18. $\frac{215}{7}$
19. $\frac{140}{13}$
20–23.

24. area: 98 cm^2; perimeter: 42 cm
25. 14
26. 61
27. 7

TECHNOLOGY

Module 4
1. Sample Response: columns A through L and rows 1 through 10
2. 100/6, or about 17 times; There are 100 rolls of 6 choices of each roll, so the expected occurrences for each number is $\frac{100}{6} \approx 17$.
3. =A13+B13+C13+D13+E13+F13
4. =A13/100
5. Check students' graphs.

ASSESSMENT

Mid-Module 4 Quiz
1. 46%
2. 68%
3. 16%
4. 50%, 67%, 17%
5. rolling an even number; rolling a multiple of 7
6. 0, 5
7. 0, 8
8. 0, 3, 6, 9
9. 0, 2, 4, 6, 8
10. 45
11. 8
12. 14
13. prime
14. composite; 3 · 5 · 11
15. composite; 2 · 2 · 2 · 5 · 7
16. prime
17. 30%
18. <
19. <
20. >
21. $2^2 \cdot 3 \cdot 5^3$
22. 2^6
23. $2^5 \cdot 3$
24. $\frac{2}{5}$

25. $2\frac{1}{10}$

26. $\frac{5}{18}$

Module 4 Test (Form A)

1. 55%
2. 0%
3. 15%
4. 60%, 0%, 20%
5. 0, 5
6. 7
7. 1, 4, 7
8. No; he missed 16, 40, 60, and 240.
9. 12
10. 5
11. 1
12. prime
13. composite
14. composite
15. =; $3^4 = 81 = 9^2$
16. >; $2^7 = 128$, $7^2 = 49$
17. <; $7 \cdot 7 \cdot 7 = 343$, $7^4 = 2401$
18. $2 \cdot 11^2$
19. $\frac{2}{5}$
20. $\frac{1}{3}$
21. $\frac{8}{27}$
22. 0.3456
23. 1.6928
24. 18.63
25. a. and b.

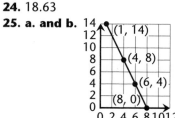

c. 10; 7
26. a. $\frac{l}{4}$ **b.** $l + l + \frac{l}{4} + \frac{l}{4}$
27. $8\frac{2}{3}$ h later (that is, at 3:40 P.M.)
28. 44
29. 13
30. 1

Module 4 Test (Form B)

1. 52%
2. 0%
3. 20%
4. 50%, 0%, 17%
5. 0, 3, 6, 9
6. 0, 5
7. 6
8. No; he missed 1, 8, 35, and 56.
9. 15
10. 1

11. 8
12. prime
13. composite
14. composite
15. <; $5^2 = 25$, $5 \cdot 5 \cdot 5 = 125$
16. <; $6^2 = 36$, $4^3 = 64$
17. =; $2^6 = 8^2 = 64$
18. $2^5 \cdot 3^2$
19. $\frac{3}{8}$
20. $\frac{1}{5}$
21. $\frac{7}{10}$
22. 5.698
23. 5.0639
24. 1.77
25. a. and b.

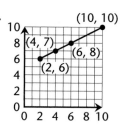

c. 9; 14
26. a. $l + 6$ **b.** $l \cdot (l + 6)$
27. 228 years later
28. 33
29. 14
30. 4

STANDARDIZED ASSESSMENT

Module 4
1. b
2. c
3. d
4. c
5. b
6. a
7. b
8. a
9. d
10. c
11. d
12. a

MODULE PERFORMANCE ASSESSMENT

Module 4

1. The ordered pairs are:

(1, 1), (2, 1), (2, 2), (3, 1), (3, 3), (4, 1), (4, 2),
(4, 4), (5, 1), (5, 5), (6, 1), (6, 2), (6, 3), (6, 6), (7, 1),
(7, 7), (8, 1), (8, 2), (8, 4), (8, 8), (9, 1), (9, 3), (9, 9),
(10, 1), (10, 2), (10, 5), (10, 10), (11, 1), (11, 11),
(12, 1), (12, 2), (12, 3), (12, 4), (12, 6), (12, 12),
(13, 1), (13, 13), (14, 1), (14, 2), (14, 7), (14, 14),
(15, 1), (15, 3), (15, 5), (15, 15)

2. The graph below shows the points plotted.

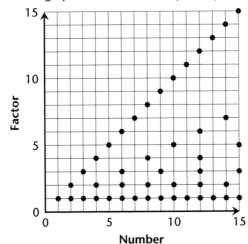

3. Answers may vary. Patterns should include the
linear relationships that appear on the graph, such as
the line produced from the number being a factor of
itself. Students may notice that non-integer values
make no sense on this graph.

4. The prime numbers only have two points. The
composite numbers have more than two points.

5. $\frac{6}{45}$ or $\frac{2}{15}$

6. 24

Name _____   Date _____

Use the Venn diagram to answer Exercises 1 and 2.

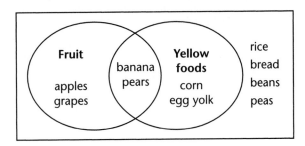

1. What yellow fruits are shown in the Venn diagram? Describe where they are located in the diagram.

2. Name all the foods shown in the Venn diagram that are not fruit.

Replace each ___?___ with the value that makes the statement true.

3. 1248 cm = ___?___ m

4. 0.45 km = ___?___ m

5. 1809 g = ___?___ kg

6. 8500 kg = ___?___ metric ton

Find each value.

7. $\frac{2}{7}$ of 42

8. $\frac{5}{9}$ of 108

9. $\frac{3}{4}$ of 180

Write each fraction as a percent and as a decimal.

10. $\frac{72}{600}$

11. $\frac{20}{50}$

12. $\frac{792}{1000}$

For Exercises 13 and 14, use the data in the table at the right.

13. Make a bar graph and a line plot for the data in the table.

14. Find the mean and median for the data in the table.

Continent	Area (millions of mi^2)
Africa	11.7
Antarctica	5.1
Asia	17.2
Australia	3.0
Europe	4.1
North America	9.4
South America	6.9

15. Find the quotient for $15\overline{)893.5}$ rounded to the nearest thousandth.

MODULES 3 AND 4 TEST   CUMULATIVE

Use the stem-and-leaf plot at the right to answer Exercises 16–18.

16. What is the range of the data?

17. What is the median of the data?

18. What is the mean of the data?

Grades for Mathematics Test

```
4 | 6
5 | 4
6 | 5 8
7 | 2 2 5 9
8 | 1 2 2 4 5 5 5 8
9 | 4 6 8 8
```

7 | 9 means 79

A normal six-sided die was rolled 30 times with the results shown. For Exercises 19 and 20 find the experimental probability of each event. Write each answer as a whole percent.

Outcome	1	2	3	4	5	6
Total	4	3	5	6	7	5

19. An odd number was rolled.

20. A number less than 5 was rolled.

21. Find the theoretical probabilities of the events in Exercises 19 and 20.

22. Find the GCF of 54, 90, and 36.

Tell whether each number is _prime_ or _composite_. If it is composite, give its prime factorization.

23. 210   **24.** 270   **25.** 37

Find each product. Write each answer in lowest terms.

26. $\frac{12}{32} \cdot \frac{4}{6}$ **27.** $\frac{3}{5} \cdot \frac{35}{60}$ **28.** $\frac{4}{7} \cdot \frac{28}{40}$

Find each product without using a calculator.

29. $2.5 \cdot 16.3$ **30.** $0.02 \cdot 180.6$ **31.** $7.09 \cdot 3.8$

32. Graph the ordered pairs in the table on a coordinate grid.

Input	2	3	4	5	6
Output	8	3	1	9	3

Find the missing number.

33. $3\frac{2}{5} = \frac{?}{5}$ **34.** $\frac{89}{7} = ?\frac{5}{7}$ **35.** $8\frac{3}{4} = \frac{?}{4}$

Answers

CUMULATIVE TEST

Modules 3 and 4

1. bananas, pears; in the area where the two sets overlap

2. corn, egg yolk, beans, peas, rice, bread

3. 12.48

4. 450

5. 1.809

6. 8.5

7. 12

8. 60

9. 135

10. 12%, 0.12

11. 40%, 0.4

12. 79.2%, 0.792

13.

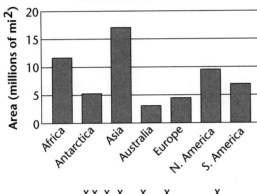

Land Area of Continents

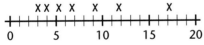

14. mean = 8.2 million mi^2; median = 6.9 million mi^2

15. 59.567

16. 52

17. 82

18. 79.45

19. 53%

20. 60%

21. 50%; 67%

22. 18

23. composite; $2 \cdot 3 \cdot 5 \cdot 7$

24. composite; $2 \cdot 3^3 \cdot 5$

25. prime

26. $\frac{1}{4}$

27. $\frac{7}{20}$

28. $\frac{2}{5}$

29. 40.75

30. 3.612

31. 26.942

32.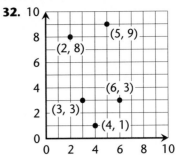

33. 17

34. 12

35. 35

MID-YEAR TEST

CUMULATIVE

Estimate each answer. Show how you got your estimate.

1. $3198 - 411$

2. $52 \cdot 39$

3. $205 + 519 + 679$

Explain how you can use mental math to find each answer.

4. $65 + 24 + 25 + 26$

5. $2 \cdot 9 \cdot 5 \cdot 8$

Find the value of each expression.

6. $4 \cdot (6 - 3) + 5$

7. $12 - 2 \cdot 5$

8. $45 \div 5 - 3 \cdot 2$

Write each decimal in words.

9. 4.18

10. 0.073

11. 15.0024

Find each sum or difference.

12. $22.42 + 3.018 + 14.16$

13. $15 + 2.62 + 14.05$

14. $\$24 - \$15.75$

15. $128.3 - 42.04$

Write each fraction in lowest terms.

16. $\dfrac{6}{30}$

17. $\dfrac{15}{20}$

18. $\dfrac{24}{36}$

Complete each pair of equivalent fractions.

19. $\dfrac{1}{2} = \dfrac{?}{10}$

20. $\dfrac{28}{40} = \dfrac{7}{?}$

21. $\dfrac{?}{25} = \dfrac{15}{75}$

Compare each pair of decimals. Use <, >, or =.

22. 0.106 ___?___ 0.13

23. 104.65 ___?___ 103.98

Write each fraction as a decimal and as a percent.

24. $\dfrac{9}{10}$

25. $\dfrac{20}{50}$

26. $\dfrac{3}{4}$

Find each product or quotient.

27. $3.5 \cdot 16.2$

28. $126.4 \cdot 0.02$

29. $8.06 \cdot 3.7$

30. $42.4 \div 4$

31. $37.3 \div 5$

32. $27.5 \div 0.02$

Write each number as a decimal and as a fraction or a mixed number.

33. five tenths

34. twenty-four thousandths

35. two and thirty-five hundredths

MID-YEAR TEST   CUMULATIVE

Find each product. Write each answer in lowest terms.

36. $\frac{3}{4} \cdot \frac{3}{5}$

37. $\frac{5}{8} \cdot \frac{4}{10}$

38. $\frac{3}{10} \cdot \frac{15}{18}$

Find each value.

39. $\frac{1}{2}$ of 18

40. $\frac{2}{3}$ of 27

41. $\frac{3}{4}$ of 104

Replace each __?__ with the correct term. Describe the rule you used to find each sequence.

42. 7, 12, 17, 22, __?__, __?__, __?__, 42

43. 192, 185, 178, 171, __?__, __?__, __?__, 143

Use the data in the table at the right to answer Exercises 44–47.

44. What is the range of the data?

45. What is the median of the data?

46. What is the mean of the data?

47. What is the mode of the data?

Maximum Speeds of African Animals	
Animal	**Speed (mi/h)**
giraffe	32
cheetah	70
jackal	35
elephant	25
lion	50
gazelle	50
zebra	40

A spinner divided into five equal parts was spun 25 times with the results shown. Write each answer as a whole percent.

Outcome	1	2	3	4	5
Total	4	5	3	6	7

48. What is the theoretical probability that an odd number was spun?

49. What is the experimental probability that an odd number was spun?

For Exercises 50–52, replace each __?__ with the number that makes the statement true.

50. 123 cm = __?__ m

51. 0.35 km = __?__ m

52. 652 g = __?__ kg

53. What is 66 ÷ 12 expressed as a mixed number with the fractional part in lowest terms?

MID-YEAR TEST

54. John, Sue, Lisa, and Fernando are student council officers. The Council has four officers: President, vice president, secretary, and treasurer. Make an organized list of all of the ways the positions can be filled by these four students. How many different combinations are there?

55. How many lines of symmetry does a square have? Draw a picture to show all of the lines of symmetry.

For Exercises 56–58, draw each figure. Then shade the part that represents the given fraction.

56. $\frac{5}{8}$ of a rectangle **57.** $\frac{1}{2}$ of a hexagon **58.** $\frac{2}{3}$ of a circle

59. Find a two-digit even number that is divisible by 5 and 3, and is greater than 75.

60. a. Graph the ordered pairs in the table on the coordinate grid.

Input	2	5	6	3	4
Output	5	11	13	7	9

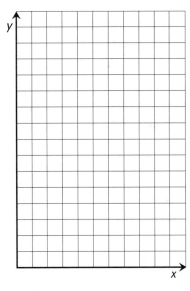

b. Use your graph to predict the missing values.

input = $4\frac{1}{2}$, output = ___**?**___

output = 12, input = ___**?**___

Answers

MID-YEAR TEST

1. 3200 − 400 = 2800 or 3000 − 400 = 2600

2. 50 • 40 = 2000

3. 200 + 520 + 680 = 1400

4. 65 + 24 + 25 + 26 = 140

5. 2 • 9 • 5 • 8 = 720

6. 17

7. 2

8. 3

9. four and eighteen hundredths

10. seventy-three thousandths

11. fifteen and twenty-four ten-thousandths

12. 39.598

13. 31.67

14. $8.25

15. 86.26

16. $\frac{1}{5}$

17. $\frac{3}{4}$

18. $\frac{2}{3}$

19. $\frac{5}{10}$

20. $\frac{7}{10}$

21. $\frac{5}{25}$

22. <

23. >

24. 0.9, 90%

25. 0.4, 40%

26. 0.75, 75%

27. 56.7

28. 2.528

29. 29.822

30. 10.6

31. 7.46

32. 1375

33. 0.5, $\frac{5}{10}$ or $\frac{1}{2}$

34. 0.024, $\frac{24}{1000}$ or $\frac{3}{125}$

35. 2.35, $2\frac{35}{100}$ or $2\frac{7}{20}$

36. $\frac{9}{20}$

37. $\frac{1}{4}$

38. $\frac{1}{4}$

39. 9

40. 18

41. 78

42. 27, 32, 37; start with 7 and add 5 to the term to get the next term.

43. 164, 157, 150; start with 192 and subtract 7 from the term to get the next term.

44. 45

45. 40

46. 43.14

47. 50

48. 60%

49. 56%

50. 1.23 m

51. 350 m

52. 0.652 kg

53. $5\frac{1}{2}$

54. 24 combinations

55. 4;

56.

57.

58.

59. 90

60. a.

b. Output = 10

Input = $5\frac{1}{2}$